YOUR M*IDDLE YEARS

Love them. Live them.
Own them.

The Authors

Paula Mee is a current member and a past president of the Irish Nutrition and Dietetic Institute, the professional body for dietitians in Ireland. Through her consultancy work, Paula provides an extensive range of nutrition and dietetic services to individuals, corporates, educational institutions and the foods industry. She is a regular contributor to Irish media (the *Irish Times* Health Supplement, RTÉ Radio 1) on nutrition matters. She was the consultant dietitian on the production team of TV3 series *Doctor in the House* and the dietitian on RTÉ series *Health Squad*.

Kate O'Brien returned to Ireland in 2013 after 18 years living and working in Asia. Through her career, Kate has enjoyed many years in the health, beauty and spa industries in London, Dublin, Singapore and Hong Kong, and has become an established writer on lifestyle and spa culture. Kate writes for *Asia Spa* magazine, *The Gloss* and *Image* magazine. She is the author of six lifestyle books.

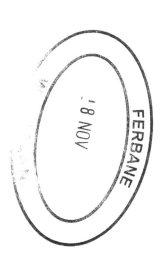

YOUR M*iDDLE YEARS

Love them. Live them.
Own them.

PAULA MEE AND KATE O'BRIEN

GILL BOOKS

Gill Books
Hume Avenue
Park West
Dublin 12
www.gillbooks.ie

Gill Books is an imprint of M.H. Gill & Co.

978 0 7171 6975 7

Designed by Tanya M. Ross, elementinc.ie
Illustrations by Eva Byrne
Printed by L&C Printing, Poland

This book is typeset in Hurme Geometric Sans 1 Light 10pt on 13pt.

The paper used in this book comes from the wood pulp of managed forests. For every tree felled, at least one tree is planted, thereby renewing natural resources.

5 4 3 2

Note from the Publisher
This book is written as a source of information only and is not intended to be taken as a replacement for medical advice. A qualified medical practitioner should always be consulted before beginning any new diet, exercise or health plan.

To all our Middle Years contemporaries –
yes, growing old is inevitable, so let's make the most of it.
Here's to the rest, and best, of our lives.

Acknowledgements

This book would not have happened without the help of our friends and family. Thank you all. Although there are far too many to mention, we hugely appreciate your support.

A special thanks to our expert contributors Prannie Rhatigan, Emily Power Smith, Mari Kennedy, Sunita Passi, Dr Rosemary Coleman, Shabir Daya, Josephine Fairley and Jackie Ryder. Thanks also to Dr Christopher-James Harvey and Troy Sing for your expertise and patience.

Thanks to Krystyna Rawicz, Una Rees, Martina Maher, Finola Mee, Aisling Grimley, Dara Morgan and all our middle years friends and focus group participants for their honesty and support and for setting us on the right track. Lastly, thanks to the great team at Gill Books, especially Sarah Liddy, Ruth Mahony, Teresa Daly and Fiona Biggs, who were ever-present and helpful along the way.

CONTENTS

Introduction

Instead of concentrating on what not to eat, move. Do things you like. Feed your inner being and you won't crave food, because you have fed yourself with life, beauty, energy, enthusiasm. Go out and love your life. Your age means nothing.

Alessandra Ferri, ballerina and former principal dancer
with the Royal Ballet

Growing old is inevitable – it's how we deal with it that matters. For many women in our youth-obsessed western world, a few lines and fluctuations in hormonal levels denote the end of fertility, the end of life as we know it and the measured approach of old age and all that accompanies it.

Thankfully, attitudes are changing and women are no longer willing to be cast aside at the first signs of ageing. We know our bodies better than ever before. We are living longer and are proving that age is no barrier to a full, vibrant life. What's more, given that scientists tell us we may actually live until we are well over 100, we have a lot of living to do. It's time to take control of our bodies and our lives and embrace the next act – the possibilities are endless.

I see lots of women around me fighting into their 60s to remain who they were. For me, I've decided I'm not who I was, only older. This is me, but it's also a new and different me. I have a grandchild, Joshua. He's 10 months old now. I have great pleasure spending time with him and being removed one step from parenting, but still being important in his life and he in mine.

My hunger for sex has declined. It's a general interest now, not a hunger that needs to be satisfied.

I've found new pleasures in the last few years – writing and painting. I've even attended a festival, Electric Picnic, invited by a group to read my poetry.

Some things are easier, some are harder. I've started gardening. That's useful in a hectic life with multiple day-to-day stresses and strains. You can't garden in a hurry. You can't be impatient or expect a plant to grow before it's ready. I keep chickens. Some days I can potter for hours, losing myself in it. Other days, I still work like a dog, 12-hour days and no breaks. I find I can fly into a rage over the most minor of aggravations. ??
– Krystana

Menopause and dry vaginas are topics that many women are still not comfortable discussing openly in these supposedly evolved times. While most of us will happily share intimate information with our closest friends, we are often too proud or too shy to admit how hormonal change is affecting us – or maybe we are hoping that by ignoring its existence, it might all just go away! There are always fillers and numerous other high-tech therapies for our faces, but once our body clock signals oestrogen's grand finale, change is imminent. In our parents' generation, menopause was kept within tight lips and rarely, if ever, discussed. Back then, the choice was stark: age visibly or have a facelift. Today we have more control over how we age and science is now proving that with the right diet and lifestyle we can look, be and feel our very best.

Menopause is not a disease; it is a normal, natural event for women the world over. Many women suffer years of immeasurable pain and anguish because of the enormous changes taking place within their bodies during these years. Others suffer little. None of us, however, is fortunate enough to retain the face of our 30s. As we watch our faces slowly become maps of our colourful lives and notice the increasing depth and dimensions of our new-found creases, we know in our hearts that this is for real. Partner this with a declining libido, sleep disturbances and a host of emotional and physical changes and it's hardly surprising that many women suffer greatly and quietly for many years.

" *There's a lot to be said about getting older and it's not all bad either. Ageing doesn't turn us into cranky old women unless we were cranky young women to begin with. In fact, research suggests that we become more emotionally settled and relaxed as we age. We mellow. That is after we have navigated our way through menopause.*

I'm feeling more relaxed now. This mostly spills into little things. The daily manicuring and preening takes much less time now. I frequently step out in comfy flats that I would have previously described as orthopaedic footwear. Don't get me wrong – I still like my lipstick and heels and won't be giving them up any time soon.

We all go through it. We don't have a say; we just have to get ready and steer our way through armed with the soundest information to guide us into the rest and best of our lives. "
– Paula

How best to deal with this biological life transition has been the subject of numerous books, many written by medical experts and all undoubtedly with the best of intentions. Most, however, are so technical that even the most scientifically-minded reader is left bewildered and uninspired.

As every woman navigating the menopausal years will attest, the profound emotional turmoil taking place in her life can completely overwhelm. Few medical experts address this and when they do, they often prescribe anti-depressants. And while most women understand menopause to be a natural transition, many also question the prescription of hormone therapy at the first sign of fluctuating hormones. *Your Middle Years* is not a hormonal prescription – it is a practical guide to help you look, feel and be your best, physically and emotionally. By succinctly combining the best of age-old eastern wisdom with natural healing modalities, practical nutrition, cosmetic science and nuggets of sound emotional sense, its pages overflow with plausible advice to inspire us to be once again at home in our bodies and minds.

To write is not hard, but to write well and with honesty and conviction can be. We are truly writing from the heart as we both navigate this challenging period. We have learned so much, but above all have realised that, to quote the ancient Persian proverb, 'This too shall pass', and that being strong and in control of our lives is paramount to alleviating symptoms, increasing energy levels and maximising our well-being.

" *My life now is clearer and more focused than it has been for many years and that must be good. I am also stronger, wiser and more confident in and about myself – one of the benefits of being older, I guess! What I have learned is that when thinking about health, you cannot separate the different parts of the body from each other; you cannot separate the mind from the body, nor people from their environment. Everything is connected.* "
– Kate

They say 50 is the new 40 and we know now that with age comes wisdom, contentedness and, most importantly, an understanding and acceptance that what we are going through is normal. It's OK. No, we can't stop the clock, but the dull haze can be lifted.

" *I'm 48. That's two years away from 50, arithmetic fans. I don't feel old. I don't feel young, either, but I don't mind about that at all, because I'd rather be the person I am now than the person I was at 25 — so anxious and unsure about so many things, so tentative. I prefer 48; plus, I'm kinder, wiser, more patient, less judgemental. These are all improvements. I genuinely feel like this is a brilliant time. Like I'm in my prime.* "
– India Knight, In Your Prime

In compiling this book, we are combining our joint expertise with renowned experts to ensure that the information offered is progressive, inclusive and, above all, useful. *Your Middle Years* is not just for the menopause years – it's for life thereafter and its objective is simple: to offer hopeful supportive advice and simple practical solutions to help women feel strong, vibrant and very much in control of their bodies and their destinies.

Embrace it or ignore it – the choice is yours – but it's one that will frame you for the rest of your life.

" I'm in my (very early!) 50s now and I need to work harder to stay healthy – my energy levels do wane and I need to eat more mindfully and push myself more than ever before to maintain some level of fitness, but I have discovered something really powerful and grounding about regular yoga practice that I haven't found with anything else. As we say throughout these pages, the hardest part is getting started, but when (not if!) you do, the rewards will be with you for what I now know can be the best part of your life. "

– Kate

CHAPTER 1

Facts

Menopause is an energy gateway – a unique chance for a woman to prepare her body, mind and spirit for a healthy, long life. It's a time when she can heal, strengthen herself, and balance and harmonize her energies. Menopause creates the opportunity for a transformation, a new beginning, as a woman becomes free to discover, pursue or complete her life's mission and touch her spirit – and the spirits of those around her – in a profound and meaningful way.

Dr Nan Lu, *Traditional Chinese Medicine: A Woman's Guide to a Hormone-Free Menopause*

The word 'menopause' is a combination of two Greek words that, when translated literally, means 'the end of the monthlies'. Menopause is a specific point in time marking the permanent end of fertility, which occurs when a woman's ovaries stop producing eggs and the hormones oestrogen and progesterone decline. We define it as a year without periods. The average woman reaches menopause at about the age of 51, although it can vary from the 30s to the 50s. Menopause can also occur if a woman's ovaries are surgically removed.

Peri-menopause means 'around menopause', and is an extended transitional state that refers to the months, even years (up to approximately 10), leading to the menopause, when physical indicators become apparent and periods become more irregular. A woman can still conceive during this time, albeit with a reduced chance of fertility.

I'm 43 and it took quite a few visits to my GP before the word menopause was even mentioned. It felt like a negative phase to move into, less creative and something we have to just get through. I didn't feel I had enough information regarding symptom management and what the heck was going on hormonally.
– Susan

While life expectancy has increased significantly during the past decades and the onset of puberty now happens earlier, the typical age at which a woman reaches menopause has not changed for centuries. While the reason for this has not yet been clearly established, two factors have been found to influence the timing of natural menopause – smoking and genetics. According to the Mayo Clinic in the US, smokers start menopause one to two years earlier than non-smokers, while the genetic link is supported by the fact that women often experience menopause around the same time as their mothers.

The World Health Organization (WHO) estimates that by the year 2025, there will be 1.1 billion women aged 50 and over. That's a lot of women going through a great deal of change, right now. In the US, for instance, an estimated 45 million women are going through menopause at any given time.

Menopause not only alters hormonal balance but also the way the brain works and the way you look at the world.

I eventually went to the doctor who confirmed that I was in menopause. I was shocked and felt devastated, especially as I had never had children and this felt like the end. The doctor put me on mild anti-depressants to help ease the symptoms, but they only made me feel more lethargic and I put on more weight. I felt like my life was over as a woman and that I was never going to have sex again and, for the first time in my life, I felt really unattractive.
– Yasmin

Each woman will experience menopause in a uniquely different way. This variation is evident different parts of the world and between women from different ethnic groups, which suggests both cultural and genetic influences. Many Caucasian women, for instance, experience hot flushes, while studies from other cultures suggest far fewer occurences of this phenomenon. Many Indian women accept the menopause as a part of the process of ageing and are less inclined to seek medical help. The Chinese Menopause Society has stated that in China 'women generally have very poor knowledge of menopause and are eager to learn more'. In Japan, some of the most mesmerising geishas are those in their 70s and beyond, women overflowing with wisdom, strength and compassion who are revered by their families and communities.

THE SYMPTOMS OF MENOPAUSE
Over 40 symptoms are associated with your middle years. Those most commonly experienced symptoms include:

▶ **Irregular menstrual periods:** The majority of women experience between four and eight years of menstrual cycle changes before reaching menopause. Bleeding may last fewer days or more days, with blood flow heavier or lighter than what was the norm.

▸ **Weight gain and body fat changes:** It is estimated that a woman can gain 0.5kg a year during peri-menopause and menopause. Body shape can change from the classically curvy pear shape (wide hips and thighs) to the apple shape, resulting in a thickening waistline and an extra layer of belly fat. This is not inevitable, however, and there is a lot we can do to minimise this 'menopot'.

Women are typically born with between one and two million eggs. By the time menopause approaches, only about 100 eggs remain. The declining number and quality of the eggs, as well as age-related uterine changes, contribute to reduced fertility, often even before signs of peri-menopause become apparent.

▸ **Hot flushes and night sweats:** Hot flushes, or, in scientific speak, vasomotor symptoms (VMS), are an intense build-up of body heat that happens as blood vessels near the surface of the skin start to dilate, increasing blood flow and giving a red, flushed look to the face and neck. In an attempt to cool the body down, a woman may start to perspire, often profusely. Hot flushes can increase in frequency and severity during stressful times and may be associated with palpitations and feelings of anxiety. As with other menopause symptoms, they follow a pattern unique to each woman and there is no way of predicting when they will start – or stop.

"I was lucky to escape the daytime hot flushes, but I regularly overheated at night. That left me sleep-deprived and pretty irritable. Everyday stuff felt overwhelming.

Personally, and thankfully, my night sweats were not relentless. Bouts of night sweats were followed by episodes of uninterrupted sleep over a two-year period. I tried meditation, yoga and massage. Layered bedclothes that could easily be removed were useful too. Unfortunately some are not so lucky and have their own internal version of global warming for years! A friend of mine used to go to bed with a packet of frozen peas tucked under her pillow. When she flipped her pillow, she had an instant cooldown!"

– Paula

▸ **Sleep disturbances:** Sleep disturbances or the inability to sleep (insomnia) may be a consequence of night sweats but can also be an independent symptom of hormonal change.

- **Vaginal dryness:** It is estimated that at least a third of women will experience some troubling symptoms in their vulvo-vaginal area (external female genitals and vagina), ranging from vaginal discharge, irritation and dryness to a painful burning sensation that can vary in frequency and severity. Changing hormone levels can also cause the tissues of the vulva and vaginal area to become thin, dry and less elastic, a condition known as atrophy.

- **Mood swings:** Many women experience tearfulness, mood swings, irritability and a general 'blue' feeling. These emotions are generally the result of actual physical surges of chemicals flooding the brain in response to fluctuating hormone levels.

- **Skin and hair changes:** Many women report physical changes to their skin and hair in particular, with loss of collagen production, slackness, dryness and overall skin thinning. Hair often becomes greyer and more brittle, and its overall texture changes too.

- **Waning sexual desire:** It is often reported that sexual desire decreases with age for many women (and men). A combination of sleep deprivation and vaginal discomfort and dryness during the menopause can severely impact a woman's sexual desire, making sex itself uncomfortable and often extremely painful. Hormonal change is an important part of this, but other factors, including changes in body image and self-esteem, difficulty in being aroused or reaching orgasm and family, medical and social concerns also contribute.

FAST FACTS ▸▸

- The years leading up to your very last period are referred to as the peri-menopause (usually from around 42 years onwards).

- The menopause is your very last menstrual period.

- When you have been 12 months without a period, you have gone through the menopause.

- After this 12-month phase and for the rest of your life, you are post-menopausal.

- During that 12 month phase you could still get pregnant, so take precautions!

"I seemed to be getting stuck further down an emotional black hole. On the recommendation of a trusted health website (victoriahealth.co.uk), I started taking essential fatty acid supplements and Sage Complex, which boosted my mood (a little!). When I eventually did go to my doctor for a routine smear test and once-over, my diagnosis was a resounding 'menopausal'. Little advice was offered, which is a shame. I didn't want HRT, bioidentical or any other form of hormone medication and the natural supplements were helping. Also, I knew then that what was happening was very normal and that it would pass – some time."
– Kate

YOUR HORMONES

Hormones are powerful. They are an indelible part of who we are as women. When we witness the teenagers of today whose erratic behaviour parents are quick to sympathise with as 'hormonal', it seems strange that society rarely recognises that adult women can be equally challenged by hormonal flux. But we are conditioned to simply stay quiet and 'get on with it'.

This hormonal unrest is not insignificant. It is estimated that once the average woman is through menopause, she will have lost all of her progesterone, up to 90 per cent of her oestrogen and the majority of her testosterone. Never underestimate how these waning levels can affect you.

As US psychiatrist Louann Brizendine says in her book *The Female Brain*, 'The menopause is the moment when the mommy brain starts to unplug, with the fallout causing physical pain, immeasurable suffering, challenging marriages, relationships and family life.'

"I'm fascinated by hormones. They have such a significant effect on just about all of our body systems – the nervous, digestive, reproductive, endocrine, musculoskeletal and circulatory systems. During peri-menopause, I can say with certainty I had physiological symptoms I had never experienced before – thankfully not all 40 of them, but a good number!

The psychological effects were interesting too. I frequently found myself scattered, unfocused and distracted at the work-desk. Productive I was not! I had seriously lost my mojo. With that came

a low-grade anxiety that sat with me sometimes for days. This ennui spilled into my personal life and into my relationships. **"**
– Paula

WHAT ARE HORMONES?

Hormones are chemical messengers that travel around the body, providing information to various tissues and organs.

Oestrogen

During puberty, oestrogen helps us develop into women. It's important for breast changes, pubic hair growth and menstruation. After puberty, this hormone continues to control our menstrual cycle, protect our bones and keep cholesterol in check.

Most of our oestrogen is made in the ovaries. We also produce oestrogen in the adrenal glands, located on top of the kidneys. Our fat cells also make a small amount.

The decline in oestrogen can happen abruptly in younger women whose ovaries are removed, resulting in a surgical menopause. But for the majority of women, there is a slower decline in this hormone during the peri-menopausal years and at menopause itself.

As the ovaries decrease their production of oestrogen, the body tries to compensate for the loss. During our middle years, we preferentially produce fat cells rather than muscle cells in a bid to counteract falling oestrogen levels. Regrettably, more fat cells means weight gain around the middle.

▶ **What to do:** Eat a well-balanced diet including phytoestrogen-rich foods. Avoid weight gain by increasing your exercise and reducing your calories.

Progesterone

Progesterone is released from a part of the ovaries called the corpus luteum. It is important for a healthy menstrual cycle and it prepares the body for pregnancy if the egg is fertilised after ovulation.

Feeling bloated and too snug in our clothes can be the result of increased water retention, often a consequence of falling progesterone levels.

- ▶ **What to do:** Avoid salty foods and hidden salt in foods which can aggravate water retention. Excessive water retention can adversely affect blood pressure.

Androgens

Women also produce small amounts of androgens male-type hormones, including testosterone and dehydroepiandrosterone (DHEA). Androgen levels influence our sex drive, as well as our mood and energy levels.

Testosterone is mainly produced in our ovaries and, to a lesser extent, by the adrenal glands. This hormone is important for sexual development and fertility. It also plays a significant role in the maintenance of bone and muscle strength.

Muscle cells are hungry and burn more calories than fat cells, so the more muscle we have in relation to fat, the higher our metabolic rate and our ability to burn calories. Unfortunately, as our testosterone levels decline, so does our ability to build new muscle cells. The consequence is a slower metabolism.

Throughout our middle years, levels of androgens gradually decline, leading to weight gain around the middle instead of around the bum and hips (where we used to deposit those extra pounds). Hence the terms 'menopot', 'muffin top' or 'middle-aged spread'.

- ▶ **What to do:** Build regular exercise and relaxation into your week. Strength training helps to maintain muscle mass in the body, which supports a healthy metabolism. Eat sufficient protein with each meal to maintain your muscle mass.

Cortisol

Cortisol is the body's stress-response hormone. It prepares the body to deal with stressful scenarios by breaking down fat stores and releasing energy. This energy can then be used in a 'fight or flight' situation. In the aftermath of stress, cortisol increases appetite to replace those calories your body thought it needed.

This means that if you get constantly stressed while sitting at your desk or in traffic, you could be driven to eat!

The presence of oestrogen helps manage the amount of cortisol your body produces. So when our oestrogen levels decline, stress levels start to rise and we are more likely to have problems. This change is believed to be partly responsible for menopausal weight gain.

▸ **What to do:** Manage stress levels with relaxation techniques and get sufficient sleep to recharge both body and mind.

Insulin

Insulin is made in the pancreas and helps to move glucose (a type of sugar) from the blood into the cells, where it is used to produce energy.

If we carry excess visceral (or abdominal) fat, we can become insulin-resistant. This means that even though the body is producing enough insulin, the hormone can't do its job and glucose stays in the blood. When the levels of glucose continue to rise, this can pose significant problems in the long term. There is an increased risk of diabetes and complications such as eye disease, kidney disease and stroke.

▸ **What to do:** Keep active, eat well and stay in shape. Avoid processed and refined carbohydrates and focus on wholegrains and high-fibre foods instead.

Leptin

Leptin is produced by our fat cells and its role is to alert the brain when body fat stores are sufficient. Normally, leptin quells the appetite. Unfortunately, too much visceral fat leads to the excessive production of inflammatory chemicals, which block leptin signals to the brain, leaving us leptin-resistant. In other words, although the fat cells may produce leptin, the hormone no longer binds to the brain's receptors. Appetite is therefore not suppressed and fat stores continue to accumulate.

▸ **What to do:** Help prevent the build up of abdominal fat by monitoring your portion sizes and exercising regularly. Eat a diet rich in antioxidants and omega-3 fats.

Ghrelin

Ghrelin is the body's hunger hormone. It is produced by the stomach lining and travels to the brain to signal that it's time to eat. Our levels of ghrelin rise before a meal and fall to their lowest level approximately one hour after eating. Women who are very overweight appear to be more sensitive to ghrelin's appetite-boosting effects.

▸ **What to do:** Eat meals at regular intervals to promote the natural rise and fall of ghrelin. Don't skip meals and never let yourself get too hungry.

Dopamine

Dopamine is a neurotransmitter that transfers signals between neurons in our brain. It is responsible for our motor functions, our motivation and our learning. It is also connected to our mood and stimulates the pleasure and reward centre of the brain.

Most drugs of abuse (such as alcohol and cocaine) and highly palatable foods (such as sugary fatty foods) spike our dopamine levels.

Repeatedly eating unhealthy foods over a period of time can desensitise you to the effects of dopamine. This makes it increasingly more difficult to get the same reward, meaning you have to eat more and more of those biscuits and bars! Overweight women with a blunted response to dopamine consistently nibble.

▸ **What to do:** The brain can be retrained. Mindfulness is one way of pressing the pause button and making more conscious food decisions. Dopamine is made from an amino acid, tyrosine. Eat tyrosine-rich foods such as poultry, eggs, fish, cheese, soya beans and peanuts regularly through the week.

HORMONE THERAPY
Is it worth it?

This is a question we simply can't answer. Twenty years ago, it was thought that the majority of women would benefit from hormone therapy (formally known as hormone replacement therapy or HRT). Then the pendulum swung to the other side and more recently it seems to be swaying back to centre.

There's no question that hormone therapy can make a significant difference to the quality of your life if your symptoms are severe. It can diminish hot flushes and sweats within weeks.

One of the major benefits of hormone therapy is that it prevents bone loss by replacing oestrogen. But the jury is still out because of the small but significant associated risk of breast cancer for some women. It seems that older women (over 60 years) also have an increased risk of cardiovascular disease when taking hormone therapy.

According to Christiane Northrup MD, author of *Goddesses Never Age*, 'healthy women who go through peri-menopause may not require any additional hormone support. In fact, some women make all the hormones they need from their own adrenals and ovaries and they sail through the process. Others enter midlife exhausted from chronic sleep deprivation, nutritional deficiencies, difficult marriages or a lifestyle of over-giving to parents or children. Hence, these women are running on empty and their bodies lack the raw materials to produce adequate hormones.'

As every woman will experience her menopause years differently, the best advice is to discuss your options with your doctor, who should be armed with the most up-to-date facts, before deciding what approach is best for you.

On a friend's sound advice, I got a referral to a wonderful gynaecologist – I chose a woman slightly older than myself this time, having had male consultants during my pregnancies. It certainly felt easier when discussing symptoms. I left her office with a complete understanding of what was going on in my body and my options of care, both medical and complementary.
– Sally

▸ Hormone therapy (HT) is an umbrella term for oestrogen therapy or oestrogen–progesterone therapy. The old-fashioned term 'hormone replacement therapy' or HRT is no longer in vogue because the objective is to provide only enough of the hormone to relieve symptoms, not to replace the amounts your body produced before menopause. After all, it is normal for hormone levels to diminish.

▸ Bioidentical hormone therapy (BHT) offers hormones that are chemically identical to those made by our bodies. Despite all the interest in these, there doesn't seem to be sufficient evidence to show that they are safer or more effective than traditional hormone therapy. However, you should discuss this along with other possible therapies with your doctor.

What's the alternative?

It's worth noting that you can significantly reduce your risk of heart disease and stroke without hormone therapy. Instead, with the right diet and a regular exercise routine, you can look after your waistline, your blood pressure and your cholesterol levels, all of which will influence your heart health. What's more, the combination of weight-bearing exercise and what you eat will either be a solid foundation for strong bones or a weak support that will prematurely age you. Ultimately the choice is yours.

WITH THE MENOPAUSE CAN COME RENEWED CREATIVE ENERGY, FEELINGS OF ASSERTIVENESS AND A STRONG SENSE OF SELF – ALL TESTAMENTS TO EXCITING TIMES IN STORE!

Plummeting hormone levels can negatively impact our immune systems. Autoimmune diseases such as coeliac disease, rheumatoid arthritis and type 1 diabetes are more prevalent in older women, which indicates a central role for oestrogen in their development. There are well over 20 different micro-nutrients necessary for immune health. Incorporating these in your diet will positively support your natural defences.

The 30-plus years that potentially stretch before you are the best reason to take charge and be prepared now. So name, claim and tame those hormones!

CHAPTER 2

Food

One cannot think well, love well, sleep well if one has not dined well.

Virginia Woolf, *A Room of One's Own*

Personally, we haven't come across any woman who was totally unaware of symptoms in the lead-up to her menopause and thereafter. But apparently they are out there. Completely symptom-free! The lucky few! For the rest of us, these years bring with them an assortment of symptoms. Luckily, the vast majority can be managed with the right nutrition regime.

MORE OR LESS? YOUR CHANGING NUTRIENT NEEDS

Our need for energy or calories reduces as we age. This is seriously unfair after all the hard work we have put in to stay in shape throughout our 40s! The average active younger woman needs approximately 2000 kcal per day. However, this is not the case when we reach our 50s. Our basic energy needs start to decline and drop as low as 1800 kcal by age 75.

Although this means that if we want to prevent weight gain, we need to eat less, our requirement for vitamins and minerals remains largely the same. In fact, we need slightly more protein and the same amount of vitamins and minerals as we always did. Iron is an exception, as we need less of this nutrient once menstruation ceases. We need to eat fewer calories but to include more nutrient-dense foods in our meals.

And there's more. If we are less active than we used to be, our calorific needs plummet, in some cases by as much as a further 200 kcal a day. So post-menopause, our daily requirements may drop by as much as 400 kcal in total. And we seriously miss those calories. We don't want to make do with less, but there's really no way to sugar-coat the truth!

FAST FACTS ▸▸

Post–menopause, we need less:

- ▸ Iron, because we no longer menstruate

- ▸ Folic acid, because we can't get pregnant

- ▸ Calories, because our metabolism slows down and we don't burn off the energy. If we are less active than before, we need even fewer calories still!

Instead, we need more:

- Protein
- Vitamin D – over 65 years 10μg/day
- Nutrient-dense food packed with vitamins and minerals.

TOP MENO-FOODS

The law requires that for a food to be described as 'a source of' a vitamin or mineral, it must supply at least 15 per cent of the reference intake (RI) in 100g. For a food to qualify as 'high in' a vitamin or mineral, it must supply 30 per cent of the RI in 100g.

Eggs

Eggs don't contain carbohydrate. The calories come from protein and fats. Two-thirds of the total fat in eggs is healthy unsaturated fats. A medium egg (59g):

- Contains 87 kcal, 7g protein and 6g fat
- Is high in vitamin B12
- Is a source of iodine and vitamin D.

Vitamin B12 contributes to a reduction in tiredness and fatigue.
Iodine contributes to normal thyroid function and to the production of thyroid hormones.
Vitamin D contributes to the normal functioning of the immune system.

Seeds

Pepitas or dry-roasted pumpkin seeds are high in phosphorus, iron, magnesium and zinc.

- A dessertspoon (10g) of pumpkin seeds contains 58 kcal, 3g protein and 5g fat.

Chia seeds contain omega-3 fats and are high in calcium, iron, magnesium and zinc.

- A dessertspoon (10g) of chia seeds contains 44 kcal, 2g protein and 3g fat (almost 2g of which are omega-3 fats).

Phosphorus contributes to the maintenance of normal teeth.
Iron contributes to the reduction of tiredness and fatigue.
Magnesium contributes to normal muscle function.
Zinc contributes to normal skin, hair and nails.
Calcium is needed for the maintenance of normal bones.

Mix any seeds you like (flax, sunflower, hemp, poppy). Scatter over salads or add to your home-made bread, granola or smoothie. All seeds contain good mixes of essential vitamins and minerals. However, you need to eat about 30g of seeds as a snack in order to get a significant amount of nutrients. A dessertspoon would not contribute much to your nutrient requirements in comparison to a serving of broccoli. As always, there really is no substitute for green vegetables.

Quinoa

We're big fans of baby potatoes in their jackets (good potassium, vitamin C and fibre content) and brown rice (we love the nutty texture and flavour), but there are alternatives. Quinoa is a gluten-free seed that is prepared in much the same way as rice. It is delicious mixed with roasted vegetables and it contains more protein than many common wholegrains, even brown rice.

The seed is a good source of amino acids such as lysine, methionine and cysteine. It is a source of riboflavin and niacin and is high in phosphorus, iron, magnesium and zinc. Because of its protein and fibre package, it's a quick and filling replacement for refined carbohydrates.

*Both **riboflavin** and **niacin** contribute to the maintenance of normal healthy skin.*

Legumes

Legumes, or pulses, contain a wide variety of essential nutrients including protein, carbohydrates, dietary fibre, minerals and vitamins. They are higher in protein than most plant foods and are naturally low in fat. They are gluten-free and have a low glycaemic index rating for blood sugar management. The glycaemic index is a measurement of the effect of carbohydrate-rich foods on blood glucose (sugar) levels. They are good fibre providers as well as containing B vitamins and phytonutrients. High in resistant starch, they help the good bacteria in our large intestines to thrive and promote digestive health.

Beans, peas and lentils are all different types of legumes or pulses.

Beans

Legumes include all types of beans (butter, black, haricot, cannelloni, adzuki, borlotti, pinto, kidney), but soya beans (edamame) and foods made from them (tofu, tempeh, miso, soya milk) are particularly nutritious and can help manage certain menopausal symptoms.

FAST FACTS ▶▶

▶ Soya beans are a source of folate, biotin, iron and magnesium.

▶ They are high in phosphorus.

▶ 100g soya beans contains over 140 kcal, 14g protein and 8g fat.

Biotin contributes to the maintenance of normal healthy skin and hair. *Folate* contributes to normal psychological function.

Assortments of canned no-sauce and no-need-to-soak beans line our supermarket shelves today and offer us a convenient shortcut in the kitchen.

Peas

Versatile fresh or frozen garden peas can easily be included in the diet as an accompaniment to most main course dishes.

▶ **Green peas** coated in wasabi make a good crunchy roasted snack.

▶ **Egyptian peas or chickpeas** are easily included in salads, soups and casseroles. They can also be roasted to produce a crunchy nut-like snack. Hummus is another chickpea snack option.

Lentils

The great thing about lentils is that you don't have to soak them, unlike dried beans.

▶ **Yellow and red lentils** are small and round. They add body and protein to soups and curries.

▶ **Green lentils** are larger and flattened in shape. They are sturdier and withstand slower longer cooking and add texture to burgers.

▶ **Puy lentils** are a much darker green in colour. With their nutty flavour, they hold their shape when boiled and look great in salads or in casseroles.

Greek yogurt

Greek yogurt is a delicious and versatile ingredient used in Mediterranean-style cooking. It is a source of vitamin A, vitamin B12, calcium, iodine and phosphorus.

Vitamin A contributes to the normal function of the immune system and the maintenance of normal vision.

Greek yogurt is made when yogurt has been strained to remove the liquid whey, leaving behind a thicker and creamier yogurt. Greek yogurt has less carbohydrate than other varieties, since much is removed with the liquid whey. This makes it very useful for people with diabetes or anyone who is weight watching. It also contains less lactose, making it particularly convenient for women with a lactose intolerance.

Greek yogurt contains more protein than ordinary yogurt. Be aware that some varieties are made with skimmed milk and have little fat, while others have added sugar and/or fat to make them more appealing.

Eaten plain or with fresh fruit, Greek yogurt is perfect as a snack. It makes an excellent healthier alternative to cream or mayonnaise in many dishes. We like to mix Greek yogurt with lemon juice and capers to make a sauce for smoked or fresh salmon.

An occasional indulgence is fine, but if you're choosing yogurt for its health benefits, it should contain fewer calories than a dessert! All it takes is a few extra minutes to read the label.

Calorie content

PER 100g	NATURAL GREEK YOGURT, 0% FAT	NATURAL GREEK YOGURT	NATURAL LOW-FAT YOGURT	SINGLE CREAM	FULL-FAT MAYON-NAISE
ENERGY (kcal)	58	119	57	193	691
PROTEIN (g)	11	10	5	3	1
TOTAL FAT (g)	0	7	1	19	76
SATURATED FAT (g)	0	5	1	12	11
CALCIUM (mg)	136	142	162	89	8
SUGAR (g)	4	4	8	2	1

Kefir

Probiotics are often found in yogurt but kefir is another good source of these friendly bacteria. Making a water- or milk-based kefir allows you to enjoy this affordable fermented product. It's simply a matter of adding kefir grains to water or milk in a big glass jar and leaving it, covered, at room temperature for one or more days. The culture works its magic and you can get the consistency you desire with a little trial and error. Initially it looks a bit lumpy and bumpy!

Numerous health claims are made about kefir, but additional and larger studies are needed before any can be verified. You can buy the grains online and there are numerous YouTube videos explaining how to make and flavour kefir.

I left Prannie Rhatigan's sea kitchen in the west of Ireland with some interesting sea vegetables and a lidded jam jar. Prannie heaped a dessertspoon of chalky-coloured grains strained from her kefir into the sugary contents (water and molasses) of my jam jar. I have been straining them every few days and making large batches of water kefir as they thrive.

The end product reminds me of the fermented taste of kombucha. I think I'll flavour it with vanilla for a change next week. It's a far better taste than many other fermented foods I've tried and an interesting drink! Not sure I'm loving it yet though.
– Paula

Nuts

Nuts have it all. They are a good mix of plant protein, healthy fats and fibre.

100g of mixed nuts provides approximately 600 kcal and 27g protein. Most of the fat (88 per cent) is healthy unsaturated fat. They are high in vitamin E, thiamine, niacin, folate, biotin, pantothenic acid, magnesium and phosphorus. Mixed nuts are also a source of vitamin B6, zinc and iron.

Vitamin E contributes to the protection of cells from oxidative stress.
Thiamine contributes to the normal function of the heart.
Pantothenic acid contributes to normal mental performance.

▸ Brazil nuts contain the highest levels of selenium.

▸ Walnuts contain the most omega-3.

▸ Almonds have the highest vitamin E levels.

▸ Peanuts are a good source of the B vitamin folate.

Sea vegetables

Nutritionally, sea vegetables are as good as any land vegetable and can often be superior in their vitamin, mineral, trace element and protein content.

Sea vegetables are generally low in calories and mineral-rich. A snack of dried wakame is a source of many nutrients, including vitamin C and zinc. It is high in iodine, iron, magnesium, calcium, vitamin B12 and phosphorus. Women with poor thyroid function and sluggish systems can snack on this low-calorie option, as long as their blood pressure is normal (it's pretty salty).

EXPERT OPINION: SEA VEGETABLES ◂

Prannie Rhatigan, seaweed expert (www.irishseaweedkitchen.ie)
Seaweeds and sea vegetables contain important nutrients for all life stages. They don't just taste great and add texture to foods; they also help us to decrease water retention, balance hormone levels and maintain strong bones and a healthy heart.

Too much salt is bad news for health, so substitute your table salt with dried, ground sea vegetables. You can dry and grind a variety of seaweeds yourself or buy a jar of ready-ground seaweed and sprinkle it over your

The people of Okinawa in Japan regularly live to well over 100 and are renowned for their healthy hearts and low cholesterol levels. They have an ancient saying: 'Food is the key to health.' As well as practising mindfulness and having good social structures, they eat a wide variety of vegetables and fish and enjoy small amounts of seaweed as an important part of their diet.

Of course, it is only one factor in their healthy lifestyle, but increasingly research is showing that consumption of some sea vegetables may be beneficial to heart health. There are two seaweeds thought to be particularly beneficial – laver or porphyra (also known as 'nori' in Japan), and eastern wakame. Claims that these sea vegetables can lower cholesterol and improve blood flow are being investigated in Japan, and are showing very promising results.

meal. It contains potassium salts, so it tastes salty and it's much better for you. An added bonus is that other heart-friendly minerals such as magnesium are also present, as are iodine, selenium and calcium, which benefit the body in so many ways.

You can buy a variety of sea vegetables fresh from local delicatessens or fishmongers. Dried seaweeds are also available from most health food shops or can be purchased online.

My mantra is: eat small amounts of a wide variety of seaweeds.

OUR ESSENTIAL NUTRIENT NEEDS

Well-balanced meal plans look after both your general health and your waistline.

As abdominal or visceral fat builds up over time in us all, our risk of heart disease, type 2 diabetes and certain cancers increases. To eat well, we need to ensure that we get both the quantity and the quality of our calories right!

Your individual energy (calorie) requirements will vary depending on your age, metabolic rate and your level of activity and exercise. Remember that calories come from the three main nutrients in our food.

FAST FACTS ▶▶

▶ 1g carbohydrate (starch or sugar) contains approximately 4 kcal.

▶ 1g fat (any type) contains 9 kcal.

▶ 1g protein contains 4 kcal.

▶ 1g alcohol contains 7 kcal.

Vitamins and minerals have no calorie content, but they help us to release energy from fats, carbohydrates and proteins.

There are certain nutrients that we need to pay particular attention to during our middle years.

Plant and animal proteins

Protein is made up of a variety of building blocks called amino acids.

Some amino acids are essential as the body can't make them itself. While proteins from animal sources contain the complete mix of essential amino acids, few plants do. Soya, quinoa and hemp are a few of the plant foods containing all the essential amino acids. Most plant proteins provide varying combinations of these muscle-building blocks, so eating a mix of animal and plant proteins over the course of a week is a good way to ensure you meet your essential amino acids requirements.

- **Enjoy fish and shellfish at least twice a week.** A minimum of one portion of oily fish a week is recommended (salmon, sardines, mackerel, herring, trout, tuna). You can use canned fish but fresh is best. One portion of white fish is also recommended (sea bass, whiting, sole, haddock).

- **Eat lean cuts of red meat** (beef, lamb, venison, pork) approximately three times a week. The recommendation is to eat less than 500g of cooked lean red meat each week, so it might be a good idea to weigh your usual cooked portion.

- **Include poultry** such as chicken or turkey (free-range).

- **Include several eggs** each week (frittatas, omelettes, scrambled, poached, boiled). An egg a day is OK.

- **Include milk and milk products** (yogurt, kefir, cheese).

- If you're vegetarian, **include protein-rich alternatives** to meat, for example Quorn.

- Most importantly, **eat less processed meat** (salami, chorizo, sausage), cured and salted hams and more plant protein instead, such as:

  - Beans, peas, lentils (chickpea hummus, lentil soups, mixed bean salads)

  - Soya and soya products (tofu, tempeh, miso soup, soya milk)

  - Nuts and nut butters (cashew nut butter, almond nut butter)

  - Seeds (in breads, muesli, flapjacks, crackers, salads).

Iron

As we go through the menopause and thereafter, our need for iron diminishes.

Although red meat (beef, lamb, pork, venison) is the richest and most easily absorbed source of iron, a number of other foods can also make a significant contribution. To ensure a good intake, there are plenty of additional, everyday foods to top up your levels:

- All seafood
- Chicken and turkey
- Beans and lentils
- Leafy green vegetables
- Sesame seeds
- Nuts
- 100% wholemeal bread.

Iron is present in foods in two forms:

- **Haem iron:** Found in animal-derived foods such as lean red meat (beef, lamb and pork) and in poultry, oily fish like salmon, tuna and mackerel, liver and kidneys. This type of iron is very well absorbed by the body.

- **Non-haem iron:** Found mainly in fortified foods, such as breakfast cereals and breads, and naturally occurring in dark green leafy vegetables, peas, beans, lentils, egg yolk, nuts and even dried fruit. This type of iron is not very well absorbed.

The tannins in tea and coffee reduce the amount of iron your body can absorb from food, so take tea and coffee between your meals rather than with them. Avoid adding extra bran and wheatgerm to meals as this will also decrease the absorption of iron from plant foods.

Calcium

It's never too late to start looking after your bones. Making sure you get enough calcium is critical, particularly as you go through the menopause and for the first five years thereafter. Dairy foods (milk, yogurt, cheese) are some of the richest sources of bio-available calcium. Choosing lower-fat varieties to reduce the calorie and saturated fat content can allow you some wriggle room for a few weekly treats.

If you are not eating or drinking three servings of dairy products each day, make sure to get the equivalent calcium from:

- Soya milk, rice milk, oat milk, coconut milk or almond milk fortified with calcium
- Tofu

- Nuts and seeds

- Dried fruit

- Sea vegetables or seaweeds.

Vitamin D

Vitamin D helps the body absorb calcium from the foods we eat. It can be made in the skin through the action of sunlight. Just 20 minutes of sunlight on your hands, legs and face every day will help boost your stores of this essential vitamin. However, many of us (wearing UV protection) have to make a conscious effort to include vitamin D-rich foods in our meal plans as we cannot make enough through the action of sunlight on the skin, especially in countries that have a more northerly latitude, such as Ireland and the UK. Make sure your diet includes:

- **Oily fish**, twice a week if possible.

- **Eggs** (if your cholesterol is normal you can include seven plus per week; if your cholesterol is high reduce to between four and six per week).

- **Fortified foods** such as certain brands of soya milks, yogurts and cereals.

Vitamins B12 and B2

If you eat eggs and dairy products you probably won't run into problems with insufficient vitamin B12 and B2 intake. Vegetarians may need to top up on these nutrients by eating adequate amounts of:

- Milk, cheese and yogurt

- Eggs

- Yeast extract

- Soya milk, yogurts and desserts

- Fortified breakfast cereals.

If you are a strict vegetarian or vegan, a B-complex supplement would be beneficial.

Another B vitamin, pantothenic acid (found in wholegrain cereals, legumes, eggs, and meat), supports mental performance. Pantothenic acid, along with other B vitamins, plays an important role in maintaining emotional balance during and after menopause.

Omega-3 fatty acids

There are two types of omega-3 fatty acids:

- The long version, **docosahexaenoic acid (DHA)** and **eicosapentaenoic acid (EPA)**, found in oily fish such as salmon, sardines, mackerel, trout and tuna.

- The short version, **alpha-linolenic acid (ALA)**, found in vegetable oils. Shorter omega-3 fats may not have the same benefits as the longer ones. Although our bodies can convert some ALA into EPA and DHA, the conversion isn't very efficient.

Vegetarians and vegans can obtain omega-3 fatty acids from ALA-rich plant sources, and should aim for an ALA intake of 1.5 per cent of energy or roughly 4g per day. Good plant sources of ALA are:

- Chia seeds and flaxseeds

- Walnuts and walnut oil

- Camelina, rapeseed and soya oils.

Some brands of milled flaxseed can contain up to 6g of ALA in a 30g portion (2 dessertspoons).

If you don't like to eat fish, you may want to consider a supplement made from algae-derived DHA or a flaxseed-based supplement. Your pharmacist will advise.

Selenium, zinc and iodine

Meat, fish and nuts are good sources of selenium and zinc. If you're not eating meat or fish, make sure you include two or three Brazil nuts in your daily diet. Choose these often when you are opting for a nutty snack.

One in 10 of us is thought to be iodine-deficient, which can cause sore breasts and hypothyroidism. The best way to ensure you are getting enough iodine is to include sea vegetables, seafood and four to six eggs per week in your diet.

HOW MUCH SHOULD WE BE EATING?

While there are no hard and fast rules, the following guiding principles are set out to help you meet your basic nutrient needs. If you frequently miss these targets, the chances are there are some nutrient gaps that could cause problems in the long term. Remember that balance is all important. Eating too much or too little of any one group of foods is unwise.

Fruit and vegetables

These provide phytonutrients, vitamins, minerals and fibre and you should be aiming for at least five servings a day. Eat a rainbow of colour! Each day, aim to have at least one dark green vegetable (broccoli, cabbage, rocket, spinach) for potassium, iron and folic acid; at least one red fruit or vegetable (tomatoes, watermelon, peppers) for lycopene; at least one type of berry or citrus fruit (raspberries, blueberries, oranges) for immune-boosting flavonoids and vitamin C; and at least one orange/yellow fruit or vegetable (carrots, orange peppers, mango) for antioxidants and beta-carotene.

Choose a minimum of five servings (two fruits and three vegetables) for essential antioxidants, fibre, vitamins and minerals. One serving is any of the following:

▶ 3 heaped tablespoons cooked vegetables or salad

▶ 200ml home-made vegetable soup

▶ 1 medium fruit, for example a banana or apple

▶ 2 small fruits, for example plums or satsumas

▶ 2 tablespoons cooked fruit

▶ 150ml glass fruit juice (if you are trying to lose weight, it is best to avoid all juices, whether they are freshly squeezed with bits in or shop-bought. They all are low in the fibre which helps to fill us. Eat the fruit instead).

Bread, cereals and potatoes

These provide energy for the brain, food for healthy gut bacteria and fibre for a healthy digestive tract. Try to enjoy four to six servings a day. Eat fewer servings if you are overweight and more if you are very active. The more you exercise, the higher your energy requirements and the more carbohydrate you can enjoy. Just make sure it's fibre-rich and filling, not sugary and refined.

Start each day with two servings. Aim to have another two at lunch and two with dinner rather than excessive amounts at any one meal. Make sure you choose wholegrain varieties of bread, breakfast cereals, quinoa, pasta and rice to boost your fibre intake.

Choose your fillings and toppings carefully. Olive-based spreads and oils are good choices, and choose tomato-based sauces instead of cream-based sauces. Eat potatoes with their skins on – baked potatoes or baby boiled potatoes.

A serving is:

▶ 1 slice 100 per cent wholemeal/wholegrain bread

▶ 3 dessertspoons uncooked porridge oats or unsweetened muesli

▶ 1 medium potato, 2 baby potatoes or the equivalent weight of sweet potato

▶ 3 dessertspoons cooked quinoa, brown rice or pasta.

Milk and dairy products

This food group provides calcium for bone health, vitamins A and D and protein. Include two to three servings a day.

If you are trying to manage or lose weight, use lower-fat dairy products and choose natural yogurt, Greek yogurt and lower-fat cheeses. Swap full-fat milk for low-fat or skimmed milk in your latte or cappuccino.

A serving is any of the following:

▶ 200ml milk

▶ 125g yogurt

▶ 30g cheese (matchbox-sized piece).

If you are avoiding dairy products, make sure you use soya/nut/rice alternatives that are fortified with calcium and additional nutrients.

Protein-rich foods

These provide protein, some minerals such as iron, zinc, selenium and phytoestrogens. Include two to three servings a day. Choose seafood, chicken and turkey, eggs, pulses and beans (especially soya beans).

Beans, pulses and lentils can bulk out meals and are a valuable source of soluble fibre and phytoestrogens. Reduce red meat dinners to three times per week and cut down or cut out processed meats. Meat or fish should be grilled or roasted rather than barbecued or heavily fried.

One serving is any of the following:

- 130g cooked fish (eat a minimum of 1 oily and 1 white fish per week)
- 100g cooked lean meat or poultry
- 2 eggs
- 6 tablespoons peas, beans or lentils.

Essential fats and oils

These provide energy, essential fatty acids and fat-soluble vitamins. Fat is essential for helping the body to absorb and transport fat-soluble vitamins. It supplies us with essential fatty acids that the body can't make. Fat is also a structural component of the brain, supplies energy for body cells, produces hormones and protects and cushions our internal organs. It's the quality (or type) and the balance of different fats in our diet that's important.

Try to use as little spread and oil as possible (regardless of type) if you are trying to lose or manage your weight. You still need fat but you need to shift the balance in favour of the healthy fats by choosing oily fish, some nuts and seeds and an avocado during the week.

- **Oily fish** (salmon, sardines, mackerel, herring) twice a week will provide you with essential omega-3 fatty acids.
- **Choose camelina, olive or rapeseed oil** instead of blended vegetable oils.
- **Nuts and seeds** are also good providers of healthy fats, so snack on a handful of these a day (try to choose unsalted versions). If you are slimming, don't choose these as frequently.
- **A serving of avocado** is half an avocado.

MANAGING YOUR SYMPTOMS THROUGH DIET

Many symptoms associated with the menopause can successfully be controlled through choosing a healthy balance of the right foods, in the right quantities.

Hot flushes and night sweats

As many as three out of four western women experience hot flushes, which is at odds with our Asian counterparts (only 20 per cent of women in Japan and China report having them). Although genetic differences are a factor, their traditional food regime, which contains large amounts of phytoestrogen-rich soya-based foods, is also important. Typically their daily consumption is somewhere between 10 and 20 times the amount of soya isoflavones that we consume in the west.

Phytoestrogens are naturally occurring compounds found in plant foods. They are structurally similar to human oestrogen and can be divided into three main types: isoflavones, lignans and coumestans.

▶ **Isoflavones** (genistein, daidzein, glycitein, equol) are mainly found in soya beans and soya products, chickpeas and other legumes, nuts and nut butters and wholegrains.

▶ **Lignans** (enterolactone, enterodiol) are primarily found in seeds and seed oils (such as flaxseed oil) and legumes.

▶ **Coumestans** (coumestrol) can be found in alfalfa and clover.

Isoflavones are plant phytoestrogens. They have a similar but not identical structure to our oestrogen hormone. They are also far weaker – it's estimated that they are over 10,000 times weaker than our own oestrogen.

Source: www.bda.uk.com

Isoflavone supplements

Phytoestrogens, like human oestrogens, are complex and seem to have varying effects on tissues in the body. Interestingly, phytoestrogens can have both an oestrogenic and an anti-oestrogenic effect on our human oestrogen receptors. It seems that in some cases they may work in our favour, but in high doses they may not. Research is ongoing but it's probably wise to avoid large and potent doses of concentrated phytoestrogen in supplement form, unless you are working with a qualified herbal doctor.

Isoflavone-rich food

Eating isoflavone-rich foods can help diminish hot flushes and night sweats. Isoflavones are also thought to have positive effects on breast, heart and bone health. They are anti-coagulant, antioxidant and anti-inflammatory.

Although some studies imply that phytoestrogens have little effect on the risk of breast cancer, others suggest that high isoflavone levels are linked to an increased risk of breast cancer. Further research is necessary as this is a contentious issue.

We recommend eating foods naturally rich in isoflavones in regular and moderate quantities and to avoid mega doses of isoflavones in supplement form. Even women with breast cancer can enjoy a moderate intake of tofu and edamame beans.

Eating too many isoflavone-rich foods may have a negative effect on cognitive function as we age. High intakes may also inhibit important thyroid enzymes in the body. This is a real health concern, especially where there is borderline iodine deficiency.

Gastrointestinal changes

Fluctuating hormones can also aggravate the gastrointestinal tract and symptoms such as bloating and discomfort can occur more frequently. To keep your gastrointestinal tract in good working order:

▶ Take a probiotic after one or more courses of antibiotics.

▶ Stay fully hydrated by drinking up to two litres of water each day.

▶ Eat sufficient fibre-rich foods daily – approximately 25 g/day.

▶ If your symptoms are severe, discuss them with your doctor.

Irritable Bowel Syndrome (IBS)

IBS affects approximately one in five women. It is characterised by chronic and relapsing symptoms such as abdominal pain and discomfort, bloating, wind, distension and altered bowel habits.

Until relatively recently, we had little success in managing IBS, but pioneering research carried out in Monash University, Melbourne, discovered FODMAPs.

FODMAPs are certain carbohydrates (sugars) found in common foods that are poorly absorbed by IBS sufferers. When these FODMAPs are insufficiently absorbed in the small intestine, they continue along the gastrointestinal tract, arriving at the large intestine, where they act as a food source for the bacteria that live there. The bacteria then ferment these FODMAPs, causing the symptoms of IBS.

In many cases, FODMAPs are healthy foods and ones that we would not recommend you omit unless they are triggering symptoms. Managing them in the diet with the help of a dietitian provides great relief and a real opportunity for reducing what can be very debilitating symptoms.

FODMAPs

FERMENTABLE	The process through which gut bacteria break down undigested carbohydrate to produce gases (hydrogen, methane and carbon dioxide)
OLIGO-SACCARIDES	Fructo-oligosaccharides (FOS) – found in wheat, rye, onions and garlic Galacto-oligosaccharides (GOS) – found in legumes and pulses
DI-SACCHARIDES	Lactose – found in milk, yogurt and cheese, and anything made from these
MONO-SACCHARIDES	Fructose (in excess of glucose) – found in honey, apples and high-fructose corn syrups
POLYOLS	Sugar polyols (sorbitol, mannitol) – found in some fruit and vegetables and used as artificial sweeteners

No single approach will work for everyone, but a low FODMAP diet has been shown to be effective for up to 70 per cent of those with IBS.

In general, three consultations are required with a qualified dietitian trained in the use of the low FODMAP diet.

At the first consultation, foods high in FODMAPs are excluded from the diet (for up to eight weeks). This may seem like a long time, but many people report improvements in their symptoms after as little as two weeks.

At the second consultation, the dietitian will outline the specific method for reintroducing foods in order to identify the trigger food(s). This can take between four and six weeks.

At the last consultation, the trigger foods and related groups of foods are noted and the dietitian will recommend suitable alternatives for long-term symptom relief. The overall variety and balance of your diet may need some adjustment to ensure a full complement of nutrients.

Cravings

It's rare to hear something along the lines of 'Oh my God, I came in the door after a tough day and I was just craving broccoli, so much so that I had a massive binge on vegetables'. That's because not all food is problematic. It seems that we only struggle with the most desirable sugary and fatty foods, the ones that are the least nutritious. These are known as hyper-palatable foods. A preference for energy-dense, sweet and sometimes fatty foods can become a problem, a big, weighty problem. This in turn can increase your risk of diabetes and metabolic syndrome.

Food addiction research in still in its infancy but the need to understand our behaviour around food has never been more pressing. We live in an environment with so many opportunities to consume calories (energy) and so few opportunities to burn them off. We eat when we are physically hungry, but also to reward, soothe or comfort ourselves. For some, even when they know their food choices are not helping their waistlines and health, they can't seem to stop. They might really want to stop eating the way they do, but they simply feel they can't.

WE ARE BORN WITH A NATURAL PREDISPOSITION TO ACCEPT SWEET-TASTING FOODS OVER SOUR-TASTING FOODS – BUT AN ACCEPTANCE, PREFERENCE OR CRAVING FOR SUGAR AND SWEET THINGS IS NOT THE SAME AS AN ADDICTION.

When we eat, the hormone dopamine is released in an area of the brain called the reward centre. We interpret this dopamine signal as 'pleasure' and our brain programming makes us want to eat these foods again and again. Many of us recall times when we have rewarded or comforted ourselves with a chocolate-biscuit dopamine spike, despite the fact that we were doing our best to avoid the biscuit tin.

Dr John Menzies, a University of Edinburgh researcher who studies the neuroscience of hyper-palatable foods, argues that there's not enough evidence to show that certain foods are addictive in the same way that alcohol or cigarettes are addictive. He believes that it is more appropriate to think about it as an *eating* addiction, not a *food* addiction. This shifts the focus away from the food itself and gets us to examine our relationship with food.

Sugar is not a poison in itself. It's the dose (amount) that maketh the poison, as they say. When we repeatedly select processed sugary and fatty foods, they hijack our neural pathways and flood the brain with dopamine. Happy days – until we notice the kilos gathering around the middle.

Interestingly, some studies have found that hyper-palatable foods flood the brain with more dopamine than healthy foods like eggs or apples. Is this because we psychologically attach attributes to these foods when we are shown images? How delicious they taste, how indulgent, how rewarding, because we're 'worth it'?

Cravings seem to have little to do with real hunger. Hunger is caused by complex physiological signals in the brain that trigger us to eat. Cravings are more to do with our brain calling for reward. Ask yourself – having finished a really tough article/project/day, is this why you crave something sweet/salty/alcoholic, even when your appetite has already been satisfied by dinner?

Some women eat foods that are rich in natural sugars and distract themselves with sugar-free drinks, chewing gum or mints. Others brush or gargle with an antiseptic mouthwash right after dinner. Sugary foods don't taste good right after you've gargled. Getting absorbed in something to avoid thinking about food works for some. Yes, eating sugar can raise your serotonin levels and elevate your mood, but taking exercise can also have the same positive effect. So walk away!

Hyper-palatable sweets and treats are undoubtedly unhealthy in excess. Many contain highly refined carbohydrates and hydrogenated fats. At the same time they are very low in fibre, protein, vitamins and minerals. We all know this. Yet many sleep-deprived menopausal women armed with this knowledge find themselves digging into junk food, despite knowing better. Why some of us and not others are unable to control our intake remains a hot research topic.

Most of us know what it's like to have a longing for a food we love and simply must have! Cravings appear to be inherently linked to feelings of deprivation.

Overly restrictive diets often leave us feeling deprived. Studies suggest that avoiding certain foods altogether often makes them irresistible. Deep down, we think that if we satisfy our craving, that uncomfortable feeling of deprivation will go away. But unfortunately, it doesn't always work that way.

Cravings may be psychological, physiological or both. We just don't know. Some people believe that their cravings are linked to an innate need to supply the body with specific nutrients it lacks, but the jury is still out on the true cause of food cravings. However, many experts agree that cravings are indeed linked to brain chemistry and may occur when you don't eat enough or you go too long without eating. The hungrier you are, the more you have a yen for foods that you might not otherwise crave.

To help prevent cravings, don't skip meals. Snack between meals on low glycaemic index foods such as fruit or a small handful of nuts. If you still find yourself in the middle of a craving, you can take one of three approaches. First, you can try to ignore or suppress the craving. Second, you can give in and succumb to the craving. Or third, you can choose to neither suppress nor succumb to the craving. You can simply acknowledge the craving, sit with it (mindfully or consciously) and watch it pass.

It's a bit like a wave. Visualise yourself up to your knees in water, watching a wave start to build out at sea. You can turn your back and try to ignore it, but you won't stop that wave coming. It will simply knock you off balance as it catches you unawares. Alternatively, you can submit to it, throw yourself helplessly into it and allow it to carry you off. Or you can observe the wave approaching, eyeball it, dig your feet firmly into the sand, take the jolt but remain standing as it passes.

It helps if you find a way to enjoy the foods you like in reasonable amounts so you can stay slim. It's about giving yourself permission to eat *what* you want, but not necessarily as much as you want. If you know you won't be satisfied with small amounts of your favourite high-calorie foods (instead of one bar, you end up eating three chocolate bars and the entire packet of biscuits), then abstinence is your best policy, at least for a number of weeks, until you crack that chemical cycle.

Make a conscious effort to:

- ▸ Take a moment to appreciate what is on your plate before tucking in.

- ▸ Make an occasion of eating by setting a table for a meal.

- ▸ Eat like you are always eating in company!

- ▸ Eat meals at fixed times.

- ▸ Not eat standing up or when you're rushing.

- ▸ Not eat with a screen in the same room.

- ▸ Not eat in the car.

- ▸ Not eat for an emotional need like boredom.

Dehydration

Water is responsible for transporting nutrients in the blood as well as getting rid of waste. Without enough water, we simply don't function well and headaches can occur. You can check your hydration by noting the frequency, colour and volume of your urine. Your urine should be pale, not dark, yellow. Don't worry if it's not pale first thing in the morning. Urine is concentrated overnight and is much darker in colour first thing in the morning. Aim to drink as much water as it takes (usually one to two litres) to keep your urine pale in colour.

Alcohol

A delicious meal with a glass of red wine is something we should cherish and enjoy, but it's putting the cork back in the bottle that's the problem for many of us. It's also a problem for our hydration the following day.

A woman's body processes alcohol more slowly than a man's. This is because a woman's body contains less water and more fat. As fat retains alcohol while water dilutes it, alcohol remains at higher concentrations for longer periods of time in a woman's body, exposing her brain and other organs to more alcohol. Women have lower levels of the enzyme alcohol dehydrogenase, which breaks down alcohol in the body. All in all, women are simply not built to handle large quantities.

Reducing alcohol, rather than eliminating it, is a big challenge, especially if you have an all-or-nothing mindset. The maximum weekly recommendation is no more than 11 standard drinks.

FAST FACTS ▸▸

▸ A standard drink equates to about 10g pure alcohol. Your liver can detox approximately one standard drink each hour.

▸ A standard drink is 125ml wine or a half pint of beer. A naggin of spirits (200ml) contains six standard drinks.

▸ A glass of wine poured at home is usually much bigger than 125 ml!

▸ Alcohol is high in calories. In fact, it is second only to fat in terms of calorific content per gram. It gives us 7 kcal per gram.

▸ A 125ml glass of white wine contains 95–100 kcal.

▸ A 125ml glass of red wine contains approximately 85 kcal.

▸ A 35ml measure of gin has about 85 kcal.

▸ A vodka and Coke has about 200 kcal – but you can save about 100 kcal by having Diet Coke.

Why Not?

Career Anxiety

The Empty Nest.

The Divorce.

CHAPTER 3

Weight

Don't put anything else into your mouth, like your projects, your worries, your fear, just put the food in.

Thich Nhat Hahn, Buddhist monk

We all find managing our weight more difficult after our 20s. We have so many opportunities to eat and so few to be active, and if we don't really work at it, the weight tends to creep up as we get older and become less active. This happens regardless of our gender. Energy balance is difficult, full stop! And the landscape around us verifies that, with the majority of people in developed countries classified as either overweight or obese.

Women over 40 face some additional challenges. We might have pretty much sailed through our 30s and early 40s with only the need for a bit of tweaking to our calorie intake or exercise regime. Nothing we couldn't handle – that is, until our late 40s, when it all seems to go to pot. Menopot, that is! The waist seems to be a magnet for new fat deposits that are stubborn to shift.

IS WEIGHT GAIN INEXTRICABLY LINKED TO MENOPAUSE?

There's no doubt that many women complain about weight gain at this time. But the causes are many and it would be wrong to blame all weight gain on the menopause transition. It's important to take time to reflect on the bigger picture and how this impacts your individual body weight. We are all different.

TRY THIS ▼

Write down the reasons for your weight gain. These may include:

▸ Increased levels of stress and anxious nibbling

▸ Hot flushes, sleep deprivation and decreased energy levels

▸ Decreased activity or exercise

▸ A sluggish thyroid and slowing metabolism

▸ Side effects of medication

▸ Declining and worsening eating habits

▸ Quitting smoking.

If you need help deciphering what you need to focus on, keep a food, mood and activity diary for a few weeks and then book a consultation with a qualified dietitian· or your doctor. Together you can work through some of the issues and develop strategies to address them.

––––––––––––

For some women, hormonal fluctuations will play havoc with their waistline. But for the majority of us, it's a combination of fluctuating hormones *and* our age and lifestyle. Focusing solely on hormones leaves us with few options and little hope. Taking a wider approach allows us to make small but significant changes across the board to adjust our weight.

IS IT JUST HORMONES OR ARE THERE OTHER CONTRIBUTING FACTORS?

Age and lifestyle can also contribute to weight gain. As we age, we can experience:

▸ Decreased flexibility and suppleness

▸ Deteriorating physical activity owing to other demands on our time, lack of interest or fear of injury

▸ Slowing metabolism owing to a natural loss of muscle and an increase in body fat.

Our lifestyle changes too, often imperceptibly, resulting in reduced energy expenditure owing to:

▸ Easing amounts of work around the house and in the workplace

▸ Less intensity in day-to-day chores and more leisure time

▸ More socialising, eating out and increased alcohol intake.

It's hopeless to just surrender. Focus on what you can achieve simply by bringing your full attention to the most important issue and taking some corrective action.

Hormones affect our levels of hunger and appetite, how satisfied we feel after eating, how quickly we burn calories and how and where we store body fat. It's understandable then that we might experience weight changes as our hormone levels shift and alter before and during the menopause.

Without corrective action, many women will accumulate weight gradually, some reporting as much as 0.5kg per year during the peri-menopause years, some even more. Being aware of the effect hormones can have on weight allows us to makes choices to prevent unwanted baggage around the middle. Knowing what approach to take is only half the battle. Taking the necessary action is key.

What about your genes?

Genes can influence your weight, but they don't have to be your weight destiny. Your lifestyle and food choices have a much more significant impact on your weight.

THE IMPORTANCE OF SLEEP

If your sleep is constantly disrupted, it interferes with the normal functioning of your hunger hormone, ghrelin. This means your ability to regulate your appetite is impaired. You may find yourself picking at carbohydrate-rich snacks you would rather do without. It can also lead to a drop in satiety, which is governed by another hormone, leptin. Even if you are picking more, you're less satisfied and may continue to nibble despite your best efforts (see Chapter 11: Sleep).

“ I could barely even drag myself out of bed when the night sweats were bad, never mind going to the gym or for a walk. Sleep deprivation is torture. I've had them for the best part of five years now and am wondering will they ever let up. ”
– Anne

It's vital to pay attention to your sleeping pattern and to seek support or help if you need it. Determine how frequently you're waking and why. Is it because of sleep apnoea, restless leg syndrome, night sweats or to visit the bathroom? The latter can be helped by avoiding fluids, especially caffeinated drinks and alcohol, for four to six hours before going to bed.

A NATURAL DECELERATION IN METABOLIC RATES

We all experience a drop in metabolic rate as we age. It's true. The number of calories we need decreases as we get older. We don't want to hear that, but we must; otherwise weight gain is inevitable. This decline in calories is due to decreasing muscle mass (which burns a lot of calories) and increasing fat mass (which burns comparatively fewer calories). Some studies show a decline in basal metabolic rate of about 2 to 5 per cent per decade. The decline seems to be most rapid after 40 in men and 50 in women (see Chapter 2: Food).

With this small decrease in our ability to burn calories, commiting to an exercise and fitness programme is necessary if we are to minimise weight gain. Our bodies are designed to move, and sitting all day can be a disaster for our bodies and brains. Becoming more active is certain to benefit your mood and limbs and is the best way to avoid a sizeable decrease in your metabolic rate.

It seems unfair that just as the pace of life relaxes and our children become more independent, we can't spend more of our leisure time nibbling a sweet add-on to the latte or lunch with friends. But if you want to retain your shape and waistline, you've simply got to be clever about your meal plans!

The science bit

While factors that influence weight gain during the menopausal transition are not fully understood, a MONET study investigated changes in calories burned during menopause. Their results suggested that menopausal transition is accompanied with a decline in calories burned, mainly characterised by a decrease in physical activity and a shift to a more sedentary lifestyle. This is good news if you like exercise. If you don't, it's time to learn to like it.

There's little we can do about our genes, gender and aggravating hormones, but our lifestyles are hugely adjustable and can either work for us or against us in terms of our waistlines.

TAKING CONTROL OF YOUR WEIGHT AND HEALTH

Oestrogen levels decline during the peri-menopause years, which usually begin in the 40s (and sometimes in the 30s). There is a further decline in oestrogen and progesterone when menstruation ends. Changes to the way the body stores fat occur during the transition. We are more likely to deposit fat around the middle, in and around the organs in the abdomen in particular. This visceral fat is different from the subcutaneous fat that is found just under the skin. So not only does the menopause diminish our ability to burn fat, it also causes us to store more fat and in different places.

Think health, not weight

Weighing yourself on a bathroom scales tells you little or nothing about your health. It doesn't take into account your age, your gender or even your height. Now is an important time to stop chasing the needle on the scales and start focusing on your body composition.

BMI calculators are found on many health websites, but your BMI alone is not a particularly useful measurement either. It's only a ratio of your weight and height. When it's used as part of a wider assessment with a body composition analysis, then it can be a useful gauge to assess your risk of disease. The risk of developing diabetes, for example, becomes 10 times higher at a BMI of 30 and over when there is a high level of visceral fat or fat around the middle.

A substantial body of evidence suggests that heart disease, stroke and peripheral arterial disease are all more common after the menopause.

The question we need to ask is not 'What weight should I be?', but 'What is a comfortable weight for me? One that would help lower my risk of disease and one that would allow me the energy and vitality to look and feel my best? One where my visceral fat is not too high?'

Fat analysis

Visceral or 'deep' fat wraps around organs such as the liver and heart. It drives up the risk of the diseases listed above, even dementia. If you have a large waistline or too much belly fat, then you probably have more visceral fat than is healthy. This deep fat churns out hormones associated with insulin resistance and glucose intolerance, increasing your risk of diabetes. It also produces proteins called cytokines, which can trigger low-level inflammation and metabolic abnormalities, risk factors for heart disease and dementia.

Subcutaneous fat, on the other hand, the pinchable padding we carry directly under our skin, may look unattractive, but has not been considered a health threat. However, evidence is emerging that the danger of belly fat lies not only in the deep visceral fat, but also in our subcutaneous fat in that region. It's difficult to determine the levels of visceral and subcutaneous belly fat except by CT scanning or with a BodPod which, of course, is not cost-effective outside of research.

Callipers gauge subcutaneous fat only, so they are not particularly useful. However, many hospitals, dietitians and clinics are now using body composition analysers to help us understand what is going on inside the body. These analysers compartmentalise weight into 'muscle mass', 'percentage of body water' and 'body fat'. Estimates of visceral and subcutaneous fat are given by bioelectric impedance. Changes in weight can be tracked and this type of measurement is simple, discreet and reliable.

Before standing on the scales, ideally you should not:

▸ Eat or drink for at least 30 minutes

▸ Exercise for at least 12 hours

▸ Drink alcohol for at least 48 hours

▸ Take any diuretics, unless prescribed by your doctor.

You should urinate 30 minutes before the measurement is taken. Perhaps the simplest way to check for fat around your middle is to measure your waistline with a tape measure. Women should aim for a waist circumference that is less than 88cm. It won't give you a breakdown of visceral versus subcutaneous fat, but it's a pretty good measure of risk.

According to Dr Samuel Klein, Professor of Medicine and Nutritional Science at Washington University School of Medicine, how you lose fat is important. Klein led an interesting study that showed that obese patients could instantly lose 13.5kg or more of subcutaneous fat through liposuction. However, there were no health benefits. Blood pressure, cholesterol and glucose control were not improved by this weight loss procedure and it had no impact on visceral fat levels. Liposuction is definitely not a substitute for eating well and regular exercise.

The bottom line is that when it comes to visceral fat, the solution is not in fat-loss supplements or a few sit-ups. Crunches, the plank and sit-ups can certainly tone the abdominal muscles and improve your shape, but a tailored exercise and eating programme is unequalled.

Hormonal changes during our middle years increase the rate at which women store visceral fat. When our oestrogen levels falls below a certain threshold, it switches on the production of an enzyme, Aldh1, which plays a key role in fat formation, specifically increasing visceral fat around the organs.

▶ As our hormones fluctuate during our middle years, we are much more likely to experience weight gain and fat redistribution in our bodies.

▶ Unfortunately, a normal feature of getting older is a slowing metabolism, setting the stage for weight gain. Women approaching menopause have particular cause for concern – that muffin top!

▶ Women typically begin picking up about 0.5kg each year during peri-menopause if they suffer from aggravating symptoms.

▶ With conscious effort, we can fend off those additional kilos. By focusing on some of the lifestyle factors that lead to weight gain such as unmanaged stress, reduced physical activity, poor eating habits, excessive alcohol consumption and disrupted sleep, we don't have to submit passively to an increase in dress size.

WANT TO LOSE WEIGHT? CHANGE YOUR BEHAVIOUR

We all know that by changing eating and activity habits, it is possible to change our weight. Patterns of eating and activity are learned behaviours and we can change them if we have a mind to do so. In order to sustain these changes in the long term, the environment around us must change too.

Examine your eating and activity patterns carefully.

▶ **Recognise the stressors in your life** and think about how you can manage them (you are time-starved, rushed each morning, eat no breakfast, grab a quick snack with more calories and less nutrition than a proper breakfast).

▶ **Think of a stimulus that triggers you to eat** (you stop for a coffee-to-go, smell the fresh baking aroma and buy a croissant without intending to!). The trigger and the learned behaviour must be un-paired.

▶ **Be solutions-oriented.** If you believe it's all downhill after that mid-morning junky snack, what can you do to prevent it happening?

▶ **Work around the challenges** in new ways. Instead of beating yourself up and being self-critical, reduce your negative thinking and focus on finding a positive outcome/action (you buy a good travel mug, fill the kettle the night before, be as ready as you can to grab and go).

▸ **Set yourself little tests** in self-control when you're ready (you stop to buy a coffee but you only buy the coffee).

▸ **Find some support.** Ask a friend to help you make the change. Their encouragement is always good to have and they may even join you in your quest for a healthier start to the day.

▸ **Find comfort and gratitude in other things** (massage, music, writing, open fire, reading, photography, nature, etc.).

Are you motivated and ready?

You can have the desire to change but it may not be matched by the appropriate action. 'Wanting' is the easy part. Your motivation for change comes when you identify a discrepancy between where you are and where you would like to be: 'I don't like being so overweight. I used to be 18kg lighter 10 years ago.' Your readiness to change will be influenced by:

▸ How important you perceive the change to be

▸ How confident you feel in making and maintaining the changes.

Are you prepared to put the work in?

Plan and prepare! There is no shortcut to success. First, write down your SMART goal:

1. Specific and to the point

2. Manageable and realistic

3. Achievable given your circumstances

4. Relevant to your value system and guiding principles

5. Time specific. You can make a short-term, interim and a long-term goal.

Then, identify personal saboteurs (your negative thought processes, your freezer contents). Finally, self-monitoring with a food diary can help you examine things that are going well and things that require further attention.

Write down the change you want to make:

▸ List positives and negatives for you.

▸ List positives and negatives for others (partner, children, friends).

Play close attention to the negatives. These can be barriers or stumbling blocks. Find ways around these or they may sabotage you.

The positives will help you stay focused. They can motivate you when times get tough!

Write out two clear goals – one on your eating habits and one on activity. Think of answers to the following questions:

▸ Why do you want to reach this goal?

▸ What are you prepared to do to get there?

▸ How will you know if you succeed?

▸ What could get in your way?

▸ How could you handle that obstacle?

▸ What steps do you need to take to achieve this goal?

▸ What will your reward be for reaching that goal?

▸ What, if any, help will you need?

▸ Who will help you?

▸ When will you start making the change?

▸ When will you review your progress and how often?

MAKE YOUR THOUGHTS COUNT

We all have negative thoughts at times. These are generally unhelpful and self-defeating. Learn to question, challenge and pick holes in your negative thoughts.

You might think, 'I'm never going to lose this weight. I've tried everything and it just won't budge from my middle! I eat healthy food.'

▸ Is there another way of viewing the problem that might be more helpful?

- Is the thought really accurate? What evidence do you have for the thought? Would that evidence stand up in court?

- Try to come up with a more helpful positive alternative. How would you advise a friend who was thinking that way?

Your alternative thought might be, 'Hmm – my old approach to shifting excess weight isn't working any more. I probably need a fresh approach but not a gimmicky one. And there are things I've never really tried, at least for any decent time frame. Maybe I could get an exercise plan from a personal trainer. I thought I was active enough but maybe I'm not. I could start monitoring my steps and work-outs with a smartphone app. I can run first thing in the morning now that it's getting lighter.'

THE POWER OF POSITIVE THINKING

The way we think about losing weight affects how we feel about slimming. This in turn affects how we respond to or behave around food. It can influence you in a positive way and help keep you on track.

TRY THIS ▼

Think out some positive coping thoughts for the following negatives:

- It's no good. I'll never be able to make myself exercise.

- I'm hopeless. I've had five chocolate bars already this week. I just can't say no!

- I can't not go out with friends! I've been invited to dinner and it's Friday. I know there will be too much wine, lovely food and a gorgeous cheeseboard. It's hopeless.

- I'll never be able to wear jeans with confidence.

- I know I'll feel hungry.

- I'm always tired in the evening. I'll never be able to prepare healthy meals.

- I'm useless. I know I need to lose weight. My doctor says my cholesterol, blood pressure and back pain will improve but I've no will power. I'll never be slim again.

Ask yourself these questions:

- Are overweight people really hopeless, useless, worthless, lazy?

- How many people do you know who really agree with that appraisal?
- Do you really believe you can measure your self-worth in kilos?
- Is it really fair to validate yourself solely on the basis of your body size or shape?

Most importantly what are the things you like best about yourself, the things that instinctively make you know you're more than just your weight? How would your friends and family answer that question?

Supporting yourself in your thoughts is not the same as letting yourself off the hook but allowing yourself to make mistakes!

- You don't have to be perfect in order to keep going with your plan.
- Of course you would prefer not to lapse but if you do, it doesn't mean that you or your change plan are a total failure.
- You can use a slip-up as a chance to learn how to deal with risky eating situations in the future.

What is the effect of thinking the way you do?

Many self-defeating thoughts have some sort of pay-off. This is why you keep having them. Maybe they allow you to avoid situations that you find difficult.

Don't give up before you even start.

Self-defeating thought: 'This is hopeless. I should be able to manage making changes to my diet by now. I'm never going to get on top of this.'

Positive answer: 'What I want to do is control my eating and improve my health. Thinking this way is not going to help me to do that. It's no good telling myself I should be doing better. I need to practise more. If I keep putting myself down I will give up instead of trying. Yesterday was a good day. What really helped me then?'

Don't condemn yourself.

Self-defeating thought: 'I just can't control myself. I ate everything I was served in the restaurant last night, even though I'd already planned what I was going to have. I'm just weak.'

Positive answer: 'If one swallow doesn't make a summer, than one slip doesn't make me a weak person. I really got it right at the party last week. In fact, my partner keeps telling me how strong I am for sticking with things so far. I need to move on and remember that 6 kilos I've already lost. I'm nearly there.'

Look at your strengths.
Self-defeating thought: 'The only reason I'm losing weight now is because I'm attending the dietitian. Once I finish the seven-week programme, I'll never keep things going.'

Positive answer: 'Yes, attending the dietitian has helped me to start making changes, but it's me that's doing all the hard work. It will take determination to keep going but I've proved to myself that I have the know-how and motivation now. No one is going to hand me self-control. I have it within me. I can decide to use it or not – it's my choice.'

Don't expect to be perfect.
Self-defeating thought: 'I'm never going to eat chocolate again. It's evil.'

Positive answer: 'It's just not helpful to tell myself that. Of course there will be some occasions where I choose to eat chocolate. Saying 'never' is just setting myself up for failure. But just for now, so that I feel in control, I'm going to limit it to two bars a week – or maybe I'll cut it out for six weeks altogether. I can make a conscious decision to eat it again when I'm ready.'

Change is difficult, but not impossible.
Self-defeating thought: 'I already know all this nutrition stuff. I've heard it before at the local slimming club. It didn't help me then, so I can't see how it's going to help me now.'

Positive answer: 'Yes, I know a lot about what changes I need to make, but this is also helping me think about how to make these changes. If I'm willing to give it a go because I know deep down I need a balanced and sustainable approach, maybe I could surprise myself. It will be very gradual but it won't be short-term. It may be slow but if I persevere, the result will be permanent this time.'

What could others do to help?

Are there people who can help you achieve your behaviour change?

▸ A friend or sister who could exercise with you?

▸ A friend who won't constantly tempt you with just the one glass of wine too many?

▸ A partner who could avoid bringing home treat foods until a weekend night?

What if you are hungry all the time?

If you are hungry – eat! But first, make sure you know what you are hungry for. Often it's not food we are hungry for but:

▸ Relief from boredom

▸ Affection

▸ A way to relieve anger or sadness

▸ A way to deal with loneliness or stress.

Your brain is in charge. The body follows. It's not the other way around. You see and smell food. You salivate. You feel the desire to eat. You overeat. Your body feels stuffed rather than satisfied. Then your brain starts rationalising and justifying. Your blood sugar was too low. Your body needed to eat. Your appetite and hunger signals were too strong. You tell yourself, 'There was no avoiding that binge'.

When you are consciously aware, your body and mind are involved together in the decision process. Your body's hunger is acknowledged. You eat. The brain checks in too. 'When is my next meal time? If I have just a snack now, could it keep me going until then? Do I need more than a snack? Could I push dinnertime forward and hold the snack till the evening? Is what I'm eating now really helping me get to where I want to go?'

Just because we feel hunger doesn't mean we should lose ourselves in it. A little hunger is fine. It's to be welcomed. Your body is adapting to fewer calories and a new eating plan. It's just letting you know it has noticed. Sit with your hunger. Take the edge off it if you can with a nutritious snack or a large glass of water.

It's important not to let hunger get too strong. If you ignore it, it will eventually make you eat everything around you. If you notice it, be curious about it. Get to know it. Learn how to satisfy it, not give in to it. This means your mind needs to engage. You need to coach yourself through the change. Telling yourself you should know better or that you're a hopeless case is a complete waste of head space and a missed opportunity.

Tactics to help
There are a few things you can do to help yourself deal with feelings of hunger.

- ▶ Never skip meals.
- ▶ If you know mid-afternoon is your low time, build a protein-rich snack into your meal plan.
- ▶ Think through the coming week and decide on your meals in advance.
- ▶ Plan your shopping (weekly or online).
- ▶ Be flexible – don't panic if the plan changes.
- ▶ Identify your real treats, apart from food – new lipstick, flowers, a manicure?
- ▶ Identify, apart from food, what else distracts and absorbs you – a crossword, a walk, music, playing cards, planning holidays?
- ▶ Avoid being the perfectionist!

The concept of 'conscious eating' really helps me. I remind myself I have choices and that my choices have consequences. Finding the pause button and asking myself the question 'Is what I'm eating now really helping me?' allows me to tap into my awareness. And sometimes I still go on to eat another slice of cake, but I do so without guilt and with the intention of fully enjoying it!
– Paula

Obstacles to get your mind around
Although you know you should be eating less, you may subconsciously sabotage your efforts.

- ▶ 'Others eat like me and stay slim!' This is probably because they're more active or have a different genetic or biochemical make-up. Avoid comparing yourself to others.

- While consciously you know you want to lose weight, subconsciously you may resent the need to change. Remember, nothing changes if nothing changes – especially weight!

- Comfort eating has no impact on your emotional needs and too much impact on your shape. Overeating never satisfies your emotional hunger.

Rewrite the rules

When you start making changes to your eating pattern, you really need to focus. This can be exhausting as you have to plan all those little things you used to do on autopilot. Older habits are easier, so you have to be attentive to the new ones you are building. You can save energy by establishing some rules to help you stick to your eating plan. Think of them as a positive, as they are really saving your brain power. Construct them with a view to making your life easier. They are not there to make you miserable. Reset them if you need to.

These rules can make life easier:

- No biscuits at meetings in the office.

- Just one latte a day, not two.

- No alcohol from Monday to Friday.

- No more than two glasses of wine at an event.

- A maximum of two slices of wholemeal bread at only one meal in any day.

Coaching yourself and changing your negative perceptions is vital to ensuring that the internal environment (your mind) is helping and supporting you. Structuring your external environment (the kitchen/workplace) can help you avoid temptation.

TRY THIS ▼

Try keeping a food diary. Write it by hand, use an Excel sheet or a good smartphone app. It doesn't matter what you use, just do it! Tracking and monitoring is hugely beneficial and helpful and will allow you to see the bigger picture.

- It logs what you are doing well and reinforces good behaviour.

- It highlights gaps in nutrition and where there is work to be done.

- It gets you to pause and consider your choices and creates self-awareness.

- It is transparent so there's no denial. It is a personal log of what you have eaten.

Your food diary can give you information about:

- When you eat and if the gaps between meals are too long.
- What you were doing prior to eating that might have triggered you to eat.
- How and where you eat, for example absorbed in a TV programme in the kitchen.
- With whom were you eating. Some people can encourage us to eat well.
- How you felt before and after eating.
- Your thoughts or emotions while you were eating.

―――――――――

Identify the steps you need to take to change your eating habits and improve your life.

- Stop 'fad' dieting – think long-term change.
- Reflect on your external environment.
- Reflect on your internal environment.
- Focus on health, not thinness.
- Focus on natural, wholesome, fresh food.
- Think nourishment, not punishment.
- Honour your hunger.
- Indulge without overindulging.
- Learn to fail and have slips.

WHICH APPROACH SHOULD YOU TO TAKE?

There is little point in losing weight, then going back to your old ways and putting the weight back on again!

Make whatever approach you take all about *you*: the type of activity that suits *you*, a plan that incorporates some of *your* favourite foods, meals that fit *your* pocket.

It shouldn't be all about the numbers – the number of kilos you *should* weigh, the number of calories you *should* eat, the number of foods on the blacklist.

Choose the right diet for you

A BBC *Horizon* series *The Right Diet*, headed by a team of Oxford and Cambridge experts, studied the effect of biochemistry, psychology and genes in overweight people. They divided 75 overweight subjects into three groups in an attempt to help them lose weight over three months. The volunteers exceeded the target of losing five per cent of their weight in that time.

Those in the Constant Cravers (CC) group were constantly grazing. Their genes made them feel hungry all the time. Feasters (F) had a glitch in a gut hormone that blunted their ability to feel full. The third group, the Emotional Eaters (EE), ate for psychological reasons, turning to fatty, sugary foods when they were anxious, stressed or feeling down.

Each group was put on a specific diet tailored to support them. Meal plans and recipes were available and the scientists composed a questionnaire to help anyone interested in losing weight to determine the best group and approach to follow. Their emphasis was on turning the diet into a lifestyle.

Individuals in the EE group benefited most from cognitive behavioural therapy and group work. The support they received from each other really helped them steer weight loss. Their meal plans were low in sugar and fat.

The F group followed a plan that was high in protein and low glycaemic index carbohydrates. The glycaemic index of a food is the measure of how quickly it raises your blood sugar after eating it. Low glycaemic index foods give you a nice steady blood sugar level, which can keep you feeling fuller for longer. Increased protein boosted the production of gut hormones such as GLP-1 (glucagon-like peptide 1), which increases the feelings of fullness – in other words, a natural stop button!

Those in the CC group felt hungry most of the time. They followed two days of restricted eating (600–800 kcal/day and no carbohydrates)

Smaller plates means less food! Studies show that if we change the size of our plate from 30cm to 25cm, we eat 22 per cent less food.

each week to ensure an overall calorie deficit. For the rest of the week, they enjoyed an unrestricted Mediterranean-type diet of fresh unprocessed food with a portion of protein at each meal.

So finding the right approach may mean getting to know yourself a little better. When you understand how you relate to food and how you gained weight in the first place, it gives you some options as to what approach might be best suited to you.

Three mindsets

Weight-watchers tend to fall into one of three camps:

▸ The 'out of sight, out of mind' group

▸ The 'absence makes the heart grow fonder' believers

▸ The 'in-betweeners'.

'One of the most powerful factors that determines the amount you eat is how much food is placed in front of you,' according to David Levitsky, PhD, a professor of nutrition and psychology at Cornell. He points to published data that showed that if you eat while blindfolded, you eat significantly less than when you can see your food. We're not suggesting you buy a blindfold, but it's interesting research.

Susan Roberts, PhD, director of the Energy Metabolism Laboratory at Tufts University, says studies at Tufts suggest that 'out of sight' is helpful for some people: 'Having things around you just keeps temptations more firmly in your mind.'

While 'out of sight, out of mind' might be the best policy, there's a difference between keeping a food out of the house and forbidding it completely. Marlene Schwartz, PhD, from Yale's Rudd Center for Food Policy and Obesity, says, 'The key is that you aren't saying that ice cream is evil, but rather that it is best enjoyed under certain circumstances, and those circumstances make it easy to control portion sizes and frequency.' In other words, it's OK to enjoy an ice cream for dessert when you're eating out, but not every evening after dinner.

There's no single approach that works best for everyone. There's no simple answer.

Jackie Ryder, personal stylist

The good news is that we can help to keep ourselves looking good by dressing slimmer. It doesn't require the will power and effort of a healthy diet, nor the energy and motivation to exercise. But as our bodies have changed shape subtly or not so subtly, what might have suited us in the past may not look and fit so well now! This is the time to get rid of clothes that no longer flatter us and start to build up a well-chosen range of clothes to suit our figures. Good foundation garments are essential. Our busts may have increased and sagged over the years, so have yourself properly measured for a bra with uplift and invest in some tummy control underwear. I advise my clients to buy their first set in skin colour and build up a collection over time. Getting everything in the right place keeps us feeling confident.

MEASURING SUCCESS

Once you have found an approach that suits you best, there are many ways to measure your success. The bathroom scales is only one of those and really not the best. Take a broader approach to evaluating the benefits of the change you have invested in. It will help you to see that health and happiness goes far beyond the scales. Reliable indicators of success include:

▶ Increased energy levels

▶ Feeling stronger and more resilient

▶ Looking fresher and fitter

▶ Improved mood and feeling more positive

▶ Normal blood pressure levels

▶ Lower blood cholesterol levels

▶ Improved blood sugar levels

▶ Decreasing waist circumference

▶ Better-fitting clothes

▶ Increased confidence.

WHAT TO EAT

Eat a mix of plant and animal proteins throughout the day. Make sure you spread your intake over the day rather than having most of your protein at one meal.

Pay particular attention to protein at breakfast. Tea and wholemeal toast is not enough. If you stabilise your hormones, you'll stabilise your hunger. Protein is better than carbohydrate or fat at controlling the hunger hormone ghrelin. Try Greek yogurt, eggs, nut butters and mixed seeds at breakfast.

Eat regularly and prevent surges in appetite hormones. Enjoy foods rich in omega-3 fats such as salmon, mackerel and sardines; chia seeds and flaxseeds; walnuts and walnut oil; and camelina oil. Omega-3 fats are anti-inflammatory and may help improve insulin and leptin sensitivity.

Move away from the fridge and look for pleasure elsewhere. Music, tai chi and yoga also increase dopamine levels, lighting up the pleasure centre of the brain.

Commit to regular exercise. Physical activity not only burns calories but can reduce stress and increase certain satiety hormones.

PAULA'S WEIGHT LOSS TIPS

▸ Remember that **motivation doesn't come from will power**, it comes from having a clear and compelling vision of where you're going.

▸ **Visualise yourself as the new you**, doing the things you won't do now because you are overweight. Repeat this exercise regularly – it helps to see yourself as who you want to be.

▸ Make life easier by making sure that your personal **trigger foods are out of reach** and not accessible.

▸ **Realise that you always have choices.** Make them consciously, not on automatic pilot. Find the pause button that allows you time to think. Weigh up the consequences of your food decisions and then choose. This will help you avoid a lot of guilt.

▸ Remember, **a lapse is not a collapse.** You are perfectly imperfect. That's what makes you human!

▸ As a general guideline, **1500 kcal per day** is usually effective to support weight loss.

1500 CALORIE
MEAL PLAN

1500 CALORIE **MEAL PLAN**

DAY 1

BREAKFAST

Scrambled egg muffin
1 large orange
417 kcal

EARLY SNACK

3 Brazil nuts
99 kcal

LUNCH

Butternut squash salad
200ml low-fat milk
381 kcal

LATE SNACK

1 kiwi fruit
1 low-fat probiotic
yogurt
100 kcal

DINNER

Grilled salmon steak
with 4 boiled new
potatoes, steamed
mangetout and baby
sweetcorn
521 kcal

TOTAL CALORIES:
1518

DAY 2

BREAKFAST

1 multigrain bagel
60g smoked salmon
30g light cream
cheese
351 kcal

EARLY SNACK

1 slice fresh pineapple
1 slice mango
56 kcal

LUNCH

Spicy chicken and
bean wrap
200ml low-fat milk
463 kcal

LATE SNACK

30g wasabi peas
130 kcal

DINNER

Moroccan lamb with
apricots, almonds, mint
and couscous
577 kcal

TOTAL CALORIES:
1577

DAY 3

BREAKFAST

40g unsweetened
muesli
1 low-fat probiotic
yogurt
handful dried fruit,
e.g. cranberries and
blueberries
271 kcal

EARLY SNACK

Orange, mango and
lime juice
166 kcal

LUNCH

Warm chicken salad
600 kcal

LATE SNACK

3 Brazil nuts and 1
sharon fruit
148 kcal

DINNER

60g couscous tossed
with a selection of
finely chopped salad
vegetables of your
choice, 60g cubed
feta cheese and fat-
free dressing
380 kcal

TOTAL CALORIES:
1565

DAY 4

BREAKFAST

2 slices wholemeal
toast
1 poached egg
1 grilled tomato
1 low-fat probiotic
yogurt
381 kcal

EARLY SNACK

Oat-based cereal bar
2 mandarin oranges
230 kcal

LUNCH

Marinated fig and
mozzarella salad
364 kcal

LATE SNACK

Banana
95 kcal

DINNER

Prawn creole
250ml glass low-fat
milk
416 kcal

TOTAL CALORIES:
1486

1500 CALORIE **MEAL PLAN**

DAY 5

BREAKFAST

2 slices wholegrain bread
150g baked beans
1 low-fat probiotic yogurt
358 kcal

EARLY SNACK

30g mixed unsalted nuts
182 kcal

LUNCH

Smoked salmon and cream cheese wrap
380 kcal

LATE SNACK

Banana
95 kcal

DINNER

Sea bass with fennel and wild rice
443 kcal

TOTAL CALORIES:
1458

DAY 6

BREAKFAST

2 scrambled eggs
2 slices wholemeal toast
with 1 level tsp low-fat
spread
1 grilled tomato
321 kcal

EARLY SNACK

Handful soya beans
130 kcal

LUNCH

Smoked trout and pea pasta
445 kcal

LATE SNACK

1 apple
2 mandarins
77 kcal

DINNER

Chicken biryani with basmati rice
617 kcal

TOTAL CALORIES:
1590

DAY 7

BREAKFAST

40g porridge oats
made up with
low-fat milk
Handful mixed
berries
223 kcal

EARLY SNACK

Handful wasabi peas
130 kcal

LUNCH

Broccoli, cherry tomatoes,
feta and hazelnut salad
with dressing
2 wholegrain crackers
385 kcal

LATE SNACK

150g low-fat natural yogurt
1 banana
193 kcal

DINNER

Grilled lean pork chop with
1 jacket potato, cauliflower,
French beans and fat-free
gravy
510 kcal

TOTAL CALORIES:
1441

CHAPTER 4

Bones

Take care of your body. It's the only place you have to live.

Jim Rohn, author

Osteoporosis is probably the most serious debilitating disease associated with menopause. It weakens bones and increases the risk of unexpected fractures. The word itself means 'porous bone' and the condition often progresses without your knowledge and without any symptoms or pain.

Once established, the disease can give rise to chronic back pain and fractured bones. The knock-on effect is that it can severely affect the quality and enjoyment of your life. That's why it's so important to take a proactive approach – don't sit and wait for osteoporosis to arrive!

Bone is a living tissue. It is continuously regenerating itself, losing old cells and building new ones. A healthy skeleton requires a balance of osteoclasts (cells that break down bones) and osteoblasts (cells that make new bone).

Researchers found that active, non-smoking women aged 80 (BMI of 25) lost approximately 30 per cent less bone than thin women of the same age who smoked and were sedentary. There is such a thing as being too thin!

We naturally begin to lose more bone than we can make in and around our mid-30s. Generally speaking, there is a slow and steady loss of bone mass every year from the mid-30s to the onset of menopause.

The pace then quickens for the first 10 years after menopause. As oestrogen levels drop to 10 per cent of what they were, the bone-diminishing osteoclasts live longer than their counterparts, the bone-building osteoblasts. This imbalance leads to weaker and weaker bones. One in three women aged 50 to 65 and one in two women over 65 will develop osteoporosis.

You can see why it's dubbed the silent epidemic. You can be sailing through the menopause, minding your own business and completely symptom-free, until you trip and fracture your hip, wrist or spine.

Symptoms of osteoporosis:

▹ Stooped posture and a loss of height

▹ A feeling of tenderness or pain in the bones

▹ Neck, spine and lower back pain

▹ Broken bones

▹ Gum disease and tooth loss.

FACTORS OUTSIDE YOUR CONTROL

Risk factors that seriously influence your bone health may not be alterable but it's still good to know about them. You can use them to remind yourself of your overall risk profile.

▶ **Gene pool:** Researchers have estimated that as much as 80 per cent of the age-specific variation in bone turnover and bone density is genetically determined. So if your parent (especially your mother) or grandparent had osteoporosis, then you are at a higher risk yourself.

▶ **Age:** As you get older, your bones become more and more fragile. Ideally you want to get to menopause with sufficient bone density to minimise subsequent losses.

▶ **Body type:** If you have a slight build, you are also more at risk. Overweight women put more weight on their bones as they move. This is a good work-out for the muscle and skeleton and keeps them strong. There are, of course, too many health-related downsides to being overweight, so it's not advisable to expand your waistline in order to benefit your bones!

▶ **Gender:** After menopause, oestrogen's protective effect on bones is no longer there. At a particularly high risk are:

• Women who went through menopause before the age of 45 years

• Women who have had a hysterectomy

• Women who had endometriosis or irregular or no periods for more than four months, not due to pregnancy.

Your risk of osteoporosis may be higher if you have or have had any of the following:

▸ Endocrine disorders, including high levels of prolactin, cortisol or thyroid and parathyroid hormone problems, diabetes, Turner's Syndrome, etc.

▸ Eating disorders.

▸ Gastrointestinal disorders, including coeliac disease, Crohn's disease, ulcerative colitis or primary biliary cirrhosis.

▸ Rheumatoid arthritis and steroid treatment for the condition.

▸ Chemotherapy or radiation: any woman who has received or who will be receiving either of these should have a DEXA scan and be treated preventively.

▸ Medications that can increase the risk of osteoporosis, including corticosteroids such as prednisolone, prednisone or cortisone, some anticonvulsants and post-organ transplant therapy.

Source: www.IOS.ie

There is nothing you can do about your age or your family history, but you can make lifestyle changes.

THE IMPORTANCE OF CALCIUM

Calcium is vital for bone health. It is necessary not only during the younger years when bones grow the most, but also later in life so that as much bone mass as possible can be retained. You don't need to eat any special or expensive foods, but you may identify some improvements or changes you would like to make.

Ninety-nine per cent of the body's calcium is stored in the bones and teeth, where it supports their structure and function. It also plays a role in:

▸ Contracting and dilating healthy blood vessels

▸ Muscle function

▸ Nerve transmission.

Less than 1 per cent of our total body calcium is needed to support these crucial functions.

Adult women are advised to eat enough calcium-rich foods to provide 700–800mg of this essential bone mineral each day. That is just three servings of calcium-rich dairy or the equivalent of fortified soya-/nut-/rice-based products (see Chapter 2: Food).

Other food sources to top up your calcium levels

Aside from milk, yogurt and cheese, there are other sources of calcium in food which help if eaten regularly.

▸ **Canned fish**, including their soft bones (particularly sardines and salmon).

▸ **Green vegetables** (spinach, broccoli and kale) provide some calcium, although these plant sources contain oxalic acid and phytic acid which interfere with the absorption of calcium.

▸ **Calcium-enriched and -fortified foods** (breakfast cereals, fruit juices, soya, nut and rice drinks).

▸ **Tofu** is a great phyto-oestrogen – and calcium-rich plant protein.

Your shopping basket of calcium-rich foods

FOOD/DRINK	PORTION size	CALCIUM (mg)
Full-fat milk	200ml	236
Low-fat milk	200ml	240
Long-life calcium-enriched	200ml	
Goat's milk	200ml	200
Low-fat yogurt		
Low-fat Cheddar cheese	25g	210
Cottage cheese		
Baked beans	200g	106
Dried apricots		
Brazil nuts	30g	51
Tofu, cooked	100g	510

TRY THIS ▼

Try these easy ways to boost your calcium intake:

▶ Mash natural yogurt into sweet potato.

▶ Add milk or natural yogurt to soups and sauces.

▶ Mix fresh berries or banana with yogurt and top with a tablespoon of granola.

▶ Mix hot or cold milk with a high-fibre breakfast cereal for supper.

▶ Make custard with milk instead of using cream with dessert.

▶ Add grated cheese to a baked potato or frittata for lunch.

▶ Chop small chunks of Brie or feta cheese into a salad and top with seeds.

▶ Make a vegetable bake topped with mozzarella cheese.

▶ Have a frothy cappuccino or hot chocolate as an occasional treat!

What if you are lactose intolerant?

Some women develop lactose intolerance as they get older. Great-tasting lactose-free milks are now available in all big supermarket chains. The level of lactose in hard cheese is minimal and the bacteria in yogurt help break down and digest lactose, so these dairy foods are not normally a problem.

Alternatively, you can buy lactase enzymes that will help you digest dairy foods. The important thing is to ensure adequate calcium and other bone minerals in your meals throughout the week.

Some women will choose a nut, rice or soya milk that has been fortified with calcium and other nutrients. The problem is that they don't generally drink enough of these alternatives to ensure an adequate intake of calcium. Make sure you can consume enough of the alternatives or try a combination of dairy and non-dairy alternatives.

What about calcium supplements?

More than the recommended intake of calcium is not necessarily better for us. Up to very recently, women over 50 were recommended to take at least 1000–1200mg/day to prevent fractures, and many took calcium supplements to help increase their intake. But recent trials have raised some concern over the safety of calcium supplements.

There is currently little or no evidence to show that increasing calcium above 800mg (either in additional foods or by taking supplements) prevents fractures. Indeed, recent research shows that unless your food intake is low, increasing calcium intake has insignificant effects on bone density.

An overview of the literature highlights the fact that taking calcium supplements can have an unfavourable risk:benefit outcome for some women. This means that the overall benefit is outweighed by some serious side effects. Taking a supplement of 1000mg daily is associated with an increased risk of heart attack, stroke, kidney stones, constipation and hospital admissions as a result of gastrointestinal symptoms.

So while it is sensible to increase your calcium intake with calcium-rich foods, it is now thought that more is not necessarily better.

What if you are already taking calcium supplements?

It's difficult to know how much calcium each of us needs as it varies from one individual to another. If you have been taking calcium supplements for some time, it might be a good idea to review your bone supplements with your doctor. New studies and insights suggest that we should reconsider and revise our approach.

Your doctor may still advise you that you need a total intake (dietary and supplementary) of 1000–1200mg/day, so you may want to take a daily calcium supplement of 500mg together with calcium-rich foods. Supplements containing calcium with vitamin D3 (as opposed to calcium on its own) seem to have the safest profile. Take your doctor's advice on board.

VITAMIN D

Vitamin D helps us absorb calcium and plays a vital role in bone health. Vitamin D receptors are located on fast-twitch muscle fibres, which are the first to respond if and when we are about to fall. It may be that vitamin D increases muscle strength and helps prevent falls. Not only is vitamin D an essential nutrient, it's also a hormone our bodies can make through the action of the sunlight on our skin. That's why it is sometimes referred to as the 'sunshine vitamin'.

However, in Canada, North America and northern European countries in the months between November and March, there is an insufficiency of both the quality and quantity of sunlight necessary for the body to produce adequate vitamin D. Moreover, with most women working indoors and using sunscreen when outside, vitamin D intake from sunlight exposure has decreased.

Darker-skinned women living in northerly latitudes are particularly at risk, as they require over 10 times more sunlight to produce sufficient vitamin D.

FAST FACTS ▶▶
Vitamin D deficiency is higher in:

▶ Elderly women confined indoors

▶ Women who don't eat oily fish

▶ Women who cover themselves for religious or cultural reasons

▶ Women with malabsorption problems and kidney disease.

Why is vitamin D important for health?

Without sufficient vitamin D, we can absorb no more than 15 per cent of the calcium we consume. When this happens, the body must take calcium from its stores in the skeleton, which can weaken the existing bone, potentially resulting in porous fragile bones.

Recent research has also looked at vitamin D's role in a variety of diseases other than bone health. Epidemiological studies have highlighted an association between low vitamin D levels and cardiovascular diseases, diabetes, certain cancers, cognitive decline, depression and autoimmune diseases. These studies suggest that the role of vitamin D far exceeds good bone health.

Recommended intake of vitamin D

The recommended daily allowance (RDA) for adults is 0–10μg, depending on what you make from the action of sunlight on your skin. However, we know that many of us can't make enough from sunlight, and a significant proportion of 18–64-year-olds have low vitamin D intakes. A large national study found that over 70 per cent of women have a daily vitamin D intake of less than 5µg.

Food sources of vitamin D

Very few foods are naturally good sources of vitamin D. Oily fish, including salmon and mackerel, are the best sources. You need to eat oily fish at last twice a week to ensure an adequate intake. Eggs contain a small amount. Fortified foods are a good source. Vitamin D is added to some milks and other dairy products, orange juice, soya milk and fortified cereals. Check the food labels to see if vitamin D has been added to your staple foods.

Have a blood test to determine your levels and take a supplement if your blood levels are insufficient or too low and your dietary intake is poor.

Vitamin D-rich foods

FOOD	PORTION SIZE	VITAMIN D (µG)
Salmon, steamed	100g fillet	5.7
Mackerel, smoked	100g fillet	8.0
Sardines, canned in tomato sauce	100g	5.0
Tuna, canned in brine	100g	4.5
Low-fat buttermilk	200ml	4.0
Bran flakes	30g	1.3

TRY THIS ▼

Here are some easy ways to boost your vitamin D intake:

▸ Have a weekly Fishy Friday and enjoy oily fish regularly – salmon, trout, mackerel, herrings, sardines and fresh tuna are good choices.

▸ Choose canned fish (salmon, sardines and tuna) for lunch and eat the bones!

▸ Include a couple of egg omelettes or scrambled egg lunches each week.

▸ Spend 15–20 minutes outside in sunshine two or three times each week without suncream (if appropriate).

▸ Discuss supplementation with your doctor if you can't meet your intake through diet alone.

Vitamin D supplements

Overall, the evidence is strong in support of supplementing with vitamin D3 to prevent osteoporotic fractures and falls. There are two forms of vitamin D used in supplements:

▸ Vitamin D2 (ergocalciferol)

▸ Vitamin D3 (cholecalciferol).

Vitamin D3 is the preferred one. Chemically it has more similarities to the form of vitamin D produced by the body and is more effective than vitamin D2 at raising the blood levels of vitamin D.

Since vitamin D is fat-soluble, take it with a snack or meal containing fat so that it can be effectively absorbed with the healthy fats consumed in food.

MEETING YOUR DAILY NEEDS

Calcium:

▸ 200ml milk in cereal for breakfast – 240mg (30% RDA)

▸ 1 low-fat yogurt at 11.00 a.m. – 203mg (25% RDA)

▸ 25g Cheddar in sandwich at lunch – 210mg (26% RDA)

▸ 100ml milk in tea/coffee – 120mg (15% RDA)

Total: 773mg (96% RDA)

Trace amounts of calcium in other foods can also boost your intake.

Vitamin D:

▸ 100ml fortified milk – 2µg (20% RDA)

▸ Serving of fortified breakfast cereal – 1.5µg (15% RDA)

▸ 1 egg – 1µg (10% RDA)

▸ Salmon cutlet (twice a week) – 2.5µg (25% RDA)

Total: 7µg (70% RDA)

You may still need a vitamin D3 supplement to ensure adequate vitamin D levels.

- **Breakfast:** Porridge with 200ml fortified milk and sliced banana

- **Snack:** Low-fat yogurt and an apple

- **Lunch:** 2-egg omelette with 25g grated reduced-fat Cheddar cheese, slice of wholegrain bread and large side salad (plus vitamin D3 supplement if necessary)

- **Snack:** 30g unsalted cashew nuts and 2 satsumas

- **Dinner:** Steamed salmon, brown rice, carrots and broccoli

" *In my late 20s, early 30s, I worked in the National Dairy Council. At the time, we were involved in initiating the Irish Osteoporosis Society with Professor Moira O'Brien and securing its charitable status. As a gesture for compiling patient leaflets on diet and bone health, I was offered a bone scan in the Human Performance Laboratory, Trinity College Dublin. It housed the first DEXA machine of its kind in Ireland at the time. My results were scary! I had osteopenia. I knew then, all those years ago, I was a candidate for osteoporosis. I couldn't do anything about my genetic predisposition to bone disease as it's very much part of my DNA. But it made me more aware of the things I could influence – what I ate and the importance of resistance exercise.* "
– Paula

DEXA SCAN

If you think you have one or more risk factors for osteoporosis, it is recommended that you speak to your doctor about the possibility of a DEXA scan. It measures the amount of minerals in bones. Bone density is measured on a point scale, known as a 'T' score. Based on your results, you can then make decisions.

Early diagnosis is essential for the best prognosis. A DEXA scan of your spine and hips is the gold standard for diagnosing osteoporosis and is highly recommended if you are at risk. Heel scans are not recommended for the diagnosis of osteoporosis.

Women who have a family history of osteoporosis or other risk factors should have their first bone density test during the peri-menopausal years. If you have a low risk of osteoporosis, you can discuss the best timing for a bone density scan with your doctor.

TREATMENT PLAN

A treatment plan will be based on:

▶ Your risk of fracture or re-fracture

▶ Your DEXA results

▶ Why you developed osteoporosis

▶ Your age

▶ Your medical history.

The best way to avoid the painful and debilitating bone fractures that come with osteoporosis is to prevent the disease before it takes hold. Of course going back in time to the teenage years when bone growth is feasible is not a possibility. However, there are still ways to limit the rapid destruction of bones common in menopausal women, before osteoporosis becomes a problem.

Food sources of bone-friendly vitamins

Like every part of our body, our bones are continuously regenerating themselves. They rely on calcium, magnesium, phosphorus and other bone minerals as structural materials. A deficiency of calcium and vitamin D can increase the risk of diseases like osteopenia (a reduction in the protein and mineral content of the bone) and osteomalacia (a softening of the bone). You will also need an adequate intake of:

▶ **Magnesium foods** (Brazil nuts, peanuts, pecan nuts, red kidney beans, black-eyed beans, aduki beans, halva, seaweeds, wholemeal spaghetti, brown rice, rye bread, lentils)

▶ **Phosphorus foods** (bran and wheatgerm, sesame seeds, fennel seeds and sunflower seeds, Brazil nuts, cashews and almonds, soya beans, cheese, eggs, sardines)

▶ **Omega-3 foods** (see Chapter 5: Immunity)

▶ **Zinc foods** (see Chapter 5: Immunity)

▶ **Manganese foods** (see Chapter 5: Immunity).

Things to avoid for good bone health

▸ Drinking tea and fizzy, carbonated drinks with meals.

▸ High-protein fad diets.

▸ Smoking.

▸ Sitting all the time. Exercise is vital for preserving bone health.

▸ Excessive alcohol consumption.

If you have already been diagnosed with osteopenia or osteoporosis, discuss treatment options with your doctor. But don't forget to feed your bones. It's not a case of drugs verses diet, the combination of both may be necessary for skeletal health.

FAST FACTS ▸▸

▸ The number of women versus men who develop osteoporosis:

  • 1 in 3 women over 50

  • 1 in 2 women over 65

  • 1 in 5 men over 50

▸ The average stay in hospital after hip replacement is 17 days.

▸ Secondary complications of a hip fracture include blood clot, pneumonia or infection.

▸ Only 30 per cent of people aged 60+ who fracture a hip regain their independence.

CHAPTER 5

Immunity

Natural forces within us are the true healers of disease.

Hippocrates

estrogen levels at menopause can have a negative impact on our immune system's ability to work well. Autoimmune diseases (coeliac disease, rheumatoid arthritis, type 1 diabetes) are more prevalent in post-menopausal women, making scientists reflect on oestrogen and its function in regulating the immune system. The exact role of oestrogen is muddied by the undeniable influences of genetics and environmental triggers. Until research gives us some critical insights, we can use key foods to help support our immune system, particularly under stress. With well over 20 different micro-nutrients necessary for the immune system to function properly, we can help you make the right food choices to strengthen your defences.

YOUR GUT

You share your body with over 100 trillion bacteria. That's right. It's thought that over a thousand different species grow in the gut, most of which we know little or nothing about. This great ecosystem is called the microbiome, an ecological community of microorganisms that literally share our body space.

We live in a complex symbiotic relationship with some of these microbes. We provide them with indigestible carbohydrates (resistant starch from plant fibres) and a space to flourish. And we, in turn, benefit enormously. These good bacteria, such as certain bifidobacterium and lactobacillus strains, derive energy from the fermentation of our otherwise indigestible waste. In return, they provide us with biotin, vitamin B12 and vitamin K, although not in sufficient amounts to meet all our requirements. The good bacteria also act as a physical barrier and secrete anti-microbial proteins that prevent the harmful, or pathogenic, bacteria from getting the upper hand.

A healthy digestive and immune system depends on us keeping the good bacteria thriving and outnumbering the not-so-good bacteria. Reduced levels of good bacteria can arise as a result of one or more of the following factors: stress, broad-spectrum antibiotics, diarrhoea, ageing, active inflammatory conditions such as colitis or gastroenteritis, fasting, a poor fibre intake and the consumption of contaminated food or water.

FAST FACTS ▸▸

Optimum levels of good bacteria are required to maintain a healthy digestive and immune system. They can:

▸ Reduce the growth of harmful bacteria

▸ Reduce the risk or impact of diarrhoea

▸ Reduce symptoms of IBS

▸ Increase tolerance of lactose in those with lactose intolerance

▸ Help reduce the complications associated with ulcerative colitis

▸ Help reduce the risk of colon cancer

▸ Improve the symptoms of colic in infants

▸ Help reduce allergic conditions such as atopic dermatitis

▸ Help support the natural defences.

Source: www.indi.ie

Good bacteria in food

When we talk about good bacteria in food, we usually refer to them as probiotics, or 'friendly' bacteria. The word probiotic is derived from the Greek word for 'pro-life', as opposed to antibiotic or 'against life'. According to the United Nations Food and Agriculture Organization and the World Health Organization, probiotics are live micro-organisms, which, when administered in adequate amounts, confer a health benefit on the host.

Probiotics can be found in some live yogurts, fermented milk drinks and other dairy produce. Different products contain different species of live bacteria, so they are not all the same and don't all have the same effects.

The potential of probiotic food products is enormous as diet is considered to have a critical impact on the microbiome. Research into probiotic use in food and tablet form is growing. Certain probiotics are being used to treat IBS. Some help prevent lactose intolerance. It's unclear whether the presence of specific bacteria is a contributor to obesity or is a consequence of obesity, but there is compelling evidence to suggest a strong association.

Research has shown that the brain sends signals to the gut, which is why stress and other emotions can cause gut symptoms like pain or butterflies in your tummy. Recent research shows that signals travel the opposite way as well, a two-way gut-brain communication that had been suspected and has now been confirmed. The growing potential for probiotic foods to impact on mental health is a dynamic area of research.

Feeding your gut bacteria

Certain foods naturally help our good bacteria to thrive in the gut. These are called prebiotics and include foods like bananas, oats and wholegrains, onions, garlic, leeks, artichokes and soya beans. Prebiotic ingredients such as inulin (from chicory) are now being added to other foods to fortify them. This results in a symbiotic product, which means that both the food for the good bacteria and the specific strain of probiotic you want to flourish are combined in one product.

More research is needed to ensure that specific strains are effective and safe, especially for vulnerable groups such as women with compromised immune systems.

If you are considering trying probiotics, choose products from reputable companies, especially those that have been tested in research studies. Reliable products should list the probiotics they contain, as well as how many live organisms a single dose provides. Speak to your doctor before taking any new supplement.

SUPPORTING YOUR IMMUNE SYSTEM

The immune system is vulnerable to attack by parasites, bacteria, moulds, yeast, fungi and viruses. We have three tiers of protection against such attacks.

First, we have natural physical defences. These include the skin and the mucus membranes in the lungs and digestive tract. Tears, the presence of hydrochloric acid in the stomach and resident friendly bacteria in the gut also play a role in protecting our systems from foreign substances that could harm the body.

Second, we have what is called the innate immune system. When you cut through skin, a group of white cells called macrophages rushes to the wound site to engulf and destroy any harmful bacteria that could enter the cut and cause inflammation and swelling.

Third, we have the adaptive immune system. If the innate system is overwhelmed or ineffective at repelling an invader, this line of defence comes into play. It is a highly sophisticated system, which protects us against more complex assaults, by viruses, for example.

What we eat can support our immune system and help to ensure that it's in good working order. Making the right food choices, getting enough exercise and managing our stress can help us cope during our middle years.

Vitamin D

Immune cells contain vitamin D receptors. The cells are activated to fight infection when necessary – vitamin D has a role in regulating the immune response, helping to suppress pro-inflammatory cells. It protects the lungs and respiratory system from infections by increasing the secretion of anti-microbial immune cells and natural killer cells.

We need to ensure that we include adequate vitamin D-rich foods, such as oily fish (salmon, tuna, sardines and mackerel), eggs and fortified foods (milk, yogurts and cereals) in our diet.

Selenium

This trace element is crucial to the normal functioning of the immune system. A deficiency results in a weakened immune response and a diminished ability to fight viral infections. Brazil nuts are the richest natural sources of selenium (although this is soil-dependent), followed by fish, shellfish, offal, meat, chicken and game.

Probiotics

In order to be of benefit, probiotics must reach the intestine in sufficient quantities and so resist the effects of stomach acids. Certain strains of probiotics have been shown to reduce the duration of respiratory infections. Other strains balance the intestinal microbiome, which helps support normal digestive and immune health. You can boost friendly gut bacteria by including low-fat probiotic milk, yogurts and other dairy products in your daily diet.

Zinc

The mineral zinc helps develop white blood cells, the immune cells that fight off foreign bacteria and viruses. A zinc deficiency can greatly increase risk of infection.

Zinc is found in abundance in oysters and shellfish. Lean red meat is another good source but vegetarians have to rely on other foods such as pumpkin and other seeds fortified cereals and low-fat yogurt and milk.

Vitamins A, C and E

The protective vitamins, minerals and other components found in fruit, vegetables, herbs and spices are called phytonutrients. A steady and consistent intake of these phytonutrients helps to keep the immune system working properly. Aim to eat at least two pieces of fruit and three servings of vegetables a day to get a complete complement of the vitamins and minerals needed for immune health.

Mushrooms provide compounds that help to produce white blood cells. Research suggests that the phytonutrients found in mushrooms such as shiitake and maitake can actually help white blood cells to act more aggressively against foreign bacteria.

Broccoli and other cruciferous vegetables such as cabbage, kale, Brussels sprouts and cauliflower are good sources of vitamins in general. Broccoli also contains glucosinolates, which help to stimulate the body's immune system. Vitamin B2, also found in broccoli, is vital for growth and vision and a healthy immune system.

Omega-3 fats

Essential omega-3 fats work by increasing the activity of phagocytes, the white blood cells that destroy bacteria. These fats also help strengthen cell membranes, thereby speeding up healing and strengthening resistance to infection in the body. Eating two servings of omega-3-rich oily fish (salmon, mackerel, tuna) each week is good for heart, joint and your immune function. Tinned salmon, sardines and tuna (albacore) count, although the omega-3 in some tuna brands is destroyed though processing. Check the nutrition label.

Weight

Maintaining a healthy weight can help your immune health too. Carrying excessive weight around the middle has been associated with compromised immune function, chronic inflammation and an increased risk of infection (see Chapter 3: Weight).

FIGHTING FATIGUE

Exhaustion breaks us down physically and emotionally. It can also affect our food choices and disrupt our immune system, making us more susceptible to illness and infection. At this time of our lives, many of us need an energy boost to enable us to deal with the challenges of busy work and home lives. Unfortunately, many things can rob us of our energy. Try to make sure that you have more energy boosters than robbers in your life.

ENERGY BOOSTERS	ENERGY ROBBERS
Carbohydrate-rich breakfast • Porridge with fruit and low-fat milk or wholemeal toast, nut butter and chopped banana.	**High sugar foods** • Provide energy with a surge of glucose into the blood. After the surge comes a slump, because this type of energy is not sustained.
Protein-rich lunch • Tuna or chicken salad with wholegrain crispbreads • Hummus/falafel with cherry tomatoes and lettuce in a warm wholegrain pitta bread • Omelette with roasted veg and rocket leaves • Bean or lentil veg soup with rye crackers.	**Alcohol** • Your weekly intake should be between 0–11 standard units per week. • Aim for two or more alcohol-free days a week. • Avoid binge drinking. As we get older we simply can't metabolize large volumes of alcohol.
Evening meal • Seafood/poultry/lean meat stir-fry with wholegrain rice and generous portions of iron- and folate-rich green leafy vegetables/legumes.	**Stress or depression** • These can lead to loss of appetite or binge eating/drinking. • They can cause gastrointestinal upset and IBS. • Increase your intake of B-complex and omega-3-rich foods.
Energy-boosting snack • Oatcakes with edamame dip • Banana, orange or grapes • Carrot sticks with guacamole • Greek yogurt and peach chunks • Handful of nuts, seeds and edamame beans.	**Anaemia** • Check recent test results to ensure ferritin/iron levels are not low. A lack of iron leads to anaemia and fatigue. • Check for vitamin B12 deficiency. This causes pernicious anaemia and fatigue. • Check for low folate levels. This causes megaloblastic anaemia and fatigue.
Healthy living (exercise, rest and sleep) • Routine exercise boosts energy levels; do whatever suits you best! • Meditation or yoga can keep you grounded. • Adequate sleep recharges your batteries. • Drink 1–2 litres fluid throughout the day. Try green tea or red bush tea.	**Underlying illness** • Food allergies can result in fatigue. • Food intolerances such as coeliac disease can result in malabsorption of iron. • Thyroid problem can lead to low energy levels and fatigue. • Gather reliable medical energy testing.

THE IMMUNE-FRIENDLY DIET

A good spread of nutrients throughout the day is essential for a strong immune system. This offers protection from seasonal illness such as common colds and the flu, as well as other more serious diseases including arthritis and cancers.

Our immune system helps protect us from cancers. We know that a third of all cancers are diet- and lifestyle-related. Excesses of some foods might increase our risk of cancer. We can reduce the risk by focusing on increasing our consumption of certain foods while limiting our intake of others.

Red and processed meat

Red meats include beef, lamb and pork. Processed meats are meats that have been smoked, cured, salted or had chemical preservatives added. They include poor-quality sausages, ham, salami, pastrami, hot dogs, frankfurters, chorizo and rashers.

Meat is rich in valuable nutrients like protein and iron, but when taken in large amounts, it can increase your risk of certain cancers. Therefore, you should:

▸ **Limit your intake** to a maximum of 500g cooked lean red meat per week (beef or pork). Think about having more legumes instead of red meat if possible.

▸ **Cut out or avoid eating processed meat altogether.** Choosing not to include processed meat in your diet can make a difference to your risk of cancer. A diet high in red and processed meat is linked to bowel cancer in particular.

Flaxseeds

Just like oily fish, flaxseeds are a source of omega-3 fats. They also contain lignans — compounds that may have a weak oestrogen effect.

▸ **Include a tablespoon of flaxseeds** in your daily diet. The toasted seeds can be sprinkled into salads, yogurt or over wholegrain cereal.

Lycopene

Lycopene makes tomatoes red and gives orange fruits and vegetables their colour. Processed tomatoes such as tomato sauce or soup have the highest amounts of lycopene, but watermelon and fresh tomatoes are also good sources. Some studies suggest that eating processed tomatoes with some oil or fat makes it easier for your body to absorb lycopene, compared to drinking raw tomato juice.

Lycopene is a powerful antioxidant.

▸ **Eat more tomato-based sauces** instead of cream-based sauces.

Immune-supporting meal plan

Supporting your immune system through diet couldn't be easier. This sample one-day meal plan is simplicity itself.

Breakfast:

▸ Apricot and walnut porridge – soak oats overnight with 3 chopped dried apricots. Add 3 chopped walnuts before serving.

▸ A thin slice of wholemeal toast topped with Manuka honey.

▸ Cup of green tea or red bush tea.

Mid-morning:

▸ Berry good smoothie (see page 216).

▸ Cup of green tea or red bush tea.

Lunch:

▸ Mango and avocado salad with chicken (see page 238).

Mid-afternoon:

▸ A probiotic yogurt with a dessertspoon of chia seeds or 3 Brazil nuts and 3 almonds.

Evening meal:

▸ A roasted salmon parcel seasoned with lemon juice, ginger or chilli, served with your favourite roasted vegetables and sweet potato.

Evening:

▸ 2 tbsp home-made fruit and cinnamon compôte with a swirl of low-fat Greek yogurt.

▸ Cup of green tea or herbal tea.

AUTOIMMUNE DISEASE

A vitamin D deficiency may contribute to autoimmune diseases such as multiple sclerosis (MS), type 1 diabetes, rheumatoid arthritis and autoimmune thyroid disease.

Studies have found that people with the highest vitamin D concentrations had a 62 per cent lower risk of developing MS versus those with the lowest concentrations.

FAST FACTS ▶▶

Phytochemicals are compounds that are produced by plants. They are found in fruits, vegetables, grains, beans and other plants. Some of these phytochemicals are believed to protect cells from damage that could lead to cancer.

THE ORGANS OF THE IMMUNE SYSTEM

Bone marrow: All cells of the immune system are derived initially from the bone marrow.

Spleen: This is an immunologic filter for the blood.

Thymus: This produces mature T-cells.

Lymph nodes: These serve as filters for foreign substances.

Gut tissue: This mucosal tissue comprises 70 per cent of the body's immune system.

Some of the most beneficial phytochemicals identified include:

▶ Polyphenolic compound in teas

▶ Sulphides in garlic and onions

▶ Flavonoids in soya beans, chickpeas, grains, vegetables and fruits

TRY SOYA BEANS (FROZEN AS A DINNER COMPONENT) OR ROASTED EDAMAME AS A SNACK.

▶ Carotenoids, including beta-carotene, in bright orange vegetables and fruits

▶ Isothiocyanates in cruciferous vegetables, including cabbage, bok choy, broccoli, kale, mustard greens and cauliflower.

So far there is no conclusive evidence that any phytochemicals will help reduce the risk of getting cancer or help get rid of cancer if you have it. However, fruits and vegetables are lower in calories, naturally low in fat and high in fibre. By making sure we eat plenty of fresh food, we also cut down on processed highly refined foods which are high in calories and low in nutrients.

Bear in mind there is no evidence that taking phytochemical supplements is as good for you as eating the whole fruits, vegetables, beans and grains that contain them.

CHAPTER 6

Heart

Ageing is not lost youth, but a new stage of opportunity and strength.

Betty Friedan, writer and activist

Many of us tend to think of heart disease as a men's issue, but it's now the leading cause of death in women over 50. The risk of high blood pressure and high blood cholesterol increases after the menopause. When oestrogen levels decline, the harmful LDL increases and the good HDL cholesterol decreases. Fatty cholesterol deposits develop and harden within the blood vessels. As a consequence, blood flows under increased pressure through narrowed vessels. When there is a complete blockage, oxygenated blood is prevented from reaching the brain and a stroke occurs. If the heart muscle is deprived of oxygenated blood, a heart attack ensues.

Keeping cholesterol and blood pressure levels as near normal as possible is really important, particularly post-menopause. A regular annual cholesterol and blood pressure test is a good idea, especially where there is a history of cardiovascular disease in the family.

HEALTHY CHOLESTEROL LEVELS

Your risk of having a heart event can vary considerably depending on what fraction of cholesterol is pushing up the total cholesterol level. A high HDL (think of H for healthy) is protective because HDL carries cholesterol away from the arteries and back to the liver, protecting against its accumulation on artery walls. A low HDL can put you at risk of heart disease.

The following levels are generally regarded as desirable. However, if you already have high blood pressure or heart disease, then you need to aim for even lower levels of LDL cholesterol.

▸ **Total cholesterol (TC): 5.0 mmol/L or less.**

- Low-density lipoprotein (LDL) cholesterol after an overnight fast: 3.0 mmol/L or less.

- High-density lipoprotein (HDL) cholesterol: 1.2 mmol/L or more.

- TC/HDL ratio: 4.5 or less, that is your total cholesterol divided by your HDL cholesterol. This reflects the fact that for any given TC level, the more HDL the better.

- Triglycerides: 1.8 or less.

Stress can increase your LDL cholesterol. Talk to your doctor about your overall risk of heart disease. You may be prescribed medication to help control your blood cholesterol or blood pressure. However, further and fundamental changes to what you eat and other lifestyle changes will alter your risk of disease.

FAST FACTS ▸▸

▸ Cholesterol is a waxy, fat-like substance.

▸ Some cholesterol is essential, but too much of the wrong kind is unhealthy.

▸ Nearly two-thirds of your body's cholesterol is made by your liver. What we eat contributes to the remaining third.

CHOLESTEROL IN FOOD

Cholesterol is found in some foods (eggs, liver, prawns, crab and lobster), but this type of dietary cholesterol has little effect on your blood cholesterol. Most women can continue to enjoy moderate amounts of these foods (between four and six eggs per week), even if their blood cholesterol results are high. A very small group of women may be asked to further restrict these foods on the basis of their risk profile.

The more important sources of cholesterol come from trans and saturated fats. These types of fat are largely found in cakes, biscuits, pastries, muffins, doughnuts, scones and baked desserts, processed meats, butter and cream. Eating too much of these fats and not enough unsaturated fats can lead to imbalance and may increase your risk of heart disease and stroke.

THE EVIDENCE OVERALL SUGGESTS THAT WE SHOULD LIMIT SATURATES TO LESS THAN A THIRD OF ALL THE FAT WE EAT.

Recent research suggests that not all saturated fats are the same and not all of them have the same effect on our heart health. The saturated fats in cocoa and dark chocolate are a case in point, and make a good indulgent alternative in biscuits, cakes and other baked goods.

▸ High in saturated fat means that there is more than 5g saturated fat per 100g of the food.

▸ Low in saturated fat means that there is less than 1.5g saturated fat per 100g of the food.

Unsaturated fats

These are also known as 'good' fats. They are better for your heart than trans or certain saturated fats. Unsaturated fats usually come from vegetable or seafood sources and are divided into monounsaturated and polyunsaturated fats. Olive oil, rapeseed and other seed oils, walnuts, Brazil nuts, almonds, hazelnuts (and nut butters), avocados, sunflower seeds, sesame seeds, pumpkin seeds and chia seeds are all sources of unsaturated fats.

Omega-3 fatty acids are a type of polyunsaturated fat. They can help lower triglycerides and assist in protecting the heart and joints. Oily fish is the best natural source of omega-3 fatty acids. Types of oily fish include salmon, trout, mackerel, herring, sardines, kippers and fresh tuna. Fresh, frozen and canned varieties can be enjoyed, although the canning process can almost halve the omega-3 levels so check the label. Aim to eat two portions of oily fish every week.

Trans fats

Trans fats increase LDL levels and lower HDL levels, cause inflammation and increase the tendency for blood clots to form inside blood vessels. The recommended intake is no more than 2g of trans fats a day. Less is better.

It's very difficult to tell how much is in our food as manufacturers don't have to declare it in the nutritional information on the label, although you will see 'hydrogenated' or 'partially hydrogenated' fat in the ingredients list if trans fats are present in the food.

▸ **Fat**, no matter what the type, **contains twice the number of calories** as carbohydrate or protein per gram, so it's easy to eat a lot of calories in high-fat foods. It doesn't have the same satiety as protein.

▸ **Eating too many fats, carbs or proteins** means consuming excessive calories. Eating more calories than you burn increases your weight and your susceptibility to disease. Eating excessive amounts of trans fats increases your risk factors for heart disease.

▸ It is important to **get the balance of your dietary fats right.** This means replacing trans fats and certain saturated fats with healthier polyunsaturated (omega-3 and omega-6) and monounsaturated fats (omega-9).

▸ Simply cutting out all saturated fats and replacing them with processed and refined carbohydrates, seems to be as bad, if not worse, for your health. This is the reason why **'low-fat' diets seem to be more harmful than healthy** for many women. Simply choosing refined carbohydrates to replace the lost calories from fat is not the right strategy.

HOW CHOLESTEROL IS LOWERED

Some foods deliver soluble fibre, which binds cholesterol in the digestive system and removes it from the body before it gets back into circulation. Others contain plant sterols and stanols, which prevent the body from absorbing cholesterol.

Include these top cholesterol-lowering foods regularly:

▸ **Oats:** Enjoy an oat-based cereal for breakfast such as porridge, muesli, home-made granola or oatcakes.

▸ **Barley:** Barley, like oats and oat bran, contains beta-glucan which can help to lower cholesterol. Try adding some as a thickener to soups, stews and casseroles. You need to include at least 3g beta-glucan in your daily diet to help reduce cholesterol. 140g cooked pearl barley contains approximately 2.5g beta-glucan. Each of the following will give you the remaining 1g beta-glucan:

- 2 tbsp oat bran

- 3 tbsp (30g) porridge oats

- 3 oatcakes

- 1 oat breakfast biscuit.

- **Pulses:** All pulses are especially rich in soluble fibre. With so many choices — from soya to navy and kidney beans to lentils, chickpeas, black-eyed beans and beyond — and so many ways to prepare them, pulses are very versatile.

- **Aubergine and okra:** These two low-calorie vegetables are particularly good sources of soluble fibre.

- **Nuts:** Studies show that eating almonds, walnuts, peanuts and other nuts is good for the heart. Eating 30g a day may lower LDL slightly. Nuts have additional nutrients that protect the heart in other ways.

- **Apples, grapes, strawberries and citrus fruits:** These fruits are rich in pectin, a type of soluble fibre that lowers LDL.

- **Soya:** Eating 25g soya protein a day (280g tofu or 600ml soya milk) can lower LDL by 5 to 6 per cent.

- **Fibre supplements:** Supplements offer the least appealing way to get soluble fibre. Two teaspoons a day of psyllium, which is found in some bulk-forming laxatives, provide about 4g soluble fibre.

FUNCTIONAL FOODS

The term 'functional foods' is used to describe any food that contains an ingredient that gives the food health-promoting properties over and above its usual nutritional value. The active ingredients in functional foods (such as spreads and little shot bottles) are usually plant stanol or sterol esters. These are naturally-occurring substances found in many grains such as wheat, rye and maize. They have a similar structure to cholesterol and so they compete with it in the gut and inhibit its absorption back into the body. These functional spreads and shots may be helpful for people with raised blood cholesterol levels if they are used to substitute a standard spread and eaten as part of a healthy diet. Some brands lower blood cholesterol by 10 to 14 per cent.

What about?

- **Dairy foods:** Foods like milk and yogurt are important sources of calcium so choose lower-fat versions. Don't cut them out.

- **Cooking:** Start grilling, boiling and baking to reduce the need to add fat. Try steaming and choose rapeseed oil or olive oil when roasting.

- **Coconut oil:** This popular oil is high in saturated fat. It is claimed that the type of saturated fats found in coconut oil may not have as adverse an effect on cholesterol levels as we once thought. But for now the advice is to stick with olive and rapeseed oil as we have the evidence for their heart-protective health effects.

▸ **Flaxseeds:** There are three main types of omega-3s (DHA and EPA, found in fish, and ALA, found in walnuts and flaxseeds). Although ALA does have some benefits, the main benefits from omega-3s come from EPA and DHA. However, nuts and seeds are rich in healthy fats as well as vitamins and minerals, so they are great foods to include in meals and as snacks.

MANAGING HIGH TRIGLYCERIDES

If your triglycerides are high, follow the cholesterol-lowering advice on page 94 and take the following additional steps.

▸ **Reduce sugar and sugary foods.** These increase triglycerides. Cut back on sugar-sweetened drinks, soft drinks and fruit juice. Stop adding sugar to tea and coffee and cut back on cakes, biscuits, sweets and chocolate.

▸ **Reduce alcohol.** If you have high triglycerides, have just one drink on any one occasion and try to have three alcohol-free days each week.

▸ **Eat a dinner serving of oily fish** such as salmon, trout, mackerel, herring or sardines twice a week.

BLOOD PRESSURE

Blood pressure is the force of blood against the artery walls. It rises and falls during the day.

It is recorded as two numbers: systolic pressure (as the heart beats) over diastolic pressure (as the heart relaxes between beats).

A healthy blood pressure is 120/80 millimetres of mercury (mmHg) or lower.

If your blood pressure stays elevated over time, this is high blood pressure. The condition is dangerous because it makes the heart work too hard and the force of its blood flow can harm arteries.

A high blood pressure is over 140/90 (or 140/80 if you have diabetes).

If uncontrolled over time, it can lead to heart disease, kidney disease and stroke.

How to lower blood pressure

Many women combine dietary and lifestyle interventions in conjunction with blood pressure medication as necessary.

▶ Take blood pressure medication as prescribed.

▶ Drink alcohol in moderation.

▶ Follow a low-salt DASH plan (see below).

▶ Maintain a healthy weight.

▶ Stop smoking.

▶ Be more active.

DASH

DASH stands for the Dietary Approaches to Stop Hypertension and is a great way to adapt what you eat to help manage your blood pressure.

The DASH eating plan contains very little saturated fat, red and processed meat, desserts and sugary drinks.

Eating less salt is a vital part of reducing your blood pressure. The DASH approach replaces foods that are high in salt with foods that contain potassium, calcium and fibre. The diet includes wholegrains; small servings of lean fresh meats, lots of fish and poultry; nuts and beans; low-fat dairy; and large quantities of fruit and vegetables.

The original DASH eating plan lowers cholesterol and makes it easy to lose weight. It is a healthy way of eating, designed to be flexible enough to meet the lifestyle and food preferences of most people, and it contains all the healthy foods found in the traditional Mediterranean diet.

Newer versions of the DASH plan have been created as dietary science learned that it was not the total amount of fat but the kind of fat that made a difference to health. To obtain more detailed eating plans, see www.dashdiet.org.

Principles of the DASH plan (low in salt and saturated fat, but high in magnesium, potassium, calcium and fibre):

▶ High in fruits and vegetables

▶ Includes only wholegrain products and low-fat dairy

▶ Includes fish, poultry and nuts

▶ Low in red and processed meat, sweets and sugared beverages.

If you're trying to lose weight, you can use the principles of the DASH eating plan – but watch your calorie intake. Losing even 5 to 10 per cent of your weight can lower your blood pressure.

WARNING!

While the DASH plan is suitable for most of us, it may not work for everyone, as it contains more potassium than usual. Always discuss your approach with your doctor before embarking on major changes.

REDUCING SALT

The more salt we eat in food, the more we develop a taste for it. The average daily salt intake is high — approximately 10g, about a dessertspoon. Although we need some salt, this intake is well in excess of what is essential. The short-term target is to reduce daily salt intake to 6g. Adjusting to a lower salt intake can take up to eight weeks, so persevere and give yourself time.

Remember that approximately 70 per cent of salt comes from processed packaged foods. Review your food basket. When you're checking the back of your food packets, keep an eye out for these ingredients, which are actually salt (or salt-based elements) under another name: brine, rock salt, sodium chloride, sea salt or Himalayan pink salt.

Salt substitutes

Many of us are aware that too much table salt can raise our blood pressure, but there are substitutes. For women who are not on medication and who have no known co-existing medical problem, Low-Salt (potassium chloride) is suitable. Sea salt, pink Himalayan salt and kosher salt are all similar to table salt and so are not suitable substitutes.

How much salt is in your food?

Changes to labelling regulations are helping to clear up some confusion surrounding the salt content of foods. Sodium levels were often given in the past without the salt equivalent. It is now mandatory for salt, not sodium levels, to be declared per 100g of a food. This will make similar foods and meals easier to compare if you have high blood pressure.

6g salt = 2.5g sodium. To convert sodium to salt, multiply the sodium figure by 2.5.

So what's 'a lot' of salt and what's a 'low-salt food'?

▶ 1.25g salt (equivalent to 0.5g sodium) or more per 100g of a food is considered a lot.

▶ 0.3g salt (equivalent to 0.12g sodium) or less per 100g of a food is low-salt/sodium.

▶ 0.1g salt (equivalent to 0.04g sodium) or less per 100g of a food is very low-salt/sodium.

Simple food choices can either enhance or diminish our health. Eating well can reduce the risk of developing high blood pressure and lower a blood pressure that is already too high.

Salt reduction and the cost of health care

In 2010 a paper in the *New England Journal of Medicine* estimated the projected effects of dietary salt reductions on the future incidence of cardiovascular disease. It concluded that the benefits of reduced salt intake were on a par with the benefits of population-wide reductions in tobacco use, obesity and cholesterol levels. A reduction of 3g per day (½ teaspoon) was estimated to save between $10 and $24 billion in annual health care costs in the US.

LESS SALT DOESN'T HAVE TO MEAN LESS TASTE. YOU CAN CREATE DELICIOUS, HEALTHY MEALS WHICH ARE NATURALLY LOW IN SALT. THAT'S GREAT NEWS FOR YOUR BLOOD PRESSURE – AND YOUR TASTE BUDS TOO!

Some women succeed in enjoying their favourite foods, but look for healthier ways of preparing and cooking them. Try brushing thick-cut chips with olive oil, season with herbs or spices and baking rather than frying. You could also simply reduce your portion size or eat a particular food less frequently. These changes often include eating less processed food with added salt, drinking alcohol in moderation and losing weight.

WARNING!

It is important to continue taking your blood pressure medication while making changes. As the diet lowers blood pressure, some people can experience side effects such as dizziness. This may mean that your blood pressure medication needs to be adjusted to reflect the improvements in your meal plans and the weight loss you have achieved.

TRY THIS ▼

Try the following to shake the salt habit:

▶ Add little or no salt when cooking. Avoid adding salt to water when cooking porridge, rice, pasta or potatoes — no matter what the pack says! Learn to adapt recipes and flavour food instead with black pepper, herbs, garlic, spices or lemon juice.

▶ Have the black pepper mill on the table always. In time you won't miss the salt.

▶ When shopping, avoid the obvious highly salted foods such as crisps, popcorn, salted nuts, anchovies, smoked fish, bacon/other processed meats and ready meals.

▶ Salt is also present in cheese, soups and sauces, and even in some foods in which you may not expect to find salt — bread, breakfast cereals and biscuits.

▶ Buy lower-salt versions of stock cubes, soy sauce and Worcestershire sauce.

▶ Choose no-added salt or lower-salt versions of canned foods such as sweetcorn and baked beans. Buy tuna or salmon canned in olive oil or spring water rather than brine.

SUPPLEMENTS FOR HEART HEALTH

The promise of heart health comes in an increasing variety of nutritional supplements. Investing in individual nutrients and dietary components rather than food is not recommended. Good foods provide a variety of phytochemicals, vitamins, minerals, bioactive compounds and fibres that are not commonly found in supplements.

The American Heart Association recently reviewed its recommendations on common supplements to drive home the message that there is 'no substitute for a balanced diet that limits excess calories, saturated fat, trans fat and sodium'. Their recommendations on supplements are as follows:

► **Patients with heart disease should consume about 1g omega-3 fatty acids EPA and DHA.** This should ideally come from fish. If you don't eat fish, a supplement is necessary. As always, consult with a physician first.

► **If you have elevated triglycerides,** try to get 2-4 g EPA+DHA per day.

► **Don't take antioxidant vitamin supplements such as A, C and E.** Scientific evidence does not suggest these can eliminate the need to reduce blood pressure, lower blood cholesterol or stop smoking.

► **Do not rely only on supplements.** There isn't sufficient data to suggest that healthy people benefit by taking certain vitamin or mineral supplements in excess of the daily recommended allowance. Some observational studies have suggested that using these can lower rates of cardiovascular disease and/or lower risk factor levels. However, it's unclear in these studies whether supplements caused these improvements.

Source: www.heart.org

Taking dietary supplements of calcium, magnesium and potassium is not recommended for reducing blood pressure. Eat nutrient-rich food instead. Supplements don't substitute for other important lifestyle changes such as losing excess weight, building more exercise into your week, taking blood pressure medication as prescribed and reducing the salt content of your diet.

CAFFEINE

Drinking a lot of caffeine can raise blood pressure.

- ▶ If you drink a lot of coffee, tea, energy drinks and cola drinks, you should try cutting down. Diet fizzy drinks often have the same caffeine content as sugary ones; try sparkling water instead.

- ▶ The total restriction of coffee or caffeinated beverages is unnecessary, even if you have hypertension. A moderate caffeine intake (300mg/day) is recommended.

WEIGHT

Being overweight increases the risk of high blood pressure approximately threefold.

- ▶ The risk continues to rise as your weight increases to very overweight (obese BMI>30).

- ▶ Systolic and diastolic blood pressures drop an average of 1mm Hg for roughly every 0.5kg of weight lost, although the actual amount varies widely from person to person.

If you already have high blood pressure, it's not a question of medication or lifestyle changes. Regardless of what medication you are taking, you will also need to make lifestyle changes to manage your blood pressure. These include eating less processed food with added salt, drinking alcohol in moderation, making time to exercise, quitting smoking and losing weight.

PAULA'S PICK OF HEART-FRIENDLY FOODS
Avocado

Many slimmers shy away from avocados, but calorie for calorie they offer a super array of nutrients. Avocados are a good source of potassium, which helps to balance sodium levels and regulate blood pressure. They are also a source of the antioxidant vitamin E and contains healthy monounsaturated fat.

Avocados contain more protein than other fruit and are a satisfying addition to salads and sandwiches. Half an avocado contains about 135 kcal.

Try adding diced avocados to eggs or omelettes before cooking, putting sliced avocados in wraps or sandwiches and adding to fruit salads or smoothies, etc.

Nuts and seeds

Nuts are high in calories but contain healthy monounsaturated fat, essential vitamins, minerals and fibre. Walnuts, flaxseeds and chia seeds are also sources of omega-3 fatty acids.

Studies suggest that eating a small handful of nuts a few times a week can help reduce the risk of heart disease, satisfy food cravings and help control weight. To avoid excess calories and weight gain, nuts should replace other saturated and trans fats in the diet.

As they are so nutrient-dense yet high in calories, you only need small amounts to get all the benefits – a small handful or about 30g contains almost 200 kcal.

Olive and rapeseed oils

Olive oil is a main ingredient in the healthy Mediterranean diet. Its protective effects are essentially due to two fundamental components: monounsaturated fatty acids and antioxidant substances.

Extra virgin olive oil is extremely versatile and a little goes a long way. Each tablespoon provides about 120 kcal. It's best used for dipping and salad dressing as its smoke point is not very high and the healthy fats can be destroyed by high heat.

Rapeseed oil is a fantastic economical cooking alternative to extra virgin olive oil, with similar health benefits. Its higher smoke point makes it ideal to use when cooking, and you can also add it to mashed potatoes or use it in a salad dressing.

Coconut oil

Even though over 85 per cent of the total fat in coconut oil is saturated, some of it is in the form of medium chain fatty acids, which don't appear to have the same adverse effects on health as other saturated fats. Coconut oil is easily digested and as it is mostly saturated, the fats are not easily damaged by heat. This makes it a possible occasional alternative fat for baking in particular. Use very moderately and don't use it instead of olive and rapeseed oil when cooking in general. More research is needed to scope out the effects of different saturated fats on health.

Camelina oil

A new oil on the shelves, camelina's nutritional profile of healthy unsaturated fat is often compared to flaxseed oil, but it has the added benefit of a higher vitamin E content and a longer shelf life. Its taste is nutty in flavour and it has a high smoke point, making it another great choice for cooking and roasting if you want an alternative to rapeseed oil. You can also use it in salad dressings, pesto and marinades.

Bananas

Bananas are not high-fat fruits. They may be higher in calories than many other fruits but their calories come from carbohydrate, excellent for refuelling before, during and after exercise.

Bananas are a rich source of potassium and also contain vitamin B6, important for healthy skin and hair and reducing fatigue. They are also prebiotics, which means they can help feed the 'good' bacteria in the gut. They are a great alternative to a high trans or saturated fat snack when you are feeling peckish.

Alcohol

There is evidence that moderate drinking has some health benefits, as long as there is no personal or family history of alcoholism, mental health, mood disorders or liver disease.

A large number of studies have documented an association between moderate alcohol consumption and a lower risk for coronary artery disease and stroke.

Polyphenols, found in red wine (such as resveratrol), have received a lot of attention in this regard. Scientists believe that these compounds reduce the risk of heart disease by preventing the oxidation and hardening of cholesterol on the inside of the blood vessels.

It seems that the quantity of resveratrol in grape skins varies with the grape cultivar and its geographic provenance. The total fermentation time a wine spends in contact with grape skins also impacts its resveratrol content. Consequently, white and rosé wines generally contain less resveratrol than red wines.

The sweeter the wine, the more calories and fewer protective flavonoids it contains. The benefits of red wine may extend beyond resveratrol and other flavonoids, of course. A Danish study found that people who buy wine are also likely to buy heart-healthy foods such as olives and olive oil, whereas beer drinkers are more likely to buy crisps and fizzy drinks.

- ▸ Try white wine spritzers (half a glass of white wine topped up with sparkling water).
- ▸ Try an alcohol-free, reduced-calorie beer.
- ▸ Try a Virgin Mary with plenty of Tabasco sauce or a Mock-ito.

Oily fish

Eat oily fish such as salmon, trout, fresh tuna, sardines, herring and mackerel twice a week. The protective omega-3 fats in oily fish keep the heartbeat regular, reduce triglycerides and prevent blood clots forming in the arteries by making the cells less sticky.

An analysis of 20 studies involving hundreds of thousands of participants indicates that eating approximately one to two servings of oily fish a week reduces the risk of dying from heart disease by 36 per cent. Be sure to consume the brown flesh as this contains most of the oil.

WARNING!

These are foods to watch out for:

- ▸ Grapefruit and other juices: Grapefruit juice inhibits the metabolism of many medications, including antihypertensive medications. It is recommended that individuals taking medication to treat coronary artery disease and its complications avoid grapefruit, citrus and apple juices and Seville oranges.
- ▸ Black liquorice: Consumption of liquorice can increase blood pressure and cause adverse effects.
- ▸ Seeds: Chia seeds and flaxseeds can interact with the medication warfarin.

THE MEDITERRANEAN DIET

We can learn a lot from the traditional Mediterranean diet (MD) of the 1960s. It was abundant in seasonal plant foods such as grains, beans, nuts, dates, vegetables and fruit. People typically consumed dairy in moderate amounts and drank a glass of wine with meals. In coastal regions, fish was a staple. Red meat was consumed only very occasionally. Olive oil was widely and freely used. Dessert was usually fruit-based.

Compared to other western diets, the traditional MD is considered somewhat of a paradox. Although fat consumption was high, the prevalence of heart disease, stroke, obesity and cancer was lower in the countries of the Mediterranean than in other European countries. Rather than limiting total fat intake, the MD focused more on the enjoyment of healthier fats.

On the menu were monounsaturated fats, found in olive oil, nuts and avocados, and polyunsaturated omega-3 fatty acids, found in oily fish. If you were to follow this diet today, limiting your intake of processed and packaged foods would ensure a better balance of fats and a lower intake of unhealthy saturated and trans fats.

In a meta-analysis published in the *British Medical Journal*, which collectively included more than 1.5 million participants, the researchers found that greater adherence to a MD resulted in significant improvements to health, including a 9 per cent drop in overall mortality, a 9 per cent drop in mortality from cardiovascular disease, and a 13 per cent reduction in the incidence of Parkinson's disease and Alzheimer's disease.

Unfortunately, the food and meal patterns of these Mediterranean countries have changed considerably over the last number of years. In Crete, for example, people consume less fruit and olive oil than they did historically. They also eat more meat, including processed meats. With these dietary and lifestyle changes, low rates of heart disease are no longer prevalent.

A weekly Mediterranean-style shopping list has few processed foods, but is big on colour and flavour. Try to include the following:

▶ **Shellfish:** Clams, crab, lobster, mussels, scallops, prawns

▶ **Fish:** Anchovies, halibut, salmon, sardines, bream, sole, tilapia, trout, tuna, swordfish

▶ **Fruits:** Citrus fruits, berries, cherries, dates, figs, grapes, melons, apples, peaches, pears, pomegranates

▶ **Vegetables:** Artichokes, asparagus, avocados, beetroot, peppers, broccoli, courgette, carrots, celery, corn, aubergines, fennel, French beans, green leafy vegetables, olives, onions, potatoes, radishes, squash, tomatoes

▶ **Grains:** Barley, brown rice, buckwheat, bulgar wheat, oatmeal, polenta, quinoa, wheat berries, whole grains, stone-ground breads, tortillas, pasta

- **Nuts:** Almonds, cashews, hazelnuts, walnuts, pecan nuts, pine nuts, pistachio nuts

- **Seeds:** Sesame, sunflower, pumpkin, flaxseeds

- **Legumes:** Cannellini beans, borlotti beans, broad beans, black-eyed beans, chickpeas, kidney beans, lentils, butter beans, split peas

- **Herbs and spices (fresh or dried):** Basil, chillies, cinnamon, cloves, cumin, dill, garlic, ginger, fennel seed, marjoram, mint, nutmeg, oregano, parsley, pepper (black or red), rosemary, saffron, sage, tarragon, thyme

- **Dairy products:** Natural and Greek yogurt, lower-fat cheeses (feta, mozzarella, Brie, camembert, goat's)

- **Oils:** Rapeseed, extra virgin olive, grapeseed, sesame

- **Chicken and duck eggs** (weekly)

- **Balsamic vinegar**

- **Red meat** (1–3 times/month)

- **Wine.**

SHOULD YOU CUT OUT DAIRY ALTOGETHER?

Because foods such as milk, cheese and yogurt are important for bone health, the advice for women in their middle years is to eat three servings of low-fat dairy every day. There is no need to cut dairy out. Just choose lower-fat options.

WHAT SPREAD SHOULD YOU USE?

This will depend on the rest of your diet and your balance of fats overall. You could enjoy a little butter containing primarily saturated fat – as long as you don't have a muffin at 11 and a sausage roll for lunch. But 'treats and sweets' seem to be more than occasional foods for many of us and it's critical to look at the frequent choices we make to determine how that affects the overall picture. Daily habits of choosing lower-fat dairy can be useful as long as you don't replace the calories with something worse.

DOES LOW-FAT MEAN HIGH SUGAR?

There is a prevailing concern that a lower-fat version of a food must be high in sugar. This is not necessarily true. Manufacturers do not add sugar to low-fat milk or reduced-fat Cheddar. They just remove fat. Yogurt is different and you will need to read the label of ingredients to see where the sugar comes from.

The nutrition table will give you the total amount of sugar in the pot, but the ingredients list will help you understand the source of that sugar. Some of these might be natural sources, for example the lactose naturally present in milk or from puréed fruit. On the other hand, it could be added as sucrose or table sugar. Read and decide.

There's no doubt it's much more difficult to remove fat from cakes, biscuits and confectionary and still retain the flavour, mouth-feel and great taste. Sugar or artificial sweeteners are generally added to replace the fat, so don't be fooled by 'low-fat' labels here.

CHAPTER 7

Complementary Therapies

Autumn is a reminder that while the leaves die and fall, there will always be Spring, a chance to replenish and be reborn. We all have the opportunity to replenish ourselves, to be reborn.

Tao Porchon-Lynch, yogi

In an ideal world, we would get everything we need to live a healthy vibrant life from fresh, colourful seasonal foods – strawberries in the summer when at their freshest and most succulent, and leafy greens through the cooler winter months. In reality, this isn't always possible and at certain stages in life, even healthier eaters often need a little boost. The menopausal years are one such time. We know that supplements are not a substitute for a healthy diet or for conventional medical treatment, simply an adjunct to sound nutritional principles.

In Asian societies, menopause is often referred to as the autumn of a woman's life. Qi is waning, our digestive systems are weaker and our bodies crave warm, nourishing foods and more internal and mindful autumn-style exercises like tai chi, qi gong and yoga. Our middle years are also the time to call on the apothecary of traditional medicines that have been an indelible part of life in these regions for centuries. From indigenous Chinese and Ayurvedic herbs and supplements, to the myriad other Mother Nature's remedies, these may be all you need to feel healthy, strong and in control of your body and your life.

WARNING!

The information provided in this chapter is not intended to replace conventional medical treatment. Any suggestions made and all herbs listed are not intended to diagnose, treat, cure or prevent any disease, condition or symptom. Personal directions and use should be provided by a clinical herbalist or other qualified healthcare practitioner.

In her 2003 book *Women, Hormones & the Menstrual Cycle: Herbal and medical solutions from adolescence to menopause*, Australian natural health expert Ruth Trickey recommends that, where possible, dietary and lifestyle suggestions and herbal remedies should be adopted prior to the onset of symptoms: 'Ideally they should be slowly incorporated into the daily routine of women in their forties to reduce the severity of symptoms once hormone levels start to decline'.

SOME HERBAL HELPERS

Many natural health practitioners recommend the following herbs for the management of hot flushes, mood swings and other menopausal symptoms. Consult a qualified herbalist before taking herbal supplements as some may be contraindicated with specific illnesses or may interact with other medications.

Black cohosh (*Cimicifuga racemosa*)
Cimicifuga has been used by Native Americans, Chinese and Europeans for many years. It's made from the root of the North American black cohosh plant and numerous studies support its efficacy in treating a number of menopausal complaints, including hot flushes, irritability, mood swings and sleep disturbances.

Research in 1985 showed that *cimicifuga racemosa* contains three types of hormonally active substances, one of which suppresses the surges in luteinising hormone (LH), associated with hot flushes, with the other two showing weak oestrogen-like effects.

Dong quai (*Angelica sinensis*)
In traditional Chinese medicine, *angelica sinensis* or Chinese angelica is referred to as a 'blood tonic' and is used to treat hot flushes and lack of sexual desire in particular. It is not recommended for use in conjunction with blood-thinning drugs such as warfarin, because it may cause bleeding complications.

The first writings regarding the female lifecycle are believed to have appeared in the Chinese Yellow Emperor's *Classic of Internal Medicine*, dating back to 220 BC. The cycle was described as proceeding in seven-year increments, in accordance with specific biological markers that best describe the natural ageing process (men have an eight-year cycle). During early youth (seven years or thereabouts) a girl's secondary teeth erupt. Menses starts about 14 years (7 x 2) and this cycle characterised by secondary sexual development (breasts, pubic hair and widening of the hips). The reproductive stage lasts for about 30 years. Peri-menopause is the stage before a woman's last menstruation at about 42 (7 x 6), with menopause at about 49 (7 x 7). Back then, it was believed that men continued to grow in wisdom until death but that a woman's useful years ended after childbearing. Today, as we know, the culmination of this seven-year cycle heralds the dawn of the wise woman.

Chaste tree berries (*Vitex agnus-castus*)

The use of vitex as a medicinal herb is believed to date back to Hippocrates (450 BC) who recommended it as a treatment for injuries, inflammation and to help women expel the afterbirth from the uterus. These dried berries have a peppery taste and were reportedly used in monasteries during the middle ages as a condiment to suppress the libido. Even today, the herb is often referred to as 'monk's pepper' or 'cloister pepper' and is prescribed to help regulate the female reproductive system and ease menopausal symptoms. It is not a fast-acting herb and needs to be taken for a minimum of six months and up to 18 months or so for benefits to be noticed.

Sage (*Salvia officinalis*)

The ancient Egyptians are believed to have used sage as a fertility drug, while the Romans considered it sacred and would gather it with ceremony. Sage's active ingredient, thujone, comprises about 30 per cent of the volatile oil content and its leaves, roots, seeds and essential oil (clary sage) are all used fresh or dried as tinctures, compresses, tonics and infusions. A 2011 Swiss study demonstrated the clinical value of fresh sage leaves in the treatment of hot flushes and associated menopausal symptoms.

Red clover (*Trifolium pratense*)

Red clover is a perennial plant that grows wild in meadows throughout Europe and Asia. The red flowers have been used for centuries as a blood cleanser and as a poultice for acne, ulcers and bronchitis. More recent scientific tests have shown that red clover contains isoflavones with oestrogen-like effects that may help relieve hot flushes and other menopausal symptoms. It is a useful source of nutrients including calcium, chromium, magnesium, niacin, phosphorus, potassium, thiamine and vitamin C.

" I had great support from my naturopath, who recommended supplements and dietary adaptations to minimise my symptoms. I had some hot flushes over a 15-year period, often putting my foot out of bed to see if someone had turned the heating on. However, this wasn't a big problem for me when my periods finally stopped, although friends of mine have said otherwise. Omega-3 supplements every day, a good multivitamin, adding turmeric to

my cooking and sage tea all helped. When I had sleepless nights, calcium/magnesium supplements helped, along with a dose of acceptance and meditation. Little did we know that in the middle ages, it was normal to have a 'first sleep', then a period of night-time wakefulness, before a 'second sleep'. Anything that normalised my experience was helpful. **"**
– Krystana

THE CHINESE WAY – TRADITIONAL CHINESE MEDICINE (TCM)

The TCM World Foundation states that the word 'menopause' is not part of the traditional Chinese medical vocabulary. It calls the various disturbances a woman experiences when her monthly cycle is coming to an end as simply 'menstrual cycle-ending symptoms'. Many experts say these years often pass unnoticed because women traditionally prepare early for this time in their lives through diet, herbal prescriptions and indigenous Chinese therapies like acupuncture, moxibustion, cupping and many others. As with all Asian cultures, change is generally managed preventively.

To the Chinese, the transition to this autumn phase in a woman's life offers the opportunity to capture the essence of life and strengthen and harmonise her body, mind and spirit. This is a hugely positive time, a time of creativity and new beginnings and a time when a woman can find a more confident voice. There is also a genuine acknowledgment of the wisdom acquired in earlier years and a feeling that these experiences can be put to use in many ways in the future.

" *Longevity is related to sufficiency of Qi.*
If the Qi is strong, life is long. **"**
– Wong Chong, Essay on Balance, *4th century*

The philosophy of yin and yang is refined into the theory of the Five Elements of wood (mu), fire (huo), earth (tu), metal (jin) and water (shui), with each nurturing, supporting and, where appropriate, controlling one another to keep the body in balance and harmony. Everything in the universe corresponds with one of the five elements and helps to explain the effect of sounds, smells, food, the planets, seasons and emotions on the body.

When a person is in good health, the movement of qi and blood through the body is harmonious. However, if qi or blood is blocked or slowed, the organs, tissues and cells will be deprived of the power needed to function at their best. Traditional therapies like acupuncture, moxibustion, acupressure, reflexology and tui na and exercise routines such as qi gung and tai chi help remove blockages and encourage a smoother flow of qi. These ancient practices continue to be encouraged not only as therapy but also as an essential component of daily life to preserve vitality and positive health, most especially as we grow older.

In Chinese medicine, as with other eastern therapies, wellness is all about keeping the body, mind and spirit in balance. Using a combination of the five elements, yin-yang theory and a targeted physical examination, a skilled TCM practitioner will discern a unique pattern from which a highly individualised therapy will be prescribed, based on the needs of each patient at that particular time. This is unique to tradtional Chinese medicine. For example, one woman's hot flushes may be worse at night and accompanied by profuse sweating, restless sleep and dry eyes, while another may have hot flushes that appear randomly during the day accompanied by low back pain, poor memory and vaginal dryness. So while both women present with hot flushes, they will be treated very differently. Rather than trying to restore hormones to the levels

Taoism, the fundamental philosophy of the world's oldest civilisation, is as relevant today as it was in classical China. Traditional Chinese medicine embodies Taoism's holistic and preventive approach to health by focusing on diet, movement and spiritual and emotional well-being. It treats the body as a whole and aims to prevent illness by maintaining overall health and balance.

In Taoist belief, the universe exists as a unified whole, comprising two opposing yet complementary forces known as yin and yang (the moon and sun, female and male, night and day respectively).

The small dots within each of the two energies (represented by black and white) symbolise that there is always some yin (black) within yang (white) and vice versa.

It is the interplay between these interdependent forces that governs qi, the vital energy or life force that powers the universe and suffuses every living cell. The ancients believed that getting vital air or qi to the tissues and cells through a continuously circulating blood supply was the basic physiological function of the body.

of a younger woman, the goal of TCM therapy is always to nourish the organ systems and rebalance the body through a combination of acupuncture, herbal formulas and lifestyle changes.

From a woman's early 40s, yin's cooling feminine energy starts to wane, with knock-on effects on her levels of fluidity, moisture and sleeping patterns, among other consequences. As these qualities decline (much like the deterioration in oestrogen levels that, in western thinking, keep body tissues fluid and moist), the balance between yin and yang is disturbed, so much so that many women post-menopause discover their more yang (energetic, often aggressive) nature, while, as men grow older, they tend to exhibit their more yin (passive, yielding) side.

Menopause represents a natural decline in kidney qi in particular. This is the energy that powers numerous functions in the body and has a huge impact on female fertility. In fact, TCM experts believe that kidney qi deficiency is the root cause of many menopausal issues. For example, a younger woman showing signs of deficiency in kidney yin (insomnia or heart palpitations) will be deemed likely to have a more difficult time at menopause unless this imbalance is corrected preventively. So in addition to a nourishing plant-based diet rich in phytoestrogens, targeted Chinese therapies and lifestyle advice, the practitioner will recommend a tonic formulated specifically to nourish her waning kidney yin. Stress is a big contributor too – in overload, our it further depletes the body's yin. In essence, our autumn phase is all about capturing and storing the yin – much like the ancient farmers who gathered and stored the harvest for the bleaker winter months ahead.

Chinese herbal medicine

Many of the most valuable Chinese herbal medicines are tonics formulated to nourish qi, blood, yin and yang. These can be consumed on a regular basis (often over a long period) with no adverse side effects. Single herbs are not nearly as strong in their effect as herbal formulas, so when treating deficient yin, for instance, a combination of cooling and warming herbs such as rehmania and Chinese wild yam is used to capture waning yin and subtly rebalance and invigorate the body.

High-impact exercise is not recommended as a woman grows older, as it is believed that muscles slowly start to atrophy with age and strenuous exercise puts undue pressure on her body, hence the move to a lower-impact, more meditative lifestyle.

Chinese therapies

There are many centuries-old indigenous Chinese therapies that are still widely used today but the following are those most appropriate for women entering this autumn stage of life.

Acupuncture

When qi is disrupted, the job of the acupuncturist is to nudge it back to equilibrium by inserting needles at specific points along the body's energy lines (or meridians) and pulsing the body with a low electric current to free this blocked energy. While western medicine remains unsure of exactly how acupuncture works, we do know that in certain situations it does so by producing measurable changes in the brain. While acupuncture doesn't actually capture the yin essence as such, it helps regulate qi and can help reduce hot flushes, improve sleep patterns and restore the balance of yin and yang in the body.

A WOMAN'S MIDDLE YEARS ARE THE TIME WHEN MORE INTERNAL AND MINDFUL EXERCISES COME INTO THEIR OWN, WITH FAR-REACHING BENEFITS PHYSICALLY, MENTALLY AND SPIRITUALLY. THIS IS WHERE MOVEMENT BECOMES SO CLOSELY INTERTWINED WITH MEDICINE IN THERAPIES LIKE QI GONG AND TAI CHI CHUAN (TAI CHI), WHICH DIRECT THE FLOW OF ENERGY TO KEEP THE BODY IN BALANCE AND HEALTH. WHEN PERFORMED CORRECTLY, THESE EXERCISES WILL BUILD DYNAMIC AND POWERFUL INTERNAL STRENGTH.

A 2015 meta-analysis assessing the effectiveness of acupuncture in women going through a natural menopause found that those who underwent acupuncture experienced a reduction in the severity and frequency of hot flushes for up to three months. Furthermore, the treatment appeared to have a beneficial effect on hot flushes regardless of the number of doses, sessions or duration of treatment received.

Moxibustion

The burning of the herb moxa (Artemisia vulgaris) can be traced back to Chinese peasants who burned herbs around parts of their body to relieve pain. The most common form of moxa used today is the moxa stick, a compressed moxa leaf resembling a mini cigar. When lit and rotated above the skin of the affected area, it stimulates the circulation of blood and qi through the body. Acupuncture and moxibustion can also be combined to enable the heat and curative effects of the herb to be distributed through the body via the meridians.

Cupping

Cupping has a long history in TCM, both on its own and as an adjunct to acupuncture to relieve a range of complaints including menopausal symptoms. The technique involves the strategic fixing of small glass jars at targeted points on the skin, using a pump to create a vacuum. The suction created increases the local circulation of qi and blood and dispels cold and dampness from the body. Cupping is suitable for joint stiffness and pain and for relieving swelling, and is often practised in conjunction with acupuncture and massage.

Tui na

Literally translated as 'press and rub,' tui na is the oldest and most common form of Chinese acupressure massage. There are over 20 different tui na techniques, all of which involve deep digital stimulation of vital points along the body's meridians. It is excellent for treating colds and headaches, insomnia, intestinal upsets, menstrual irregularities, low back pain and stiff neck, and can be used on its own or combined with acupuncture for more powerful results.

EXPERT OPINION: THE INDIAN WAY – AYURVEDA ◄ ·······················

Sunita Passi, Ayurvedic specialist, meditation teacher, journalist and founder of Tri-Dosha (www.tri-dosha.co.uk)

Ayurveda is the time-tested Indian system of healing that remains hugely popular the world over. At its heart is the concept that our bodies are a microcosm of the universe with three doshas at work: vata (air), pitta (fire) and kapha (earth). Each of us has a unique pattern of physical, mental and emotional energy that corresponds with these doshas, and although one dosha is generally dominant, we possess all three doshas in varying degrees (see the table on pages 120 to 122).

We are said to be in good health physically and emotionally when the doshas are balanced. The proper amount of vata promotes creativity and flexibility, pitta generates understanding and analytical ability, and kapha engenders stability, affection and generosity.

Imbalances in the doshas are believed to disrupt the flow of prana, the life force that enters the body through our food and breath. The key to Ayurveda is treating the body, mind and spirit as a unified whole to maintain health and harmony. Those who adopt this self-healing philosophy understand it to be a long-term lifestyle choice, with the full benefits reaped only when its core principles are adhered to in strictest Ayurvedic tradition.

When recognising the dominant dosha, a trained practitioner will prescribe a treatment and skincare programme based on each individual's unique needs. A typical regime could include a series of therapeutic massages, oil therapy, vegetarian diet, herbal tonics and a daily routine of yoga and meditation. Those in good health will also consult an Ayurvedic practitioner for preventive advice on diet, exercise and meditation practices to keep their body in balance and working at its best.

AYURVEDIC CONSULTATION

During an Ayurvedic consultation, you will be asked questions related to your body type and physical characteristics. The aim of this analysis is to determine your current dosha (body type), known as vikruti (meaning imbalance in Sanskrit).

The table that follows lists the dominant characteristics of each dosha. Work your way through the table, circling the key traits that apply to you, basing your choices on what you observe as the most consistent over a long period of time – at least six to 12 months – and not just how you feel today. If you feel that you have characteristics from more than on section, circle both or even all three.

Once you've read through the table and selected the characteristics that apply to you, add up the number of characteristics under vata, pitta and kapha to discover your vikruti dosha.

Most of us will have one dosha predominant, a few will have two doshas equal, and the odd few will have all three doshas in equal proportion.

Doshas

PHYSICAL BODY			
	VATA	PITTA	KAPHA
HEIGHT	Tall or very short	Medium	Usually short, but can be tall and large
FRAME	Thin, bony	Moderate, good muscle	Large, well developed
WEIGHT	Low, difficult to gain	Moderate	Heavy, hard to lose
SKIN	Rough, dry, thin	Warm, oily	Cold, oily, thick
EYES	Small, dry, nervous, often brown	Sharp, penetrating, green, blue or grey with yellowish sclera	Big, beautiful, loving, calm
HAIR	Dry, thin, curly	Soft, oily, red, fair	Thick, oily, wavy, lustrous
NAILS	Rough, hard, brittle, split easily	Soft, pink, lustrous	Whiteish, pale, smooth, polished
VOICE	Low or weak, quick, talkative	High or sharp, moderate, clear, precise	Slow, maybe laboured, or deep tonal
WALK	Quick, light, hurried	Medium-paced, purposeful	Slow, steady, calm

PHYSIOLOGICAL			
	VATA	**PITTA**	**KAPHA**
DISEASE TENDENCY	Nervous, sharp pains, headaches, eczema, dry, rash, gas/constipation	Inflammation, rashes, allergies, mucus, heartburn, ulcers, fevers	Fluid retention, excess mucus, bronchitis, sinus, asthma
ELIMINATION	Irregular, constipated, hard, dry	Regular, loose	Slow, plentiful and heavy
SWEAT	Minimal	Profuse, especially when hot	Moderate, but present even when not exercising
TEMPERATURE PREFERENCES	Craves warmth, dislikes cold and dry	Loves coolness, dislikes heat and sun	Dislikes cold and damp, prefers heat
APPETITE	Variable, small	Good, regular	Slow, steady
DIGESTION	Eats quickly, delicate	Strong, can eat almost anything	Eats and digest slowly
ENDURANCE	Minimal	Moderate	Excellent
SLEEP	Poor, disturbed	Moderate but sound	Heavy, prolonged, excessive
DREAMS	Frequent, can't remember on waking	Vivid, often in colour, easy to remember	Only remembers highly significant, clear dreams

PSYCHOLOGICAL			
	VATA	PITTA	KAPHA
EMOTIONS	Enthusiastic, outgoing, changeable ideas and moods	Strong-minded, purposeful, thrives on challenges, expresses opinion	Calm, placid, good-natured, easy-going, reliable
MEMORY	Poor long-term, quick to grasp but forgets	Sharp and clear	Slow to learn but never forgets
STRESS	Anxious and nervous	Angry, irritable	Fear and anger if pushed
WORK	Quick, imaginative, active and creative thinker, bored with routine	Natural leader, efficient, planned routine, perfectionist	Keeps things calm, caring, enjoys regular routine
FINANCES	Poor, spends rapidly	Moderate, buys luxuries	Rich, thrifty
HOBBIES	Travel, art, philosophy	Sport, politics, luxuries	Serene, leisurely types
CREATIVITY	Original, fertile	Technical, scientific	Entrepreneurial
FRIENDS	Makes and changes often	Most work-related, changes when change jobs	Long-lasting and sincere
LIFESTYLE	Erratic	Busy but plans to achieve much	Steady and regular, maybe stuck in a rut

THE WISE WOMAN

Ageing is associated with the loss of life's juice, literally and figuratively. As the body shrinks with age, the mind goes fuzzy, joints dry out and muscles lose tone. Menopause is a time of great fluctuation in the doshas, especially vata, and is most commonly recognised by a change from the pitta phase to the vata phase of life. Vata is ruled by ether (space) and the air elements, so this vata dominant stage is characterised by an overall drying out in the woman's body – the thinning of hair, nails, skin and some internal organs. Other indicators include hair shedding, sleeping difficulties, low energy levels, irregular or no periods and intense feelings of heat in the face and upper body, accompanied by an increased heart rate, dizziness, headache, weakness or anxiety.

While all women move towards vata dominance, they will undoubtedly experience some of these symptoms along with others most associated with their dominant dosha. For example, pitta women may suffer badly from intense hot flushes, often requiring regular changes in clothing during the day and bed-linen changes at night. The typical kapha woman is prone to weight gain, fluid retention and feelings of mental and physical heaviness. She may also struggle with personal relationships at this time and become more lethargic, spending longer periods of time sleeping.

AYURVEDIC HERBAL THERAPY

Indian women generally prefer to use single herbs rather than mixed formulas. Those familiar with traditional Ayurvedic cuisine will use an array of herbs and spices to stimulate the senses and keep the body strong and balanced. Below are the most commonly prescribed during the menopausal years.

Shatavari (*Asparagus racemosos*)

This is the most respected herb for treating menopausal imbalance. Thanks to its cooling, regulating and nourishing qualities, it helps balance the hormonal, nervous and metabolic systems and is widely regarded as a natural alternative to hormone therapy.

Ajwain (Carom seed)

A traditional herb known for its anti-inflammatory and curative benefits, ajwain is rich in thymol, a chemical that enhances the release of gastric juices and improves digestion. It also stimulates the circulation, eases the pain associated with arthritis and helps with menopausal imbalances. The seeds are either chewed raw (mixed with a pinch of salt for flavour) or ground into a powder and added to cooking and nourishing tonics (see the Ayurvedic home remedy on page 124).

Fennel (*Foeniculum vulgare*)

Ayurvedic practitioners prescribe fennel to treat a range of issues including constipation, diarrhoea, indigestion, urinary disorders, coughs, rheumatic pain, dull and oily skin and menopausal issues. Fennel contains a number of phytonutrients, including anethole, which is widely used as a tonic to support the female reproductive system and menopausal hot flushes in particular.

To make fennel tea, pour a cup of boiling water over 1–2 teaspoons crushed fennel seeds. Leave to stand for a few minutes before drinking.

Turmeric (*Curcuma longa*)
Another centuries-old remedy in the Ayurvedic pharmacopeia.

TRY THIS ▼

This time-trusted Ayurvedic home remedy has been passed from mother to daughter for generations. It is excellent for relieving menopausal vata imbalances, pitta-related hot flushes and the bloating associated with kapha. The ingredients can be sourced at reputable Asian food stores.

½ tsp dill seed powder
¼ tsp dry ginger powder
¼ tsp ajwain powder (the ajwain seeds are crushed to make a powder)
1 pinch asafoetida (traditional Indian powder)
1 tsp cumin seed powder
1 tsp raw sugar cane
1 glass water
1 tsp aloe vera juice

Boil all the ingredients except the aloe vera juice for 5 minutes. Filter and leave to cool, then add the aloe vera juice. Menopausal women should take once daily for 14 days. The dose can then be increased to twice a day (after lunch and the evening meal) for up to 3 months.

RENEWING LIFE'S LUSTRE

Rejuvenation or rasayana refers to the 'the path of juice' and is a trusted recipe for invigorating waning vitality. At its core is living more healthily and purposefully by eating well, refuelling vitality and renewing the skin's lustre – in other words, stimulating the body physically, mentally and emotionally.

Rasayana requires:

▸ **Foods to nourish:** Mindful eating and consumption of nourishing foods and supplements eaten in accordance with Ayurvedic principles (see the table on page 128).

▸ **Fluids to flourish:** Treatments such as pizhichil, the application of warm medicated oils over the body, and shirodhara, a method of opening the third eye in the forehead via the dripping of medicated oils onto the forehead, are a key part of the rejuvenation ritual as they help lubricate both body and mind while also keeping the skin richly nourished and the essence of life once again in full flow.

MOVEMENT

Although specific advice will vary depending on each individual's constitution, the overall aim is to nurture the body as a whole by connecting mind, body and spirit through movement. In essence, this means daily yoga or other mind/body practices such as tai chi and qi gong combined with more tailored exercises recommended by an Ayurvedic practitioner (see the table on page 128).

BREATH

Pranayama or control-led breathing is integral to a healthy Ayurvedic lifestyle at all stages of life, but most especially during life's transitions to ensure prana flows freely to every recess of the body to keep us healthier and stronger in body and mind. Correct breathing technique is also believed to help cleanse the body while also promoting sounder sleep patterns. There are many different breathing exercises but the following are those most commonly recommended.

Breath of life

Lie comfortably on the floor (either on rug or yoga mat). Bring your feet close to the buttocks and let them fall apart, bringing the soles of the feet together with your hands resting gently on the floor. If you're uncomfortable, put cushions under your knees.

Start breathing slowly and deeply into the diaphragm, feeling the abdomen slowly expand and contract. Start slowly and naturally, pausing for a second of two between breaths.

Then start to extend the breath so it comes up from the abdomen and starts to fill the chest. Continue this breath cycle, pausing between each breath.

When complete, bring your knees back together and gently stretch your legs. Relax comfortably for a few minutes before finishing.

Alternate nostril breathing (Nadi shodhana)

This wonderfully calming technique is routinely used for balancing wayward energy during this vata phase of life.

Sit comfortably with a straight back and your right hand held in what is called Vishnu mudra (the thumb and ring finger actively touching and the other three fingers relaxed).

Close off the left nostril with the right ring finger and breathe in deeply through the right nostril only (to a count of 5 or thereabouts).

Then close off the right nostril with the right thumb, release the hold on the left nostril and exhale gently through this nostril (to a count of 5). Keep your eyes closed throughout the exercise. Continue in this fashion: close left, inhale right, then close right, exhale left and so on.

Begin with 11 repetitions and increase as and when needed.

Breath of balance

Sit with your legs bent, feet comfortably crossed at the ankles, spine extended, shoulders relaxed and away from the ears, eyes closed or facing down.

Extend the arms to the side with fingertips touching the floor.

Inhale and raise both arms above your head. Bring the fingertips together above the head.

Turn the palms out and exhale as you lower the arms, bringing fingertips to the floor.

Repeat this motion in coordination with your breath as you visualise diamond white or violet universal energy streaming from the crown of your head and surrounding your body.

Continue inhaling and exhaling, moving your arms up and down for 1–3 minutes.

You can chant the following to yourself as you breathe: 'I am balanced between earth and heaven.'

" As long as there is breath in the body, there is life. When breath departs, so too does life. Therefore, regulate the breath. "
– The Hatha Yoga Pradipika

MASSAGE

Traditional Ayurvedic massage uses medicated herbal oils specifically selected based on the body's dosha. Its techniques used are designed to loosen the excess doshas, directing them towards the organs of elimination. It also enhances circulation, increases flexibility and relieves pain and stiffness. Massage can be performed by one or more therapists in tandem (Abhyanga) and techniques range from kneading to rubbing and squeezing with the hands. Shirodhara, sometimes referred to as the 'massage of the third eye', is a powerful and uniquely Ayurvedic therapy during which a steady stream of warmed medicated oil is slowly poured over the third eye in the forehead to relieve tension and calm both body and mind.

	VATA	PITTA	KAPHA
SEASONS	Increases in autumn.	Dominates late spring/early summer.	Increases in winter and lasts until early spring.
FOOD	Strengthening foods to nourish: Wholegrains, lentils, pumpkin, tomatoes, yogurt, cheese (for digestion), ghee, protein (including white meat, fish and venison to build stamina, warming teas (ginger and nutmeg)	Reduce intake of spicy foods and sour, salty and pungent tastes, which all produce heat (e.g. sour fruits like tomatoes). Use cooling and refreshing flavours like fresh coriander and dill. Use pulses (in moderation only as they can produce acidity). Eat plenty of vegetables such as asparagus, broccoli, Brussels sprouts and cabbage.	Avoid comfort eating, overeating and napping during the day, which can exacerbate weight gain. Eat foods rich in omega-3 fatty acids and replenish the body with antioxidant-rich fruits and vegetables.
HERBS/ SPICES	For the body: Warming herbs like ginger, cinnamon, liquorice, ashwagan-dha, calamus, jatamansi, dashmula In cooking: Saffron, black pepper, salt, tamari, ajwain, sage, turmeric, rosemary, fennel, cinnamon, bay leaf, cumin, basil	For the body: For sensitive skin and problematic digestion, use neem, shatavari, amalaki, fennel cardamom, mint and saffron. In cooking: Fennel, aniseed, turmeric, cinnamon, coriander, mint, liquorice, lemongrass, rose, water, saffron, peppermint, dulse	For the body: For oily/clammy skin, use neem, sage, rosemary and triphala to heat the body. In cooking: Black pepper, chilli, ginger, mustard, nutmeg, cloves, bay leaves, allspice, cardamom, cayenne, marjoram, cumin, caraway, cinnamon, basil, anise, turmeric, sage
MOVEMENT	Yoga: Spinal twist to correct neck stiffness and assist flow of prana Swimming: Breaststroke helps ground and control stress.	Yoga: More relaxing, meditative styles	Kapha is prone to being slow and sluggish so higher impact exercise will stimulate metabolism, boost the release of endorphins and prime the body for action.
BREATH	Alternate nostril breathing helps balance wayward energy.	The pranayama 'breath of fresh air' technique helps purify and recharge both body and mind.	Pranayama helps regulate, rebalance and purify kapha's internal energy.
MASSAGE	Best suited to more flowing rhythmic movements using a soothing oil blend to calm the body	Massage coconut oil into the scalp and feet in particular to cool pitta heat.	Vitality-boosting movements delivered with an energising oil blend

MIND POWER – VISUALISATION

Meditation has been shown to increase the working memory and as we move to a new phase in life, strong mental health is there to support you (see Chapter 10: Mindspace).

Shabir Daya, pharmacist and co-founder of the online health resource Victoria Health (www.victoriahealth.com)

Not all supplements are created equal – with so much misinformation on the market, the following is a guide to the best supplements for your middle years and beyond.

SUPPLEMENTS FOR MENOPAUSE SYMPTOMS
Hot flushes and other menopausal concerns

Formulated specifically for women during their menopausal years, Sage Complex by Food Science of Vermont is overflowing with phytoestrogens, including red clover, dong quai, sage extract and Siberian ginseng, which together help to rebalance hormones and reduce many of the concerns associated with menopause. In fact, supplements rich in these nutrients are useful for women post-menopause as well to maintain internal hormonal balance.

Vaginal dryness

Declining oestrogen levels are believed to be primarily responsible for vaginal dryness and the combination of phytoestrogens and herbs found in Sage Complex can favourably reduce symptoms of dryness and irritation.

A lack of polyunsaturated fatty acids can also contribute to vaginal dryness. Essential fatty acids (most especially omega-7) derived from sea buckthorn oil can help reduce dryness for many women. Omega-7 essential fatty acids are important structural components of mucous membranes which form the protective lining of internal organs such as the vaginal, digestive and respiratory tracts, as well as the surface of the eyes and mouth. Sea buckthorn oil promotes healthy regeneration of these membranes, while also providing nutrients essential for the healthy functioning of the membranes in the vaginal tract.

The active ingredient in turmeric (Curcuma longa) is curcumin, which displays potent anti-inflammatory and antioxidant properties that can help quench inflammation in the soft tissues of the body, including the vaginal area. However, the vast majority of turmeric supplements available contain low levels of curcumin, which are easily degraded by the stomach acids. Research has shown that turmeric is not water-soluble but dissolves efficiently in fats, so choose a supplement containing 95 per cent curcumin or thereabouts, coated in an enteric coating or a supplement that presents with some form of oil to ensure the greatest availability to the body (see Chapter 12: Sex for an overview of vaginal lubricants).

Anxiety and stress

Symptoms of stress and anxiety can be a feature of life during the menopause years and are most commonly associated with reduced hormonal levels. Magnolia (Magnolia officinalis) is a centuries-old Chinese medicine ingredient that is well documented for its ability to help control stress-related symptoms including irritability, restlessness, muscle tension and concentration.

Rhodiola (*Rhodiola* rosea), also known as Golden Root, is another ancient plant that herbalists call an 'adaptogen', as it can help rebalance the body.

BEYOND MENOPAUSE

As we move into our post-menopause years, taking care of our health will help keep us balanced, strong and energised. The following recommendations are an adjunct to a nutritious diet and regular exercise routine.

Multivitamins and minerals

Numerous studies indicate that by the time processed foods reach our table, their nutrient content can be seriously compromised, not just due to cooking, but also as a result of the manufacture and storage, during which antioxidant nutrients can be severely compromised. The vast majority of multivitamins on the market contain synthetic or semi-synthetic nutrients, with some using mega doses that can actually do more harm than good, so if you are taking a supplement choose wisely and don't overdose!

Krill oil

It is virtually impossible to achieve our daily targets for essential fatty acids if we don't consume at least two servings of oily fish per week and eat plenty of essential fatty acid-rich foods. Krill oil extract is prepared from a species of Antarctic krill (Euphausia superba) that shares similar fatty acid profile to fish and has an efficient delivery mechanism through the body.

It also contains astaxanthin, a powerful antioxidant that helps to protect the body against free radical damage.

Astaxanthin

It is now generally accepted that free radical damage and inflammation are key causes of ageing in the body. Astaxanthin is a member of the carotenoid family of antioxidants and is an excellent free radical neutraliser and anti-inflammatory. The best dietary sources of astaxanthin are salmon, trout and some other seafoods, but many of us find it difficult to obtain meaningful amounts from our diet alone. If choosing an astaxanthin supplement, ensure it is derived from algae (not fungus) and that the supplement contains some form of oil or essential fatty acid to enhance absorption.

Probiotics

For centuries, many cultures have included pickled and fermented foods in their diet to maintain intestinal gut health. The live probiotic bacteria in our intestines manufacture vital immune-enhancing compounds essential to health. With our stressful lifestyles and dependence on processed foods, our need for probiotics is greater than ever before. The biggest challenge, however, is maintaining sufficient quantities of these bacteria as the typical stomach environment is highly acidic and can destroy them. When taking probiotics, choose acid-resistant strains such as lactobacillus species, with a minimum of 4 to 5 billion organisms per capsule. Choose a probiotic with multiple strains of bacteria, coated enterically to protect them from the acidic stomach environment and to ensure they colonise the gut effectively (see Chapter 5: Immunity).

Vitamin D

Once associated principally with healthy bone production in the body, numerous studies now associate vitamin D deficiency with a range of chronic health concerns, including compromised immune function, diabetes, depression and cell mutation. So much so that the UK National Diet and Nutrition Survey rolling programme suggests that up to one in four adults in the UK have a low vitamin D status and are therefore at increased risk of deficiency.

Vitamin D3, the active form of vitamin D, is required for a healthy immune system, strong bones and teeth, skin health and efficient digestion and absorption, among many other functions. As vitamin D is fat-soluble, it can be difficult to absorb in the body. Some vitamin D3 supplements can be sprayed sublingually, thereby avoiding the gastric route. To ensure your vitamin D needs are met throughout the year, 25mcg is recommended from spring to autumn, with increased amounts recommended during the colder months between autumn and spring. When supplementing with fat-soluble vitamins, regular blood testing is advised.

CHAPTER 8

Beauty

There's too much emphasis on youth. I'm 58 and I don't mind telling everyone. I'm a grandma with a capital G. Because you can't be 58 and wish you were 35 – it's not going to happen. I'm going to do the best I can with what I have.

Andrea Dellal, model

Fresh, bright and healthy skin can shift that 'just OK' feeling up a gear to one of real self-assurance and confidence. As we get older, for many of us, that 'just OK' all too easily becomes our every day. But with a little effort, we can change this. For some it's a juggling act of a few needles interspersed with regular beauty treatments, while for others it's the needle-free route with the best skincare advice and regular treatments to maintain nourished, glowing skin.

We are often told that a few lines are a sign of a life well lived, but it is estimated that a woman will lose up to 30 per cent of facial collagen during the 5 years after menopause, while hormone-induced facial bone loss can be up to 20 per cent, giving the face a dull, shrunken look. This is not predestined, however, and you will find practical solutions in this chapter to some of the most common skin concerns women experience as they grow older, along with recommendations for the most effective ingredients to keep every type of skin fresh, plump and vibrant.

THE BIOLOGY

The skin is the body's largest organ, with numerous functions that go far deeper than simply being our outside selves. Through its network of sensory nerves, the skin communicates pressure, pain, temperature, odour and sexual stimuli to the brain, which responds via the blood system to maintain a relatively constant body temperature and water content.

Like a freshly ironed sheet covering a newly sprung mattress, the skin of a newborn is soft, smooth and entirely blemish-free. As the mattress ages, the sheet starts to sag. This sheet is the skin's epidermis. Just 0.02mm thick on the face, it comprises cells called keratinocytes, which are glued together by an extracellular matrix. The epidermis is continually regenerated by stem cells at its base that spawn new keratinocytes, which migrate through the epidermis before sloughing off to reveal even fresher cells underneath.

The thick mattress beneath the epidermis is the dermis, a chunky gelatinous sea of matrix and cells. Woven though this mesh are rope-like protein fibres of collagen (giving skin its firm, tensile strength) and feathery coils of elastin (to maintain resilience). While this network of collagen and elastin provides strength and elasticity, the stuffing is made of large molecules of glycosaminoglycans or GAGs, the most common of which is hyaluronic acid. These absorb water to give the dermis of young skin its jelly-like consistency and smooth, plump feel.

From the moment we are born, we begin to age, but it's only in our 20s that the effects start to become visible in the skin. During this decade, genetically-programmed chronological (or natural biological) ageing causes biochemical changes in our skin's collagen and elastin fibres and the once neat architecture starts to disintegrate. Both the epidermis and dermis begin to thin and collagen and elastin start to unravel. It is estimated that from the age of about 40, the skin thins by 1 per cent per year, with a projected 2 per cent reduction noticed in collagen and elastin, while further damage is incurred by skin cells simply drifting into 'senescence', which means they just shut down.

For many of us, one of the most disturbing signs of peri-menopause is the accompanying physical changes in our skin, with loss of collagen, slackness, dryness, increased sensitivity and overall skin thinning. Our skin's protective barrier gets weaker, leaving skin drier still and more vulnerable to environmental aggressors, while at the same time the existing fine lines seem to morph into deeper wrinkles and the density of the skin decreases, resulting in loss of overall facial volume – and a drawn, gaunt look.

Women who experienced acne during their teen years may be more prone to its recurrence during the menopausal years, especially around the lower face and neck, while others may be prone to redness, irritation and inflammation due to disturbed hormonal balance (a condition that Chinese medicine calls 'excessive internal heat'). Others still might notice hair thinning, temporary hair loss or excessive hair growth (hirsutism) in areas of the body where the hair follicles are more sensitive to androgen such as the chin, upper lips and cheeks.

At this stage in life, many women (and men) start to exercise intensely in an effort to improve their body shape and maintain a youthful appearance. Intense exercise can give rise to a skeletal and bony face – the so-called 'runner's face'. The increased energy demands of extreme exercise burn off fat beneath the layers of skin and the depletion in fatty tissue results in a loss of elasticity, the deepening of wrinkles and the pronounced appearance of facial bones. To make matters worse, hours spent running and training outdoors expose us to harmful UV radiation, incurring further damage to the skin.

As each person's genetic programme is different, so too is their rate of skin ageing, which explains why some age less visibly than others. Ethnicity also plays a role. For example, while Asian skin is generally stronger, tougher and less prone to wrinkles than western skin, it is not as supple and as the skin becomes less elastic and the underlying fat padding starts to disintegrate, Asian skin often becomes drier and start to drop.

While we can't stop much of this chronological ageing, we can act preventively to reduce its consequences and help keep our skin brighter and healthier for longer. We can also minimise much of the free radical-induced photo-ageing caused by UV exposure, while also paying close attention to what we eat and take steps to reduce the stress factors in our lives. Cigarettes are major culprits in skin ageing, with many studies showing that smokers have more wrinkles than non-smokers of the same age, complexion and sun exposure history.

The field of psychodermatology explores the interaction between the mind and the skin. There is an unquestionable link between stress levels and our skin. Once we appreciate that our skin and nervous systems come from the same part of the embryo during our development, we can understand why this is the case. So when we are embarrassed, shocked or stressed, our skin responds accordingly by blushing, flaring up or breaking out.

Stress impacts the skin through a cascade of reactions triggered by the brain, which instigates the release of hormones, including cortisol, oestrogen and testosterone, that cause blood vessels to dilate and the skin to sweat and flush. On top of this, there is a more localised stress-induced system within the skin itself that exacerbates these reactions. The permeability of the skin's protective barrier becomes more vulnerable, allowing water to escape and bacteria and allergens to penetrate, hence our skin can become dry, irritated and problematic.

MAKING YOUR SKIN WORK FOR YOU

Daily care for the skin is everything. If you are not prepared to spend the few minutes, every morning and night, that it takes to cleanse, tone and nourish your skin effectively, then read no further. Experts recommend starting in the mid-30s with age maintenance, rather than age restoration 10 years later.

All skin is different, so finding a product that works is entirely personal and can entail much trial and error. Bear in mind too that your skin's needs vary with the seasons – richer and more nourishing creams and oils are needed during colder, drier periods. So while sticking to some form of routine is wise, it's also good to switch up your regime from time to time. Our skin changes as we age, so what works now might not be as beneficial in the future. That said, the following guidelines are based on three simple steps: cleanse – tone – nourish. When performed twice daily, without fail, they will help you look and feel radiantly fresh and bright, regardless of age and skin type.

Cleanse

Cleansing the face every morning and night is an absolute must for healthy skin. A thorough cleanse – as opposed to just moving the dirt and grime over the face with a wipe – is the most important step for effective skincare.

▸ **Use a cleanser suited to your skin type** and how your skin is feeling. If, for instance, your skin feels dry and parched, an oily cleanser will give the best cleanse while also locking in moisture.

▸ **Use a clean cloth** that has been held under warm running water to wipe away cleanser. Rinse and repeat until all traces of make-up and grime are removed.

  • **Morning cleanse:** A quick clean using a small amount of cleanser (oil- or water-based) will suffice as there should not be any make-up, sunscreen or grime to remove.

  • **Evening cleanse:** This is most important as make-up, dirt and sunscreen remnants will have accumulated through the day. Oil-based cleansers are generally better at removing oily make-up and sunscreen, as the oil in the cleanser attracts the oil or excess sebum on the skin. Avoid mineral oil – it is of absolutely no benefit and can clog pores.

- **Double cleansing:** If you already use more than one product to deep cleanse at the end of the day, this is considered double cleansing and it will help remove stubborn dirt, make-up and grime from the face.

Exfoliation

A deep yet gentle exfoliation once or twice each week helps slough stubborn dead skin cells and encourage fresh cell renewal, while also allowing the skin to breathe and function more effectively. Choose an exfoliator that works for you and is not too aggressive. For example, if your skin is hormonally aggravated choose a creamy or oily product that is gentler on the skin, avoiding harsh ingredients.

For sensitive and very dry skin, a gentle exfoliation once a week will suffice, while oily and combination skin types should exfoliate two or three times a week, using a gentle enzyme-based or granular product.

Tone

A spray of mist or toner on thoroughly cleansed skin gives a dose of moisture to support the skin's protective barrier. Always choose alcohol-free toners (alcohol dries the skin). Those containing natural disinfectants like witch hazel can help remove residual bacteria and are especially useful on oilier skin. Keep a toning mist handy to spritz the skin during the day while at work, after exercise or when travelling. Let the toner sit on the skin – don't wipe it off.

Exfoliating toners are a relatively new category of toner. Often called acid toners, they use acids such as glycolic and salicylic acids to delve more deeply into the skin to slough away grime. These do not, however, replace traditional toners, but can be use as needed for a more intensive tone.

Nourish

Most traditional skin creams worked in a superficial way – the cream simply sat on the surface of the skin, creating a barrier that retained moisture. The advent of cosmeceuticals in the 1980s brought cosmetics into the medical science arena with ingredients that included alpha-hydroxy acids or AHAs such as glycolic acid, hyaluronic acid, various categories of peptides as well as antioxidant vitamins A, C and Retin-A, scientifically formulated to delve deeper into the skin and boost collagen while at the same time fight wrinkles, spider veins, pigmentation and other issues.

Creams

There are many great moisturisers on the market – some more expensive than others, some more effective. Most will do just as they say – add moisture – but few do much more. To keep older skin sufficiently nourished, some active anti-ageing armoury is also required. Hyaluronic acid, AHAs, peptides and certain vitamins formulated from natural or synthetically-derived ingredients will help stimulate collagen and elastin production while also feeding and plumping the skin. So whether you are 40, 50 or 60, ingredients like these will boost the complexion, close pores and stimulate cell renewal.

Hyaluronic acid is a hydrating substance that holds up to 1,000 times its weight in water. This basically means that it holds moisturising ingredients in the skin and prevents moisture loss from the skin. When choosing a moisturiser, check the ingredient list for hyaluronic acid (often listed as sodium hyaluronate).

Serums

Serums didn't exist in our mothers' time. They are generally more active than moisturisers and are specifically designed to treat and repair the skin. An effective serum will contain the highest level of active ingredients possible, clearly matched to the problem they are trying to address – serums designed for ageing skin, for example, will contain peptides, hyaluronic acid and vitamin A derivatives. They should not be overloaded with additional ingredients, like sunscreens, that could compromise their performance. From a practical perspective, one of the benefits of serums is that they are lighter in texture and are absorbed almost instantly into the skin, making them especially popular in hotter climates. While heavy creams can leave the skin feeling oily and weighty, serums feel soft and smooth. Always check the labels as many poorer-quality serums contain large amounts of silicone, a relatively cheap ingredient that lends a silky texture but has no added benefits. Most serums fall into two types – those packed with antioxidants to protect the skin during the day and those designed to repair the skin overnight. It is worth investing in both.

Masks

Face masks are the final weapon in our skin's armoury. These should ideally used once a week or so when enjoying a bath or long hot shower as the steam generated will encourage absorption of the essential ingredients into the skin. Many of today's masks can be kept on the skin overnight (in place of a night cream), which really gives them time to sink into the skin. Choose a brand you trust and use as directed on the product. When applying a mask, always include the décolletage area as it is especially sensitive and, if not cared for, will quickly show the signs of age.

Face oils

Oils from plants, nuts and seeds are a concentrated source of minerals, vitamins and essential fatty acids (EFAs) that have long been used as natural healers. From gently cleansing the skin of impurities to keeping it smooth and supple, these oils are the ultimate multitaskers and it seems our ancestors already knew what scientists have subsequently been able to prove – when applied directly to the skin, pure plant oils can dramatically improve the condition of the skin, strengthen nails and give hair a healthy, glossy sheen. They are perfect for exceptionally dry environments (such as when flying) and the real beauty is that they can be adapted to match our body's changing needs, be they hormonal, seasonal or stress-induced. The quality of oils used must be of a high standard, as bland mineral oils just sit on the surface of the skin, clogging pores. Buy your oils from a reputable skincare company so that you can be confident about the quality of the ingredients.

While those with oilier complexions have traditionally avoided oil-based products in the belief that they make the skin even oilier, it is now accepted that when used appropriately, oils are the gentlest and most effective cleansers and regulators of oily skin. The skin absorbs oil-soluble substances more easily than it does water-soluble substances, so when essential oils are diluted with a plant or vegetable carrier oil, they can deliver results deep within the skin. Rose and camomile, for example, when used over moisturiser or blended with moisturiser in the hand, create a barrier that prevents moisture loss, while a soothing combination of camomile, apricot kernel and evening primrose is the perfect remedy for dry and irritated menopausal skin.

Using face oils

Experienced make-up artists apply oils on the face and neck before make-up as the oil preps the skin, helping make-up last longer. Rose, either used on its own or combined with frankincense and geranium, for instance, works as an intensive skin therapy when applied under a night cream or face mask and left overnight to boost collagen and restore firmness as we sleep. Natural oils are equally beneficial when used on the hair, keeping it clean and shiny, something that Indian women have known for centuries.

▶ **Cleansing with oil:** Smother the oil over dry skin to remove make-up. Add a splash of warm water to emulsify – the milky fluid that forms will remove all traces of dirt, without stripping the skin. Rinse with warm water.

▶ **Moisturising with oil:** Simply massage a couple of drops into damp skin directly after cleansing and toning (use a little more if the skin feels very dry) until the oil is fully absorbed. Alternatively, a few drops can be added to your moisturiser before applying.

YOUR BATHROOM SHELF

Just like our body, our skin abides by a 24-hour circadian cycle. Working in sync with this will keep our skin nourished and balanced.

Dry skin

Morning: Gentle cleanse with cream/balm/oil-based cleanser, tone, antioxidant-rich day serum, moisturiser and sunscreen (UVA/B SPF 30+)

Night: Deep cleanse with oil-based cleanser or cleansing balm, tone, night serum (repair), eye cream (nourish) and moisturiser (hydrate)*

Extras: Gentle exfoliation once a week, face mask (hydrate/nourish) once or twice a week

* If skin feels especially dry, add some nourishing face oil to your night moisturiser or apply to the face before moisturiser. Oils can also be applied gently around the eye contour area in place of eye cream.

Oily skin

Morning: Light cleanse with cream/foam/gel, tone, antioxidant-rich day serum, moisturiser (light, oil-free) and sunscreen (UVA/B SPF 30+)

Night: Deep cleanse with cream/gel/oil-based cleanser, tone, night serum (repair) and moisturiser (nourish)

Extras: Exfoliate twice a week, face mask (nourishing/cleansing) for oily skin once a week

Sensitive skin

Morning: Gentle cleanse with cream/balm/oil-based cleanser, tone, antioxidant-rich day serum (brightening), moisturiser (nourish) and sunscreen (UVA/B SPF 30+)*

Night: Deep cleanse with oil-based cleanser or cleansing balm, tone, night serum (repair) and moisturiser (nourish/hydrate)

Extras: Freshen and protect throughout the day – a quick mist of toner will freshen skin that has been exposed to environmental toxins and the high-energy rays emitted from computer screens. If your skin feels super dry, a gentle application of a light, nourishing face oil (that can be kept in your handbag or at your desk) will hydrate and brighten your complexion. Reapply sunscreen if you are outdoors or driving.

*Choose products specifically formulated for sensitive skin and free from harsh extras such as alcohol, synthetic dyes and fragrances. While a skin-brightening serum is recommended, always make sure it is not too active and doesn't further irritate skin.

SAFE SUN

The last 20 years have seen profound shifts in our understanding of the impact of UV light on the skin, most importantly the realisation that UVA radiation is as harmful (if not more so) than UVB, as it hastens the progression of skin cancer and seriously ages the skin. This sector of the beauty industry, however, is prone to much confusion, as the legislation of SPF products is so varied – specific ingredients listed in a particular suncare product in the US may go under a different name or SPF number in Europe or Australia. However, it is universally accepted that by using good protection we can protect our skin from up to 90 per cent of the environmental ageing that is directly attributed to the sun.

Both the US Department of Health and Human Services and the World Health Organization (WHO) have identified UV as a proven human carcinogen. A tan results from injury to the skin's DNA; the skin darkens in an imperfect attempt to prevent further DNA damage and these imperfections, or mutations, can lead to skin cancer. That is fact. UVA is the dominant tanning ray that causes cumulative damage over time.

These skin-ageing rays, although less intense than UVB, are 30 to 50 times more prevalent and are present with relatively equal intensity during daylight hours throughout the year. UVB, on the other hand, is the chief cause of skin reddening and sunburn and plays a key role in the development of skin cancer. UVB can burn and damage skin year-round, especially at high altitudes and on reflective surfaces such as snow or ice, which bounce back up to 80 per cent of these rays so that they hit the skin twice. See www.skincancer.org for more.

Sunscreen

Sunscreen formulations have changed radically over the years with scientific advances in both formulation and UV filter technology. Sunscreen filters fall into two broad categories: chemical and physical (often marketed as 'natural'). Most UV filters are chemical (e.g. octinoxate or avobenzone) – they work by forming a thin, protective film on the skin's surface and absorbing the UV radiation before it penetrates the skin. Physical barriers (including micronised zinc oxide and/ or titanium oxide) are insoluble particles that reflect UV away from the skin. To ensure you are getting effective UVA and UVB coverage, always choose a broad-spectrum sunscreen with an adequate SPF plus some combination of UVA-screening ingredients such as stabilised avobenzone, ecamsule (mexoryl), oxybenzone, titanium dioxide and zinc oxide.

We do know that almost all active ingredients in sunscreens break apart or react with other chemicals to some extent in the sun, hence the need to reapply the product every couple of hours. Water resistance, or how well a sunscreen stays on the skin, is a factor too. No sunscreen is fully waterproof so always read the label. If a sunscreen says it provides two hours' water resistance, that's what it does and the product will need to be reapplied every two hours to maintain its water resistance.

Natural sunlight is the body's best source of vitamin D. The skin makes it in direct sunlight. New research is showing that sunlight can also stimulate the production of nitric oxide, which dilates the blood vessels, thereby lowering blood pressure and reducing the risk of cardiovascular and kidney disease. Although scientists are as yet unable to quantify how much sun is needed to achieve this desired effect on our blood vessels, when it comes to meeting daily vitamin D needs, the Cancer Council of Australia recommends two to three hours a week of direct sunlight in winter, or a few minutes a day in the strong summer sun.

The Australian SunSmart programme is an appointed WHO Collaborating Centre for UV Radiation. It recommends that we use SPF 30 or higher, broad-spectrum, water-resistant sunscreen. If used as directed, SPF 30 sunscreen filters 96.7 per cent of UV radiation and SPF 50 filters 98 per cent. When applied correctly, both of these provide excellent protection. SunSmart recommends that the average-sized adult should apply approximately 35ml of sunscreen for one full-body application; that is a lot more than half a teaspoon of sunscreen (about 3ml) to each arm and the face/neck, and just over one teaspoon (6ml) to each leg, the front of the body and the back of the body.

WE NEED TO TAKE MORE RESPONSIBILITY FOR OURSELVES WHILE IN THE SUN BY HEEDING THE INSTRUCTIONS ON SUNSCREENS AND BY WEARING A WIDE-BRIMMED HAT AND SUNGLASSES (PROTECTIVE CLOTHING IN INTENSE HEAT) AND AVOIDING DIRECT MIDDAY SUN.

While an increasing number of multitasking moisturisers and make-up products advertise some degree of sun protection, for the vast majority of us this is not adequate. SPF is powerful and can compromise the benefits of certain active ingredients in skincare so it is wise to use a separate broad-spectrum sunscreen, rather than choosing a multitasking serum/moisturiser inclusive of sunscreen protection.

The eyes and lips need protection too. UV damage can make the lips hard, dry and prone to cold sores, while predisposing the eyes to cataracts, macular degeneration and the possibility of other serious medical issues.

" The abdominal skin of an 80-year-old, which has never seen the light of day, is as smooth, thick and firm as that of an 18-year-old. Photodamage is totally under our control. "
– Dr Rosemary Coleman, consultant dermatologist

FACIAL MASSAGE

Those who appreciate the benefits of massage will know how powerful a technique it is for relieving tension and easing both body and mind. This centuries-old panacea remains as popular as ever, but it is only recently that the western world is waking up to its benefits in tightening, toning and rejuvenating the face and neck. Just as an active, fit body looks healthy and invigorated, a skilled facialist uses massage to stimulate blood circulation and bring facial muscles to life. What's more, massaging products into the skin helps work them deeper, while a more gentle massage around the delicate eye area helps drain lymph and de-puff the eye contour. So as well as seeking out a skilled therapist, why not become your own facialist? It's easy – just massage product deep into the skin around the face and neck, with more gentle movement around the eye area. As with every effective work-out, the more you put in, the more you will gain.

CARE OF THE EYE AREA

The eyes are the most delicate and expressive part of the face and the skin around the eyes is thin and delicate, so it needs to be treated extra carefully. Computers, lack of sleep, sun exposure, smoke and environmental aggressors all play their part in leaving the eyes tired, dull and lifeless.

There is an extensive range of specially-formulated eye creams and gels on the market, but they can be expensive. A nourishing facial oil (when applied gently) will also keep the eyes looking fresh and nurtured. If you are buying eye creams or gels, shop around to find a product that works for you – one that isn't too heavy (as this can lead to puffy bags) and one that works well under make-up, without pilling. Always tread lightly by using a gentle circular motion (using the third finger of each hand), starting at the outer eye, working under the eye towards the nose and then over the lid. Skin-nourishing foods and regular exercise also help keep the eye area hydrated and clear, while protective sunglasses block damaging UV light – even on cloudy days.

Don't forget your eyebrows! Like a great haircut, well-shaped eyebrows frame the face and highlight the eyes, but a combination of age and many years of plucking has left many of us with very sparse eyebrows. Keep your eyebrows well-shaped and, when time and money allow, have them professionally shaped and tinted for added impact and definition.

CARE OF THE NECK

The thin-skinned neck region has fewer sweat and sebaceous glands to protect it from moisture loss than the rest of the body, so if not adequately protected, it can become creepy and wizened-looking, making you look instantly older.

In her collection of essays *I Feel Bad About My Neck: And Other Thoughts On Being A Woman*, the late Nora Ephron summed it up succinctly: 'Our faces are lies and our necks are the truth.' While Botox, fillers and a plethora of other treatments can help tackle a multitude of facial issues, Ephron concluded that 'short of surgery there's not a damned thing you can do about a neck.' Times have changed and sadly Ephron is no longer around to experience the latest generation of non-invasive neck procedures designed to tighten and tone the entire neck area.

Sun damage can be more apparent in this region too and more difficult to repair. While shelves are overflowing with dedicated neck creams, a good face cream containing active anti-ageing ingredients can be equally effective.

" I have found that most people start taking care of their face about 10 years earlier than their neck and chest. It is as though they don't realise these exposed parts of their upper body actually exist until the signs of ageing appear. Everyone should apply SPF from hairline to cleavage every morning. I remove more skin cancers from women's chests than anywhere else on their bodies and in many cases, there will be some scarring. Careful application of skin products and SPF, together with protective clothing as required, can save a lot of medical intervention later on. When applying perfume, avoid the neck and chest areas to reduce your risk of skin pigmentation and an unsightly mottled neck. Fortunately, IPL, Fraxel, Ulthera and peels can be used to reverse some damage in this area. "
– Dr Rosemary Coleman, consultant dermatologist

What is more worrying, however, is the current prevalence of upper back and neck-related injuries. The term 'text-neck' (coined by US-based chiropractor Dr Dean Fishman) is an apt description of our life in the digital age, where the repeated neck stress caused by overuse of handheld technology and staring down at phones, tablets and laptops is increasing the risks of spine degeneration and chronic neck and shoulder problems – not to forget the minuscule creases being added to the neck area. We need to start looking up more and heed the following advice to keep our necks taut, strong and healthy:

▸ Ensure your neck and décolletage area is covered with sunscreen – or with clothing – every day.

UVA RADIATION CAN TRAVEL THROUGH GLASS AND CAN DAMAGE YOUR HANDS SO ALWAYS KEEP A TUBE OF SPF 50 IN YOUR CAR. WEAR GLOVES ON BOTH HANDS WHEN PLAYING GOLF.

▸ Look upwards whenever you can (all the more reason to do those upward dogs in yoga as they help keep the neck stretched and taut!).

▸ Ensure your computer screen is at eye level and you are sitting up straight.

▸ When exfoliating your face, extend the technique to the top of the chest, as sloughing away the dead skin layer allows the active ingredients in the serums and creams to absorb faster.

▸ Avoid very heavy or thick neck creams as they may irritate the crease lines and show up as red rings around the neck.

▸ When creaming the neck area, always sweep upwards towards the chin and up to the ears to avoid the aged 'turkey neck' look.

Dr Rosemary Coleman, MD FRCPI, consultant dermatologist (www.drrosemarycoleman.com)

We all age, but let's slow it down and soften it. It's the overall health of the skin that really matters and as we age, radiance and clarity become even more important. After all, we have all seen beautiful women in their 70s and 80s with creamy clear skin.

With the passage of time, there is a reduction in collagen and elastin in the skin. Facial fat also starts to drop, resulting in the inversion of the normal 3-D facial triangle to a 2-D shape. Wrinkles and fine lines are the early signs of ageing; sagging and skin laxity come later as the muscles weaken and start to sag, resulting in the brow dropping (brow ptosis) and the development of jowls.

It goes without saying that each person's skin concerns will change with age. A 50-year-old may have very deep wrinkles resulting from the constant movement of strong facial muscles. When she reaches her 60s, those very same wrinkles may have reduced because the muscles will be weaker; however, the brows and cheeks will also have dropped, so her needs will be different. Therefore, treating dynamic wrinkles with botulinum toxin (Botox) plays a greater role in earlier years, while volume replacement and tightening take over when a woman is older.

In my years of professional experience, a question I have yet to answer satisfactorily is at what age we allow women to go from being vain to being marvellous? A 30-year-old having Botox, fillers or other procedures is often considered vain, while at 93, a woman having her first Botox treatment is regarded as 'wonderful'. Somewhere within this time frame, we seem to give people permission to intervene and to feel better about themselves without considering them vain. Why are we so hard on ourselves? We live in a very visual society where youth and beauty are equated with success, whether we like it or not!

While no one actually needs Botox, fillers or most of the other cosmetic treatments available today (unless used as treatments for specific medical conditions), most of us can benefit significantly from their careful application. These cosmetic treatments can help relax the face, open the eyes, lift the brows and freshen the complexion, helping people look and feel better and more confident in themselves.

A consultant psychiatrist once said to me, 'The effect on morale and confidence that you can achieve in an hour can take me three years of psychotherapy'.

I use botulinum toxin and fillers to help reduce the sharp angles and shadows that come with age, thus softening the face. Botulinum toxin can also be used to lift the brow, to reduce frowning, to lift the corners of the mouth and jawline and soften neck lines, creating a more relaxed and less intense appearance. Soft tissue fillers (the best of which is hyaluronic acid) can revolumise and rebalance a dull, sagging face, bringing back youthful facial curves.

People can overdo treatments (especially Botox), in the forehead in particular, giving a flat, shiny and artificial appearance. All areas of the face should age at a similar rate, so whatever is done, do it in proportion; and while individual needs will vary, unless you are prepared to live by the basic health recommendations – eating a healthy, varied diet with appropriate nutritional supplements, using sunscreen every day (without fail!), never smoking, getting adequate sleep and exercise and managing everyday stress levels – no amount of cosmetic intervention will truly save your skin.

DR ROSEMARY COLEMAN'S TOP SKINCARE TIPS

▶ **Always wear sunscreen** and take vitamin D.

▶ Use skincare **products with active ingredients.**

▶ **Shop around to find a dermatologist** with an eye for what you want. Make sure you both have the same taste and outcome goals. If you think they themselves look odd, then run!

▶ **Think in terms of a percentage improvement** rather than an all-or-nothing approach and you will get more subtle, balanced results.

▶ **If you are choosing plastic surgery,** see a reputable consultant plastic surgeon.

▶ **Never have permanent correction** of any variety. Your face is not permanent – it is constantly changing and being remodelled by Mother Nature.

▶ **Never have implants or irreversible fillers.** Herein lies the beauty of hyaluronic acid products. They are regarded as the safest fillers in the world, with the lowest side effect risk, and they can be erased using the enzyme hyaluronidase, which, when injected, dissolves the filler and reverses the effects.

- ▸ **Never have tattooed make-up**, which ages and exaggerates facial features rather than softening them.

- ▸ **Never have tattoos on the eyebrows** – even when so-called semi-permanent – as they rarely look natural and can last far longer than expected. The eyebrow naturally descends with age so they can look very strange. Try reputable eyebrow growth stimulators instead as they will work for most people.

- ▸ **Never smoke.**

COSMETIC PROCEDURES

There are hundreds of cosmetic procedures on the market, all promising to leave you fresh-faced, line-free and glowing. While many are supported by a wealth of scientific trials and proven to be safe and effective, many others are not. If something sounds too good to be true, then it probably is. In almost every case the first line of attack is a healthy nutritious diet, effective sun protection, appropriate supplementation and a healthy lifestyle. If women are not prepared to invest in their health, desired results will be harder to achieve.

The following is a list of the most common cosmetic procedures performed by dermatologists worldwide, all designed to treat specific age-associated skin concerns. With the ongoing advances in cosmetic science, many established treatments are being upgraded to the latest state-of-the-art systems designed to deliver results faster and more precisely than ever before.

Always remember that the average time for skin cell regeneration is five to six weeks, at the end of which significant results should be apparent. The length of time the results will last varies considerably but with all procedures listed, once the skin is well nourished and protected, benefits will endure longer.

ActiveFX Fractionated Laser Skin Resurfacing

ActiveFX is a fractional carbon dioxide laser procedure that penetrates the top layers of the skin to a precise and controlled depth, creating multiple tiny invisible burns (the size of a human hair). The light energy vaporises skin imperfections while also stimulating the regrowth of collagen and elastin below the skin's surface and diminishing the appearance of brown spots, wrinkles, acne scars and other skin damage or discoloration.

Chemical peels

Chemical peels are topical applications of a peeling solution that help reduce fine lines, pigmentation, acne and other age-related skin concerns. Alpha-hydroxy acids (AHAs), glycolic acids, beta-hydroxy acids (BHAs) and salicylic acids are the most commonly used peels, suitable for the skin on the face, neck, back, hands and chest.

Enzymes from the acids help loosen the glue that holds dead skin cells together, resulting in a deep, natural exfoliation and a smoother, plumper and brighter complexion.

Cosmelan

Cosmelan is a cocktail of depigmentation agents that temporarily reduces the production of melanin by inhibiting the enzyme tyrosinase. The procedure works in conjunction with a home-care regime and is a safe and highly effective solution for long-term pigment control. After one week of Cosmelan, most people will see a significant improvement in their skin colour, tone and texture as blemishes start to disappear. After three to six weeks, skin should look brighter and healthier.

Fraxel fractional laser resurfacing

Fraxel fractional laser resurfacing technology is recognised as the ultimate 'freshen up' for tired, sun-damaged and ageing skin. Fractional lasers penetrate the top layers of the skin to a precise and controlled depth, creating multiple tiny invisible burns (the size of a human hair). The light energy penetrates and vaporises skin imperfections, while also stimulating the regrowth of collagen and elastin below the skin's surface.

Intense Pulsed Light (IPL)

IPL, or photorejuvenation, therapy, uses sophisticated light technology to deliver a range of light pulses that penetrate the skin to treat skin lesions and age-related skin imperfections. It is a safe and effective procedure that can be tailored to individual skin needs. The glass surface of the IPL handpiece is gently placed over the skin and the targeted lesion absorbs the pulses of light, without affecting the surrounding healthy tissue. Cells in the deeper layers of the skin (dermis) are heated, stimulating the production of collagen.

Jet Hydration Therapy (JHT)

JHT technology is a means of delivering water, hyaluronic acid, vitamins or glycolic acid deeply into the skin via a painless high-velocity pump that is propelled into the skin to unclog pores, exfoliate and hydrate skin cells. JHT can be used safely on the face, neck, chest, back and hands, leaving skin fresher, smoother and more radiant.

Microdermabrasion

Microdermabrasion is mechanical skin exfoliation, during which a highly controlled flow of fine, medical-grade aluminium crystals is blasted at the skin via a high-velocity air jet to remove the skin's outer layer (the stratum corneum) and stimulate collagen production underneath.

Ultherapy

Ultherapy by Ulthera is a focused ultrasound procedure that lifts, tightens and smooths the eyebrows, cheeks, neck, under-chin areas of the face, chest and décolletage.

Vein Gogh Therapy

Vein Gogh Therapy is a treatment for unwanted visible blood vessels that don't respond satisfactorily to laser therapy (like those frequently found around the nose and chin). A tiny probe is inserted directly into the blood vessel. The tip of the probe delivers a burst of radiofrequency heat energy that coagulates the blood and collapses the vessel wall. The procedure is fast and relatively painless.

Viora Reaction™

Viora Reaction™ radiofrequency skin tightening and body contouring technology uses multiple frequency energy channelling to stimulate the production of collagen and improve skin elasticity, resulting in instantly firmer and tighter skin.

YAG Laser

YAG Laser uses sophisticated laser technology to deliver a range of light pulses that penetrate the skin to treat a range of skin lesions and age-related imperfections, including pigmentation, broken blood vessels, acne vulgaris and rosacea. It has also been shown to reduce menopausal hot flushes.

Botulinum toxin (Botox/Dysport)

Botulinum toxin has been used for many years as a medical treatment for squints and nervous tics. Since 1987, it has been used to temporarily remove facial lines and to this day it remains the worldwide number one cosmetic treatment for skin ageing. Botox is injected precisely into the skin, putting the muscles in the target area to sleep. When delivered professionally, Botox is safe and effective. By attaching itself directly to the muscle, it does not travel through the body and does not cause permanent damage. The most common areas targeted are the frown lines and the marionette lines at either side of the mouth. As with other procedures, lifestyle makes a dramatic difference to the success of Botox.

Soft tissue fillers

Hyaluronic acid is naturally occurring in the body and helps hydrate and volumise the skin. It is the safest soft tissue filler on the market, with an extremely low incidence of allergic reaction or side effects. Juvéderm and Voluma are smooth hyaluronic acid gels which, when injected into the skin, dramatically reduce the appearance of wrinkles and facial scarring, giving the face a plumper, smoother and more youthful look. Juvéderm contains a combination of hyaluronic acid and local anaesthetic and the injection is virtually painless. Voluma is a thicker version of Juvéderm, most often used when greater volume is needed (for example to augment cheekbones, a wasted chin or a flat mid-face).

What to choose?

- **Advanced/deep lines and wrinkles:** IPL, Fraxel, soft tissue fillers, Active FX

- **Thinning skin:** Recommended treatments: IPL, chemical peels, Fraxel, Active FX, Ultherapy, JHT

- **Loss of facial volume and skin sagging:** Soft tissue fillers, Ultherapy, surgery

- **Skin pigmentation and age spots:** Skincare products with active ingredients, chemical peels, microdermabrasion, IPL, Fraxel, Active FX, Cosmelan

- **Facial redness and broken blood vessels in the face, neck and chest:** IPL, YAG laser, Vein Gogh therapy

- **Acne scarring:** Fraxel, Active FX, soft tissue fillers, chemical peels, microdermabrasion

- **Neck area:** IPL, Fraxel, Active FX, ultherapy, chemical peels

- **Hands:** IPL, Fraxel, Active FX, chemical peels

HAIR CARE

Our hair is delicate and should be treated gently by avoiding harsh chemicals and by not brushing or pulling it too hard. Our middle years take their toll on our hair as it becomes finer, duller and more brittle. Hair loss is an added problem for many women – it is often the result of dieting through the years, intense or prolonged stress, reduced iron levels and certain diseases and medications.

A hint of grey is no longer seen as a sign of being 'old'. Many of the world's top fashion and beauty editors have chosen to be grey. Grey hair is not coarser per se, as is widely believed, although it is less lubricated (due to reduced sebum production from the oil glands) so it can feel more brittle.

'Along with everything else in our body, hair ages too, insofar that it tends to become finer and weaker,' says trichologist Philip Kingsley. 'By simply taking some extra care these changes can be thwarted. Shampoo hair frequently to exercise the scalp (particularly if the scalp is gently massaged with a kneading motion). Follow with the appropriate conditioner and, once weekly, use a scalp and a hair mask.'

Healthy hair follicles typically go through a lifecycle with three different phases every six years or thereabouts: the growing (anagen) phase, the resting (catagen) phase and the shedding (telogen) phase.

While it is estimated that the average person typically sheds about 50 to 100 hairs per day, research is showing that an increasing number of women are experiencing hair thinning by their early 40s, primarily due to stress and fluctuating hormones. Androgenetic alopecia, more commonly termed 'female pattern hair loss' is the result of changes in hormone levels, primarily the male androgen hormones. It can be triggered by a range of factors including pregnancy, menopause and generally getting older. Telogen effluvium is the term used to describe the stress-related hair loss that can happen after the body goes through a major trauma such as illness, childbirth or other stressful events. With the right advice and treatment, hair will regrow and complete recovery is possible in this case.

There are an increasing number of hair restoring products and therapies on the market today, some of which may indeed help, but to ensure hair follicles are sufficiently nourished, the best advice is to surround them with a rich supply of blood, through a nutritious high-protein diet (see Chapter 2: Food).

Keep your hair looking its very best

- For the best style and colour, **an experienced colourist** is well worth the time and cost.

- To keep your hairstyle in good shape, experts recommend **a trim and shape every four to six weeks.** If left longer, the hair starts to lose shape and become more difficult to manage.

- **If you are suffering from hair loss,** it is wise to see an experienced trichologist.

- **Heat damage to the hair follicle can be a problem,** especially when blow-drying hair every day, so always use an appropriate conditioner and heat protector (your stylist will advise).

- Older and grey hair is more **susceptible to sun damage**, so wear a hat when in the direct sunlight and use a sun/chlorine protector when swimming.

- **If your hair is grey,** use a shampoo and conditioner specifically formulated for grey hair. These are designed to help rid the hair of yellow-orange tones and add extra gloss.

- As with our skin, **regular head massage** using natural oils helps maintain clean, sleek and shiny hair.

- **If you enjoy regular facials,** ask your therapist to include a short head massage during the facial routine.

- **Give your hair a nourishing mask once a week.** This is best done in the bath or shower where the hot steam facilitates the absorption of the oils into the hair and scalp.

BODY CARE

Many of us invested heavily in keeping our bodies fit and toned in our younger years. Why stop now? With a little effort, we can continue to radiate health and vitality.

Cellulite

Cellulite is congestion in the fat cells in parts of the body, including the buttocks, thighs, back of the arms and upper and lower back. Although much medical uncertainty exists about its actual causes, it is widely accepted that poor circulation, inadequate diet, lack of exercise and genetics all play a role. Cellulite is believed to be less of a problem in men, due to their more muscular build and body fat distribution. While our tissues start to weaken with age, other factors, including weight change, stress and smoking, will exacerbate this. Unfortunately, most topical cosmetic creams rarely, if ever, show long-term benefits as, despite what manufacturers say, they just don't penetrate deep enough into the tissues. More invasive treatments such as liposuction (the vacuum suctioning of excess fat from under the skin via a small surgical incision) and endermologie (a mechanical procedure that kneads the affected area) can temporarily improve the appearance of cellulite, but only in a fraction of people treated.

Our middle years are probably a time to accept that life is far greater than the bumps that we can do little about (and that are rarely noticed by others!) and that by moving more, body brushing our skin and paying more attention to when and what we eat, we can still look and feel vibrantly healthy.

Body scrubs and body brushing

Body brushing performed a couple of times a week before your morning shower helps enhance skin tone and boost blood and lymphatic flow. The most effective body brushes are those made from cactus bristle and are best used (before showering) in an upward direction towards the heart.

Exfoliating body scrubs help cleanse the skin by removing dead skin cells. The best scrubs are those containing natural granules like sea salt, which, when applied to damp skin with gentle circular motion, cleanse and invigorate the system.

MAKE-UP

With make-up trends changing by the week and a myriad ways to highlight our best features and conceal the flaws, getting the right look is possible at every age. All it takes is a little practice. The following tips are gleaned from interviews with some of the world's best make-up artists. Choose what works best for you.

Tips for make-up perfection

- **A fundamental skincare regime is key.** No regime – no glowing skin – end of story!

- As the skin starts to age, **less is most definitely more.** Whatever products you are using, keep them as light as possible to give a seamless look.

- If you are not comfortable applying make-up, **it is worth getting advice** or paying for a make-up lesson from a trusted expert – or asking the trained staff at make-up counters in your local department store for help.

- If you don't already own **good make-up brushes,** invest in them now. It will be worth it and you will have them for years.

- **Prep the skin with a great skin hydrator** and buy the right primers, foundations and highlighters for your skin type and colour. If you are not certain, get professional advice.

- **Perfect your eye make-up technique.** There are numerous easy-to-follow tutorials online (Lisa Eldridge, Mary Greenwell and Charlotte Tilbury are all excellent) or arrange a make-up lesson with a trusted expert.

- When buying make-up, **always test foundation on the neck** and try to match your skin colour so it blends continuously. Often two colours are needed to create the shade that best complements the skin's undertones.

- **Blend foundation** along the jawline.

- **Bronzer works** but is not for everyone, so only use it if you really need it.

- **Contouring,** when done correctly with a light hand and a good brush, adds great definition to the face. Again, if you are not sure, seek professional advice.

- **Your cheek and lip colour** should mimic your skin's natural tone to lift and radiate your complexion.

- **Replace mascara after six months or so** – it doesn't last and if not replaced will look clumpy and old. Many of the latest formulations are very flattering on older faces. Get expert advice as to what works best for you.

- **Don't make everything strong.** This look is ageing, so keep at least one feature subtle.

- **Define the brows** by creating a soft arch that's not too drawn.

- A relaxed and understated look is about **developing your own style.** Keep it simple and be confident.

EXPERT OPINION: PERFUME ◀ ···

Josephine Fairley, long-time lover of perfume and co-founder of The Perfume Society, (www.perfumesociety.org)

Have you clung to a signature scent forever? More to the point: has it clung to you? Well, a funny thing happens at midlife – scents we have loved in our younger years may simply not smell the same any more. Our hormones can play tricks with favourite fragrances, altering the way they interact with the skin. (This is also why pregnant women are sometimes nauseated by a fragrance they have always loved.) Worryingly though, a much-loved fragrance may change character without us even realising it – because there can also be a dwindling of our ability to smell, a natural process that begins in our 50s and often really become noticeable from 60 onwards.

Everyone's body chemistry is different, influenced by hormones, skin type, what you eat, medications you may take and more. Even adding a new vitamin or supplement to your well-being regime (if you have one!) can change how a fragrance smells on your skin. Several factors can alter a perfume; it might become more sour, or more sweet. The deeper, richer notes – woods and ambery ingredients, for instance – don't change as much from person to person as fresher, more volatile ingredients like citrus or lily. The bottom line is: never buy a fragrance because you like it on a friend. More than that, never buy a fragrance without trying it on your own skin – full stop.

If you can't tear yourself away from a favourite scent that seems to have 'gone off' on your skin, there are alternatives. Spray it onto hems, cuffs and collars or onto a cotton wool ball to be tucked inside your bra. (Do be careful it isn't going to stain if you're going to use it on fabric; spritz it onto a white Kleenex, and if it doesn't leave a mark, it's safe to use on pale clothing.) Or try a 'voile' of fragrance (as the French so romantically put it): simply spray fragrance into the air and walk through it, subtly perfuming your hair and your clothes. I'm also a big fan of spritzing my scarves and pashminas, creating a sort of personal 'smellprint' via the fragrances I love – which all tend to be within the same family anyway, and therefore work wonderfully well together.

The good news? Once the menopausal years are over, you can go back to wearing old favourites without any problems – if you still want to. Interestingly, a Perfume Society VIP subscriber recently commented that she'd changed the style of fragrance she wears now she's in her late 50s, 'because it isn't all about seduction any more, is it?' Well, that depends, of course. But whether you fancy becoming a cougar – and fragrancing yourself with something seriously purring – or are happy simply to wear the equivalent of a crisp white shirt (a sheer rose or an exquisite cologne), there's no point in life at which we have to fall out of love with perfume – and a good thing too, considering the huge amount of pleasure it can give us, as we spritz, splash and spray.

CHAPTER 9

Movement

Flowing water never stagnates. The hinges of an active door never rust. This is due to movement. The same applies to essence and energy. If the body does not move, qi does not flow and energy stagnates.

Spring and Autumn Annals, 4th century BC

t is now pretty much a given that regular exercise can make an enormous difference to our quality of life, for the rest of our lives. Numerous studies show that middle-aged women who exercise regularly report a higher quality of life and reduced symptoms of menopause than those who lead a more sedentary lifestyle. Fitness also makes us smarter by keeping our brains active. So although far too many women become somewhat obsessed with exercising to burn calories, its real benefit lies in its ability to help build and regenerate new tissue and get our bodies running at a higher metabolic rate.

With regular exercise, everything improves – our skin, our hair, our heart, our brain and memory – while the risk of many diseases reduces. The hardest part is getting started. Whether it's yoga, walking, weights, swimming, dancing or running – at home, in the gym or the great outdoors – once exercise becomes a part of your life, a strong, toned body and mind will be yours.

FAST FACTS ▸▸

▸ Aerobic exercise: This literally means 'with oxygen', and it describes any cardiac work that stimulates heart rate and breathing, but not so much that you can't sustain the activity for more than a few minutes. Exercises include brisk walking, jogging, yoga, swimming, dancing, tennis and many others. Many of these exercises will become anaerobic when performed at an extremely high intensity.

▸ Anaerobic exercise: Also called strength or resistance training, this type of exercise literally means 'without oxygen'. It challenges your muscles with a stronger than usual counterweight and as you use progressively heavier weights, your muscles start to grow stronger. Examples include lifting weights or working with resistance bands.

A healthy balance between aerobic and anaerobic exercise is important throughout our lives and most especially as we grow older to keep our bones strong, our muscles and joints in good working order and our blood flowing freely through our body. There is no need to pound the pavements unless you have always done so. In truth, unless you are well used to running you are probably better off not doing so – a longish, brisk walk (where you start to sweat) combined with cycling, swimming, tennis, yoga and some resistance work or other activity you enjoy is more beneficial. Most importantly, you must enjoy it – otherwise you simply won't keep it up.

Ideally, your week should include a combination of aerobic (such as walking), strength (such as dumb-bells or more strength-based styles of yoga) and flexibility (such as yoga) sessions. This is the best way to manage your waistline, stress levels, mood, metabolism and sleep. A combination of exercise types can lower your risk of cardiovascular disease and arthritis, protect your bone mass and prevent falls (especially as you grow older).

WE HAVE 660 MUSCLES THAT MAKE UP ALMOST 50 PER CENT OF OUR LEAN BODY WEIGHT. THESE MUSCLES ARE A MASSIVE RESERVOIR OF POWER – AND EXERCISE TRIGGERS REPAIR, RENEWAL AND GROWTH. SEVERAL MONTHS OF LONG, SLOW EXERCISE WILL TURN YOU INTO A HAPPY POWERHOUSE OF AEROBIC CAPACITY.

The US Women's Health Study followed 34,000 middle-aged women over 13 years to discern just how much exercise women needed to remain within five pounds of their body weight at the start of the study. They found that women who were in the normal weight range to begin with needed approximately one hour of exercise every day to keep their weight steady. This said, any increase in exercise is good and is more important in your middle years than ever before.

GETTING STARTED

Exercise is about setting yourself challenges and pushing yourself out of your comfort zone, but it's also about going at your own pace – some days that may be a fully fuelled run, other times a slow jog or calming yin-style yoga. Most importantly, however, it's about finding an exercise you enjoy and that makes you feel good. That's the key benefit, after all.

Whatever you choose, ensure it continues to challenge your strength, your breathing and your endurance. Once you start, you will find that the beginners' yoga class or 500 metres that you found quite challenging soon becomes a kilometre or a power yoga session and one day, perhaps, a 10K run or a yoga retreat. It could be one of the most exhilarating and rewarding things you will ever do.

Get the all-clear from your doctor before starting any regime. If you are new to exercise, it is advisable to work with a personal trainer to ensure you are working your body safely and in correct alignment. The following guidelines should help too:

▶ **Start slowly and build up gradually** to prevent injury and keep you motivated. In other words, don't go straight from nothing into boot camp – positive stress can so easily turn into negative stress and increase the likelihood of injury.

▶ **Begin every routine with light dynamic stretching** (leg swings, ankle and shoulder rotations, etc.) to warm and loosen your muscles. Your trainer will advise accordingly.

▶ **Work your core.** This doesn't necessarily mean planks, crunches and sit-ups, unless you like that type of work-out. More refined precise movements such as Pilates target those inner muscles you never knew you had. Measure your success. Your trainer can design a programme that will constantly challenge you against your personal goals.

▶ **Don't give up!** Results won't happen overnight, so whatever works, stick with it.

YOGA

Yoga is immensely popular now. The practice has survived the past 5,000 years and will probably survive the next five millennia. Those who practise yoga know that its real genius lies in the fact that it is not just a series of physical movements but, unlike many other forms of exercise, that it fulfils the need to find some clarity in an increasingly confusing world. The emphasis in yoga lies very much on feeding the mind and emotions as well as the body.

" *I realise this seems like an arbitrary piece of advice but I really mean it. Everyone I know who is over 50 and looks fantastic – including one woman well into her eighties – does yoga. Just do it.* "
– India Knight, In Your Prime

Yoga is all about strength and flexibility and if there was ever a time of life where it comes into its own, it's now. When you look at other middle-aged women who radiate health and vitality, chances are that yoga's downward dog is part of their exercise routine. Science supports this too, with researchers in India showing that yoga can reduce hot flushes, night sweats and sleep disturbances among women going through menopause, while also helping to sharpen their mental function. Yoga is basically strength, stamina, balance and flexibility, all in one. Often described as meditation in action, it can be an intense work-out or a more meditative experience, depending on the style chosen. Nearly all forms, however, are rooted in hatha – yoga's physical discipline that focuses on developing control of the body through a series of asanas (poses) and pranayama (or breathing) techniques. Styles popular today include the more dynamic ashtanga and bikram yoga as well as the more calming, meditative yin, sivananda and somatic yoga. Kundalini and vinyasa flow sit somewhere in the middle, depending on the asanas practised and the level of intensity. Some use props while others crank up the temperature and go for the sweat, but all are designed to align and strengthen the muscles and bones, with knock-on benefits for the functioning of the nervous, hormonal, digestive, cardiovascular, pulmonary and immune systems. No particular style is the best. It's down to personal preference, but once you begin, you will realise that one of yoga's less tangible effects is a new-found resilience and the ability to cope better with everyday stresses.

If you are new to yoga, it's best to try several classes and teachers until you find one that resonates with you. You could also explore the numerous apps and websites available, such as DoYogaWithMe. com and yogaglo.com among many others. Check the teacher's qualifications and, most importantly, their experience. Mastering the postures takes time and practice and what you may feel are small insignificant movements will make a huge difference when you're starting out. It's all about precise alignment and holding the postures. If you suffer from a bad back or shoulder problems, the faster-paced, more dynamic classes are best avoided. Try hatha, iyengar, sivananda or yin yoga instead.

" I am a firm believer in regular exercise being integral to physical and emotional health and from the vast research carried out for this book, it is clear that regular exercise helps keep us healthier, stronger and more balanced and in control. The older I get, the more important yoga has become to me. I don't pound the pavements like I once did and I know now (also from my research) that intense exercise can in fact do more harm than good. Nor do I practise ashtanga (the style of yoga I first learned and loved) – now it's vinyasa flow, somatic and the calming yin yoga that weaves its magic every time I do it. There's something really powerful and grounding about regular yoga practice that I haven't found with anything else, and with so many variants to experiment with, most women should find something that works for them. "
– Kate

RESISTANCE EXERCISE

Although strength or resistance exercise on its own does not lead to weight loss, there are many benefits for body composition, which makes it far easier to manage your weight. By slowing the visceral fat building up around your middle, you are also lowering your risk of diabetes and heart disease.

Strength or resistance training is the type of exercise that:

▶ Protects remaining muscle mass

▶ Builds new muscle mass

▶ Increases muscle strength so you can climb stairs or lift shopping bags with ease

- ▸ Tones muscles and keeps them shapely (think tighter abs!)

- ▸ Strengthens bones to help prevent osteoporosis.

Muscle is metabolically active tissue. In other words, it burns calories when it's working, repairing and refuelling itself. Fat burns very few calories. It tends to hoard them instead.

While changes in fat distribution are the result of hormonal changes at midlife, the overall weight gain that can happen during our middle years is more to do with the effects of ageing (less exercise and loss of muscle mass) than anything else.

USE IT OR LOSE IT! AS YOU GET OLDER, RESISTANCE TRAINING HELPS YOU RETAIN AS MUCH MUSCLE AS POSSIBLE.

There is no one right way to build strength, but the objective should always be to work all the major muscle groups (legs, hips, back, abs, arms and shoulders) twice a week at a minimum. This training can be varied and doesn't have to be the same, week in week out.

You can use:

- ▸ Resistance bands (long elastic bands)

- ▸ Kettle bells

- ▸ A bar weight or dumb-bells

- ▸ Your own body weight (acting as the resistance in exercises such as planks and push-ups).

One set (between eight and 12 repetitions) of the same movement each session is enough (though some evidence suggests that two to three sets may be more beneficial). It's a good idea to invest in a few sessions with a qualified personal trainer who will tailor a programme for you to follow at home or in the gym.

Recovery post-training is also important, with a rest period of 48 hours recommended between resistance sessions.

Recovery nutrition

Eating adequate protein with meals is important to promote repair and build new muscle mass. Typically we eat very little protein at breakfast and too much with our evening meal. A better distribution (about 30g protein per meal) has been shown to reduce the risk of sarcopenia, which is the loss of muscle mass and strength as we get older.

Resistance training is the best way to prevent loss of muscle mass, a major cause of disability in older women, although some see its effects as early as their late 40s.

Research shows that women over 60 have to lift weights more often than younger women to maintain their muscle mass and muscle size. In other words, the older you are, the more you may have to work to maintain your muscle. Research has shown that a mix of carbohydrate and protein promotes a faster recovery, compared with a carbohydrate-only snack or meal.

The sooner you eat after strength training, the quicker the muscles begin to replenish their energy stores. Ideally, aim to eat a carbohydrate- and protein-rich snack within 30 minutes of exercise, and no later than two hours afterwards.

A build-up of the free radicals that are generated during exercise can leave muscles sore and tired. Although regular training improves the body's defences against free radicals, you can also boost them further by eating antioxidant-rich fruits and vegetables. Bear in mind that recovery snacks contribute to your overall calorie intake for the day, so if you are trying to lose weight, you may do better to skip the snack and have a suitable meal as soon as you can after exercise. Don't be seduced into taking protein shakes and bars unless you don't have the time to eat real food.

Examples of suitable post-exercise snacks

RECOVERY SNACK	CALORIES (kcal)	CARBO-HYDRATE (g)	PROTEIN (g)
300ml smoothie: whizz 150g low-fat yogurt, handful of frozen mixed berries and 150ml fruit juice in a blender	156	29	8
3 rice cakes + thin spread peanut butter	175	18	6
A banana + 200ml low-fat milk	187	30	8
125g low-fat yogurt + 6 whole almonds (unsalted)	192	22	8
2 Weetabix + 150ml low-fat milk	210	35	10
2 slices wholegrain toast + 135g baked beans (For those with higher calorie requirements)	278	49	7

I was more of an aerobic exerciser when I was younger. I just loved those bright pink leotards and legwarmers of the 80s. In those days we motivated ourselves with 'no pain, no gain' and Jane Fonda's 'feel the burn'. More recently I'm concious of the importance of resistance exercise and for most of the noughties, I enjoyed body pump.

Today, I'm even more discerning about the type of resistance training I do. I'm concerned about lower back pain and how strength training might impact my bone health. Having osteoporosis doesn't mean I need to avoid weightlifting, but I lift much lighter dumb-bells now.

I love a good spin class too. The 'off the saddle' cycling is also a safe type of weight-bearing resistance training for me. Along with a weekly Fierce Grace hot yoga class (where I get to practise my plank), I get both the endorphin rush and the stress-relieving benefits, which is good for my bones and, more importantly, my mental health. I know now that I don't have to 'feel the burn' to keep my body healthy and strong.
– Paula

If joining a gym or doing structured resistance sessions on your own isn't for you, then look for other possibilities to strength-train during your typical week. This might include some of the following:

▶ Digging, lifting and carrying things around the garden

▶ Lugging and carrying shopping bags in and out of trolleys and cars

▶ Moving and lifting furniture around your home

▶ Lifting and unloading a heavy golf bag around the course

▶ Scrubbing and scraping, pulling and shoving as part of a hobby

▶ Doing some regular press-ups and planks at home. Check out the many apps and free online YouTube clips videos available, for example Sworkit and Mat Pilates with Amy, which will show you how to do these exercises correctly.

TRY THIS ▼

Give this sample weekly resistance training programme a try:

▶ Take five minutes to walk briskly and warm up your muscles before you start working them. Stretching for 10 minutes at the end of your session is the best way to cool down.

▶ Focus on slow, controlled movements before even thinking about a weight challenge. Get your form or technique right to minimise the risk of injury. You can then decide how much weight you need to lift (barbells, dumb-bells, kettle bells) once your alignment and form are correct.

▶ Counting out loud can help keep you on track and get a good rhythm going. Always exhale as you work against the resistance or weight (lifting, pushing, pulling) and inhale as you release or let go.

▶ The aim is to tire the muscle by the time you do the last two repetitions in a set, without losing form. Always work out in a measured and controlled manner with no jerking.

▶ If you simply can't do the last two repetitions, swap your weight for a lighter one. On the other hand, if it's not challenging you enough, you won't get the results.

▶ Increase your weights or add another set of repetitions to your session. You want your muscles to know they've been worked hard but not over-worked.

- You might work on legs one day and arms another, but ideally you need to cover all muscle groups twice a week. (Female tennis players have incredible bone density in their serving arm but dramatically decreased density in their non-serving arm.)

- Resistance work naturally causes tiny tears in our muscles. This is not dangerous. In fact, these little tears knit and mend to make our muscles stronger. However, they need time to do this, so ideally you should leave about 48 hours' recovery time until the next strength or resistance work-out.

- Be persistent. Continue to challenge muscles by slowly increasing the weight or resistance used.

Results take time. Be patient.

" Women in midlife begin to start suffering from a new STD: sitting-to-death disease. I recommend a standing desk or standing while on the phone. Setting the alarm on the computer to remind the person to stand up and walk around a bit is another way. "
– Bonnie Roill, Aspire2Wellness

MORE REASONS TO MOVE

- **Exercise makes us happier.** When we're active, our brains release feel-good endorphins that bring a more positive outlook on life.

- **Exercise gives us a goal to work towards.** With many sports, the only person you're really competing with is yourself. When you are running or practising yoga, each race or practice is an opportunity to push your endurance a little. The reward doesn't come easily, but that feeling you get when you shave a minute off your mile or beat your personal record, whatever your sport, is truly unmatched.

- **Exercise helps us sleep better.**

- **Exercise gives us a sense of belonging.** Statistics show that activities like running, yoga, swimming, tennis and many others can bring new friends and a sense of community.

- **A combination of cardiovascular and resistance work**, when done properly and consistently, engages muscles, improves joints and boosts endurance – making us stronger in every way.

CHAPTER 10

Mindspace

Here's a thought for today ... if you were attentive to your life rather than simply getting through it, then even if a doctor told you you had only six months to live, if you were awake to every minute, it would be longer than if you had 100 years to live in an unconscious state.

Ruby Wax, *Sane New World: Taming the Mind*

The concept of well-being means different things to us all – a sense of contentment, happiness, peace, calm, joy, empowerment, worthiness, comfort, ease. These words hold a different meaning for each of us at different stages in our lives. As we move through our 40s, we often begin to realise that real life is messy and imperfect. We may have become furious multitaskers working on autopilot to keep it all together and stay on top. Yet despite this, life has often not gone according to plan. At the same time, we face the menopause years, heralding more change and situations beyond our control. If our well-being is dependent on life going to plan in a world that celebrates the faultless body and always-on mode, then this time of our lives can be immensely challenging and disempowering.

It's worth bearing in mind that while a combination of poor diet, sun damage and lack of exercise can contribute to making us look and feel old and unattractive, stress and unhappiness add even more years to our face and body. Combine this with working long hours under pressure and the worrying demands of everyday life and it's hardly surprising that untreated stress can lead to overeating, overdrinking and massive sleep disturbances, the very issues that made us feel more miserable from the outset.

Neuroscience is now showing that through mindfulness we can consciously repattern our brain and transform negative habits. What's more, the more we practise, the more presence we create in our lives. As our brain changes, so too does our capacity to self-regulate in difficult situations, making us more comfortable in our own skin. Science is showing that by simply making the choice to be kind to ourselves, we can alter our brain and body chemistry. This in itself has huge implications for our mental, physical and sexual well-being and for the quality of our relationships.

This may all sound easy, but it's actually very difficult. But regular practice will help put daily pressure and anxiety into perspective, while also helping, in the words of Vietnamese Buddhist monk and author Thich Nhat Khan, 'to regain sovereignty over our own territory' and be once again in control.

" *It wasn't the night sweats or hot flushes that affected my life, but the mood swings. They were awful; I thought I was going bonkers. I didn't enjoy my 40s and am happy to wipe out the last decade.* "
– Diana

With origins in Buddhism, mindfulness and meditation is one of the eight lifestyle choices Buddha instructed his followers to practise in order to break free from the cycle of suffering and rebirth.

Meditative techniques were widespread in India by the time Gautama Buddha was born, around 480 BC. Puritans roamed the countryside, wearing rags and begging for their meals. Buddha became one of them. He famously achieved enlightenment – his insights about the causes of suffering and the way to end it – while meditating under a bodhi tree. Buddha taught his followers that practising meditation and mindfulness was crucial to preparing their minds for enlightenment. The other steps on the path are:

- Right understanding
- Right motivation
- Right livelihood (not making a living in a way that harms other beings)
- Right action (not exploiting oneself or others)
- Right speech
- Right effort (diligence)
- Samadhi or enlightenment (to be fixed/absorbed in mind and body).

The rise of mindfulness in the west is credited to Jon Kabat-Zinn, a graduate student in molecular biology at MIT in the United States. In 1965, Kabat-Zinn developed an eight-week programme called Mindfulness-Based Stress Reduction (MBSR) to help patients cope with chronic illness. The technique is now widely used in medicine to help people suffering from a multitude of issues from asthma to depression.

At its simplest, mindfulness is the practice of being fully aware, without judgement, of what is happening right now and being available for life as it unfolds at that moment. When we are in the present moment, we dwell in the space between the past and the future. Once here, we start to pay attention to what is happening and begin to notice thoughts, sensations and patterns of behaviour. As we cultivate our capacity to stay in the present, we allow things to be as they are, without becoming stressed about them, and realise that by being aware of what is arising and passing is enough. As the ancient Chinese philosopher Lao Tzu said, 'Practise not doing and everything will fall into place.'

We get brief glimpses of this occasionally when the vividness of life reveals itself, for example when the sun catches a bee buzzing around the lavender or when you hear your child laugh heartily and very happily. Any number of life events and moments can stop us in our tracks and give us the experience of being part of something much bigger – if we let them. Mindfulness offers us the capacity to be more available to these magic minutes. Study after study now shows that meditation and mindfulness training profoundly affects every aspect of our lives – our bodies, our minds, our physical health and our spiritual well-being. While not quite the fountain of youth, it's pretty close and those who practise enjoy a calmer, quieter mind. There's no right or wrong way to practise either; it's much more about learning to be still and to be in the moment. Acceptance lies at the heart of mindfulness – so accept it and be with it.

If you have not practised stopping, the years will seem to have gone. You may never have stopped for a moment to look at the moon or hold a flower in your hands. Without stopping and looking deeply, we are not able to really live our lives. The energy that enables us to stop is mindfulness.
– *Thich Nhat Hanh,* Understanding Our Mind

The capacity of the mind to change is powerful, but all too often this happens in a mindless way. Thoughts aren't facts and there is no end to where our mind can take itself if we let our thoughts become our reality. Neuroscience tells us that any thought we don't feed into has a life span of just 19 seconds. The problem is that we identify with thoughts we habituate with and start to create internal narratives that are not our reality. The answer lies in acknowledging thoughts as they arise and labelling them – planning, fixing, children, etc. – before returning to our breath. The breath acts as an anchor, and by bringing attention back to the breath time and time again and letting go of (rather than identifying with) these myriad thoughts, we gain more distance and perspective in our daily lives. Once you start to practise, you will become more aware of your breath and can use it to help control anger, stress and many other aspects of life.

It is often our reactivity that is at the root of much of our suffering. As you cultivate this capacity to stop and stay, you will soon notice that you don't instinctively rush to 'fix' something and that you are more willing to allow things to be as they are. So when something unpleasant happens, rather than getting trapped in familiar cycles of fruitless reactivity, you can simply say to yourself: 'It's OK, I can handle this.'

MEDITATION

Former Apple chief Steve Jobs was a lifelong practitioner of mediation. In his 2011 biography of Jobs, Walter Isaacson quotes him: 'If you just sit and observe, you will see how restless your mind is. If you try to calm it, it only makes it worse, but over time it does calm, and when it does, there's room to hear more subtle things – that's when your intuition starts to blossom and you start to see more clearly and be in the present more. Your mind just slows down, and you see a tremendous expanse in the moment. You see so much more than you could see before.'

Meditation is all about turning our attention inwards and listening to our body. By doing so, we increase awareness of how we feel and start being an observer of our own thoughts and emotions. Ultimately, this means we become less reactive and start to make healthier, balanced choices for ourselves and for those who depend on us. Finding that balance begins by simply allowing ourselves to sit still, to close our eyes and to re-connect with that sense of deep stillness that rests inside all of us. This is meditation, and while there are many techniques emanating from various spiritual traditions, it is focusing inwards that ignites this change (see Mindfulness Practices, page 182).

Nepal-based Matthieu Ricard is a world-renowned author, monk, photographer and close associate of the Dalai Lama. He was among the first to undergo stringent scientific evaluation of the impact of long-term meditation (up to 60,000 hours) on the brain. Results showed a degree of stimulation in areas of Ricard's brain associated with positive emotions and impulses that was previously unrecorded in scientific literature.

Significant neurological changes were noted in attention, pain control and, most notably, in the increased overall flexibility of the mind – further proof that meditation can significantly alter brain activity and can potentially bring about lasting change in brain function. Ricard has commented that you don't need to own a pair of sandals and have a Himalayan view to develop your capacity for positivity and compassion, as just 20 minutes a day of caring mindfulness meditation over four weeks was also found to alter brain activity and enhance the immune system. 'Like the arm of a clock, you don't see it [the mind] moving but it does,' he explains, 'and all of this comes from an understanding of how the mind works. The mind is the boss; speech and body are the servants. Our goal is to change the mind and to achieve this we must go to the source.'

In essence, the practice is less about sitting in silence for a few minutes every day, and much more about knowing how to use the openness of mind acquired while meditating in everyday life to help us become more rounded human beings.

"*Training the mind? It must be done thought after thought, emotion after emotion, meditation after meditation, day after day, month after month ... for the duration of one's whole life.*"
– *Matthieu Ricard, Buddhist monk*

STRESSFUL SITUATIONS

Kabat-Zinn says that when life gets challenging mindfulness provides 'a simple but powerful route for getting ourselves unstuck, back in touch with our own wisdom and vitality'.

Stress in small, short doses is good, as anyone who has performed in front of a live audience will attest. Those nervous feelings help improve memory and enhance performance. However, at certain times in our lives, we all face intolerable situations we cannot change. When overlooked, situations like these have the power to damage us both physically and emotionally. But rather than wanting things to be different, we need to accept what is, put our energy into gathering the resources needed to respond to these challenges and once again gain focus in our life.

In her book *Flourishing*, Irish psychologist Maureen Gaffney says, 'Stress disrupts your normal routine, your conditioned patterns of thoughts and reactions. But this has an upside. It allows you to break free of them, even for a while. It allows another dimension to break through. You may be feeling that the world is not as safe and predictable and controllable a place as you thought. But you also discover that, for all the stress, life goes on. The sun still rises and sets. You still enjoy the taste of fresh crusty bread, the waves still break magnificently on the shore. Children still laugh uproariously. And when you take the trouble to notice these things, you feel less alone and instead feel supported and held up by the universe'.

EXPERT OPINION: MINDFULNESS ◀ ·····································

Mari Kennedy, transformation coach, yoga teacher and mindfulness trainer (www.mari.kennedy)

I like to think of well-being as the capacity to thrive, to stay open and available to life, regardless of what is going on in our life. In our endless strive for excellence, many of us have confused well-being with perfection. This is particularly true for women. We believe we will be well when things go to plan and when life is within our control. Mostly our sense of well-being lies somewhere in the future, relying on external circumstances going right, be it the state of our finances, our physical health or the quality of our relationships being exactly as we want them. To this end, we are living in what Buddhist teacher Tara Brach calls the 'if only' mind – a mind that is never satisfied with the present moment and is constantly thinking 'if only we were healthier, thinner, richer, more successful, more appreciated; if only we had the perfect partner, a better job, a bigger kitchen – we would be happy and well.'

As with all change in our lives, we can choose to regard menopause as an invitation or a threat. Inherently it is both: it's a threat to our old youthful way of being in the world and an invitation to live from a deeper, wiser, more empowered place. Both can be dynamic, but in different ways. As humans, we tend to respond to this inevitable time of change in one of the following ways:

▶ We push through in overdrive, resisting and denying the changes happening within our bodies and minds.

▶ We give in and resign reluctantly, putting everything down to 'the change' and getting older.

▶ We transform mindfully and elegantly with wisdom, passion and resilience, embracing the invitation to live more deeply and wholeheartedly.

It is our mindset that will decide how we make this transition, and mindfulness, as a practice, offers us a way of engaging with our mind and emotions in the here and now. Mindfulness, or the inner revolution, as I like to call it, offers us a choice to become more empowered and engaged with the changes we face. When we choose to live moment to moment through these years, we can become radiant, passionate and wise women. This conscious choice can be the difference between putting up with the menopause or inhabiting the potential of the rest of our lives.

This idea of living in the moment is terrifying for most of us who have been over-functioning for years. But it is possible and will take practice. But if I – who was running to stand for the first half of my life – can do it, you can. As Tara Brach says, 'By coming into presence we experience the most profound quality of well-being.'

Paying attention in the present moment is key, but doing this with self-compassion is where mindfulness can really transform our lives.

When we are truly mindful, we are engaged and attending both to our experience and to ourselves, with kindness. This is a big ask and for the vast majority of women, unheard of! Most of us have spent the first half of our lives focusing on other people, our families and careers as well as myriad self-improvement projects, always pushing ourselves further and further. But cultivating mindful self-compassion could be our greatest gift to ourselves as we transition into and through menopause.

When we cultivate our capacity to be present with kindness towards ourselves through this time of change, yes, we will experience the grief, the sadness and self-rejection that naturally comes – but we will also have more access to the joy, relief, freedom and possibilities of leaving our youth behind. If we deny or fight the uncomfortable feelings that naturally come with any life change, we run the risk of numbing our capacity to feel the real joy that this time can bring.

Two recent Australian studies have highlighted the benefits of self-compassion during menopause. A 2014 study found that self-compassion may be a resilience factor that helps women manage hot flushes and night sweats, while a 2015 study found that self-compassion was one of three factors associated with well-being among midlife women.

MINDFULNESS PRACTICES
It is only through practice that we become mindful.

Mindful moments 1: Being present (<1 minute)
While reading this, just take a moment to move your attention into your right foot. Notice with curiosity the sensations as you rest your attention there for just for a few moments.

That's being present – and it's as simple as that! It's just that easy to remember to be present. Our bodies are always in the present moment.

Mindful moments 2: Anchoring attention on the breath (10 minutes+)
Here the breath is the anchor to the present moment as we train the mind to pay attention. If you are new to meditation, start by sitting for 10 minutes, gradually increasing this sitting time as you continue to practice.

Record the meditation on the next page into your phone and play it back to yourself or ask someone to read it slowly to you. Set a timer for 10 minutes.

Sit comfortably on a chair with your back upright, but at ease. Place your feet flat on the floor and let your hands rest on your thighs. Gently close your eyes and play the following meditation.

Bring your attention to your feet in contact with the ground.

Notice the sense of pressure and contact of your body against the chair – your tights, your back, your buttocks.

Now move your attention to the sensations of your hands resting on your thighs.

Let your attention rest on your shoulders and allow them to drop naturally with gravity.

Now focus on your jaw and allow a space between your teeth. Let the root of your tongue soften in your mouth.

Now scan your body and notice where you can feel your breath most easily. Maybe it's in your nostrils – the sensation of cool air entering and warmer air leaving, or maybe you notice your breath more easily in the upper chest area, feeling it rising and falling, or perhaps it is in the tummy – the expansion on the inhale and release on the exhale. In whichever part of your body you notice your breath most easily, let your attention rest there.

Your attention will wander and that's OK. When you notice that you have become distracted, gently and without judgement, bring the attention back to rest on your breath – your anchor. Become curious rather than judgemental as you keep returning your awareness to the breath. You *will* be distracted by thoughts, sounds, and sensations of discomfort in the body, or maybe by feelings of boredom or agitation, and as soon as you notice your attention pulling away, escort it back gently to the breath.

Mindful moments 3: Self-compassion break (1–2 minutes)

This powerful practice is taken from the mindful self-compassion programme developed by Kristin Neiff and Christopher Germer (www.mindfulselfcompassion.org).

It takes only a few minutes and can be used any time of the day or night.

MEDITATION ♨

Think of a difficult situation in your life, one that causes you continued stress. Bring the situation to mind and try to actually feel the stress and emotional discomfort in your body.

Then, say to yourself:

'This is a moment of suffering.'

Then say:

'Suffering is a part of life. I'm not alone. Other people feel like this.'

Now, put your hands over your heart, feel the warmth and gentle touch of your hands on your chest, or adopt a soothing touch that feels right for you and say to yourself:

'May I be kind to myself.'

Then ask yourself:

'What do I need to hear right now to express kindness to myself?'

Choose one or more of the phrases below that speaks to you in your particular situation:

▸ 'May I learn to accept myself as I am.'

▸ 'May I forgive myself.'

▸ 'May I be patient.'

STRATEGIES FOR COPING WITH LIFE'S CHALLENGES
Engage fully with the challenge

The invitation of mindfulness is to welcome everything that comes – the good, the bad and the ugly. This is difficult. We wonder how we can possibly welcome sagging skin, loss of sexual drive, the breakdown of our marriage or the death of a parent or dear friend. However, in making the choice to befriend the challenge, we make space for the pain, the grief, the overwhelming vulnerability and fear. In other words, we welcome and befriend whatever is true in that moment.

The mindfulness practice of RAIN developed by Michele McDonald and adapted beautifully by Tara Brach in her book *True Refuge: Finding Peace and Freedom in Your Own Awakened Heart* helps us compassionately befriend those difficult times by:

R: Recognising what is happening

It starts the minute you focus your attention on whatever thoughts, emotions, feelings or sensations are arising right here and now.

A: Allowing life to be just as it is

Allowing means 'letting be' the thoughts, emotions, feelings or sensations you discover.

I: Investigating our inner experience with kindness

You engage in a more active and pointed kind of inquiry. You might ask yourself: 'What most wants attention?' 'How am I experiencing this in my body?' or 'What am I believing?'

N: Non-identification

There's nothing more to do but rest in natural awareness.

Pause and take a deep breath

Have you ever noticed that the more stressed you get, the busier you become? Often it's a strategy of escape, because if you do stop, you will have to meet the pain or exhaustion. Mindfulness teaches us that when life gets challenging, the best action is to pause, take a deep breath and literally check in to find your centre in the flux. It's so simple but often forgotten. Try it right now by thinking of a challenge you are currently facing. Notice any tightness or contraction in your body as you think about it. Now take five long deep breaths and focus on the exhale.

Learn to sit with yourself

A daily practice of sitting with yourself in meditation creates an inner resilience and stability that can take you through tough times, while also making good times even better. By doing so, you lean into your humanity and vulnerability and uncover your true worthiness and capacity to befriend whatever arises. Think of it like sitting with a friend who listens without judgement to how you really are feeling in that moment.

... or sit with a professional

A skilled therapist or coach provides a safe space to find meaning when life feels rocky and unsafe underfoot.

Find your tribe

As women we are naturally relational beings, so surround yourself with those who support you, who can be with you in your pain and let you cry without needing to fix or heal or sort you out. Begin by spending less time in the company of those who deplete your energy and bring you down and more time with people who really listen and support you and help you feel alive.

Re-engage with the cycles of life

The 'must-be-quicker-faster-and-better' culture we live in does not value the feminine wisdom of cycles. Death, pausing, endings and darkness are feared and avoided when possible. When we hit a difficult time, we are encouraged to get on with it. The antidote to this is to learn to appreciate cycles and understand that the darker moments, those times of loss, death and sadness, are all part of the bigger natural cycle. Just think of day and night, the seasons, the moon, the cycles of birth and death. Our Celtic sisters knew that the light of new beginnings is born in the dark. It's the process of change and transformation.

Give up control

We cannot control life. It's a mystery and a process. There are no guarantees. We know tough times happen – our children will disappoint us, our breasts will head south and people we love will die or betray us. We cannot avoid or control our changing circumstances, but we can engage with the dynamic nature of our bodies and our ever-changing circumstances. So get curious, stop judging, blaming and managing everyone and everything around you. Stay open and take responsibility for your own life and your destiny. Welcome the opportunity change presents and move with it.

Find your passion. One of the great joys of this time in life is the chance to finally come into our own – our own authenticity, our own realness. We have lived and loved, lost and survived. Now we are at a time when we are closer to knowing what really matters to us. We may have played the good girl or indeed the rebel in our earlier lives, but here is an opportunity to step into a life that is more aligned to our own values and passions.

This point in our lives is a threshold. Thresholds are powerful places to pause and review before deciding how to step into the next stage. This is the time to listen reflectively to what lies at the core of our deepest desires of heart and soul. Those who have been questioning in their late 30s may now have some signposts to guide them, while others have some deep excavation work in store. For each one of us, this threshold presents the perfect opportunity to courageously inquire and listen. So start by asking yourself the following questions:

▶ What really matters to me at this point in my life?

▶ Who and what brings me alive?

▶ What do I want to create as I move into my next chapter?

▶ How do I want to feel in the next stage of my life?

▶ What legacy do I want to leave behind?

▶ What is my deepest desire?

Your answers will pave the path that you take through the second half of your life.

MINDFULNESS MEDITATION APPS

With the current boom in user-friendly mindfulness apps, there are no excuses for not finding a little calm amid life's stresses. From guided to silent meditation sessions tailored for every life situation – at home, on the run, in the car or in bed – there are sessions designed for every level, from beginners to advanced and everything in between. Some of the apps are free, while others charge a monthly or annual fee.

When starting out, it is often easier to be guided by a voice so you know what to do and where to focus. But shop around various apps to find a voice that resonates with you – one that doesn't irritate and that you will happily follow. As you become more in tune with the practice you, might switch to silent mode.

Bear in mind that even short bursts of meditation (5–10 minutes) done regularly can be more beneficial than longer infrequent sessions. Choose a time, three or four times a week (at least) when it suits you to meditate (on the bus to or from work, at lunch, while walking or in bed at night). You can even set a reminder in the app. Remember that it takes time to become comfortable with the exercise and your chosen app, so give it time. Don't give up even if it feels difficult. The rewards will be with you for life.

" *Of all the excuses we dream up to talk ourselves out of meditating, lack of time is at the top of the list. We don't have 10 minutes to meditate but we just scrolled Instagram for the sixteenth time. Kids get in the way, work gets in the way. Life gets in the way. But finding 10 minutes a day to meditate is, indeed, possible. It's a matter of prioritisation and habit. It requires discipline, and some days it can be challenging, but the benefits are infinite.* "
– Andy Puddicombe, Headspace

Headspace is one of the most popular apps on the market. Others include Imagine Clarity (Matthieu Ricard's guided meditation practice, with all proceeds benefitting humanitarian organisation Karuna-Shenchen), Calm and Mindapps.

"Meditation has been a part of my life for many years – more specifically, it has been hidden away in a little corner of my mind, regularly popping into my 'doing' brain, pleading to practise. I have tried to calm my mind and find some stillness, but rarely accomplished it. I'm always racing too much, always looking ahead to the next email, the next job, the next holiday. That was pre-Headspace.

The introductory 'Take 10', interspersed with succinct video nuggets explaining how meditation works on the mind, is ingenious. With a focus on the breath, it worked first time for me. Although it took me almost six weeks to complete the 10-day freebie, I got there and desperately wanted more. Through this process, I (albeit very occasionally) managed a few seconds of relaxed concentration (the meditative grail, I am told), interspersed with busy-mind-working-overtime syndrome. When I did lose the thread and nod off, Puddicombe's voice would interject: 'It's perfectly normal to be distracted, just bring the attention gently back to the breath.' I must confess to bending the Headspace rules a little. I know it's ideally done first thing in the morning, but with breakfast and school lunches (times three) and many other pressing issues, this was never going to work for me. I find it works best when I'm in bed at night. With his warm lilting tones, Andy tells us to sit straight and comfortably still. I do this on my bed (not sure if I'm supposed to but I reckon if it works for me, it must be OK).

I now tend to choose single sessions – to help me sleep or when I need a short burst of calm when life is feeling a little out of control – and just maybe the woman who is always too busy to be still (aren't we all?) is hooked!"
– Kate

CHAPTER 11

Sleep

My big idea is a very small idea that can unlock billions of big ideas that are at the moment dormant inside us. And my little idea that will do that is sleep. And we women are going to lead the way in this new revolution, this new feminist issue. We are literally going to sleep our way to the top, literally. So I urge you to shut your eyes and discover the great ideas that lie inside, to shut your engines and discover the power of sleep.

Arianna Huffington, editor-in-chief, Huffington Post Media Group

Life in the fast lane takes its toll and the sad fact is that in this super-connected era, our electronic lives are taking over our entire lives. So much so that technology has turned our homes from places where we rest and recharge into places to charge up our phones and our lives. We need to slow down, to sleep longer and deeper and to make time for what really matters.

(Night sweats were my most common and worst complaint. But while waking up in a clammy sweat was unsavoury, the exhaustion I experienced as a result of chronic sleep disturbances was torturous. It stripped me of capability, of competence, of confidence, of certainty. It left me feeling exposed and unable. Work opportunities I should have been delighted to accept were rejected. I simply didn't have the energy or the oomph to take them on.)
– Paula

Sleep is considered to be our most important recovery mechanism. It is a biological imperative that does far more than rest the body: it heightens the senses, sharpens the mind and mellows the spirit. It's hardly surprising then that beauty experts consistently rate sleep among their top essentials. When sufficient and deep, a good night's sleep can transform our appearance. As we grow older, even a couple of late or relatively sleepless nights can leave our minds overwhelmed and inefficient. What's more, when we don't sleep well, our bodies begin to feel more strained and release the stress hormone cortisol, with potential knock-on effects on our weight, on collagen production in the skin and on many other body systems.

The simple rationale is that the body regenerates when it sleeps. Toxic build-up is cleared; growth hormone is produced; the body's innate healing ability kicks into full gear; our immune systems are revitalised;

sensory input slows or stops; breathing and heart rate slow; cells are repaired; and our systems are rebalanced. That's a lot of work in a short time frame.

SLEEP STAGES

In *Sleep: A Very Short Introduction,* Steven Lockley and Russell Foster tell us that 'sleep is complex and, although our body is at rest, sleep itself is an active state. While we sleep, our brain moves back and forth between two phases: non-rapid eye movement (NREM) sleep, which is when the body mends and regenerates, and rapid eye movement (REM) sleep, when dreams typically happen (although dreams also occur to a lesser extent during NREM sleep). On average, about 25% of the human sleep episode will consist of REM sleep.'

▸ **NREM sleep:** Stages 1 and 2 are characterised as light sleep. Within minutes of nodding off, the brain produces alpha and theta waves and our eye movements slow down. These introductory stages are brief, generally lasting up to seven minutes.

▸ **REM sleep:** During stages 3 and 4, the body goes into deeper sleep. This is when our system detoxifies, muscles and tissues are regenerated, immune function is boosted and energy levels restored. So crucial is this stage that a lack of deep sleep is guaranteed to leave us feeling physically slow and lethargic and emotionally drained.

REM sleep plays an important role in learning and memory formation, as it is during this phase that our brains consolidate information harvested during the day storing it in our long-term memory. The body enters REM sleep about 90 minutes after initially falling asleep. During this final sleep phase, the brain becomes more alert, most dreaming occurs, the eyes dart quickly, heart rate and blood pressure increase and breathing becomes faster and shallower.

The length of sleep stages changes during the course of a typical night with the majority of deep sleep (stages 3 and 4) occurring earlier in the night and more REM sleep towards the end of the night/very early morning.

CIRCADIAN RHYTHMS

Our sleep–wake pattern is partly controlled by our circadian rhythms, and understanding your unique rhythm is important to ensure quality sleep. The lives of the ancient Chinese revolved around the natural order of day into night, with qi energy being dominant during the working daylight hours and the body entering its calm resting phase after dark. Working in tune with these rhythms is as important for health and well-being today as it was centuries ago.

The master timekeeper of our internal 24-hour clock is located in the hypothalamus region of the brain, and the rhythms generated from this control centre govern the timing of many behavioural, physiological and metabolic functions in the body, including sleep, temperature regulation, the production of hormones like melatonin and cortisol, heart and lung function, glucose and insulin levels and much more.

The sleep-inducing hormone melatonin, produced by the brain's pineal gland, is believed to be the most powerful reset button for our biological clocks. The appearance of light at dawn suppresses its production and tells us to wake up and be active. Our bodies evolved in harmony with these light signals, and sleep experts are warning us that one of the most fundamental stresses on our systems today is that we are living completely out of sync with these natural fluctuations. However, under the right conditions, our internal clocks can be reset – the trick is to listen to your body and work with it.

HOW MUCH SLEEP IS ENOUGH?

It is widely accepted that sleep patterns become more irregular as we grow older, irrespective of gender. This is believed to be partly due to changes in our body's circadian rhythms, which advance noticeably with age, resulting in an earlier sleep/wake cycle (in other words, we sleep earlier and rise earlier). What's more, the grey matter in the brain that is responsible for deep sleep (arguably the most important part of the sleep cycle) starts to thin and slowly decline with age, making this vital sleep stage more difficult to reach and maintain, while the production of growth hormone also decreases, with knock-on consequences for cellular regeneration through the body.

All in all, it's a vicious circle and although we know that that a few nights of broken sleep won't kill us, lack of sleep in the long term can accelerate the ageing process in the brain, leaving us slow, exhausted and hugely compromised in both body and mind. According the US National Sleep Foundation (NSF) website, sleep.org, women are more likely than men to suffer sleep problems such as insomnia and to experience excessive sleepiness, and further research revealed that one in five women has a bad night's sleep five days a week, compared with just 8 per cent of men.

Equally important is the quality of our sleep. It is well recognised that hormonal fluctuations affect sleep, especially as women grow older. In fact, the NSF states that about 61 per cent of women who are post-menopause and almost 80 per cent of women who are in peri-menopause report sleep problems. This is partly due to the reduced production of the sleep-promoting hormone progesterone by the ovaries and partly to the night sweats that keep many women awake through the night.

SLEEP STRATEGIES
We are old enough to know that being permanently exhausted doesn't mean we are super busy or super important – it just means we aren't prioritising! The following tips are nothing new, nor are they rocket science – just well-documented advice to help us keep more in sync with our bodies so we can sleep more soundly and deeply at night.

Get some natural sunlight
It is now accepted that sunlight entering our eyes helps regulate and reset our body clocks, so work with your body's unique rhythms by starting each day with 15–20 minutes in the natural morning light.

Exercise
Regular exercise encourages deeper sleep cycles. Although the best time to exercise is a time that works well for you, it has been shown that people are more likely to stick to a routine if they exercise first thing in the morning. Bear in mind that strenuous exercise before going to bed is a stimulant.

Create a routine
We are hardwired to rise at dawn and go to sleep at sunset and our body's ability to regulate healthy sleep patterns depends on this consistency. The production of melatonin drops off rapidly in the morning light and this sets the pace for the next 24-hour cycle, so using the weekend to make up for lost sleep will disrupt this rhythm. Try to rise at a similar time every morning (occasionally allowing up to an hour's variation if needed). If you must catch up on lost sleep during the day, nap for a maximum of 45 minutes.

Switch off

It takes time for the brain to produce the neurotransmitters needed to release melatonin, so we can't expect to go from full speed to stop without first slowing down. Take time to wind down and calm down. Switch off electronic devices and leave them charging in the kitchen, not the bedroom. Back-lit screens and devices such as smartphones, tablets and laptops emit a large amount of blue light, which can suppress melatonin production and disrupt sleep quality. Turn off the TV up to an hour before sleep and don't bring devices to bed. Why not revert to reliable old paper? If you must read on an e-reader or tablet, reduce the backlight to a minimum. Power off social media as well. You can catch up on Facebook, Twitter, etc. in the morning – you won't have missed much!

Cut out stimulants

Caffeine and alcohol are known stimulants with effects that can last many hours. If you are a coffee drinker, enjoy it in the morning. If you are experiencing problems getting to sleep, cut out all caffeinated beverages, including soft drinks, many teas (check ingredients lists for caffeine) chocolate and certain medications after midday. When taken in excess, alcohol can induce sleep – but it's not deep sleep and it doesn't last. Drinking alcohol just before bed can wake the body in the middle of the night and reduce overall sleep quality.

Do mindfulness meditations

Numerous studies report the benefits of mindfulness meditations in improving sleep quality and quantity.

▶ **Self-guided meditation:** Progressive muscle relaxation (PMR), or the 'Body Scan' as mindfulness experts call it, helps prepare the body for sleep. As you lie in bed, tense and relax your muscles in groups from the toes up to the forehead. Squeeze each muscle group for a few seconds and release, before moving on to the next, or mentally 'talk' yourself through relaxing each part of the body: 'I am relaxing my toes. My toes are relaxed. I am relaxing my knees. My knees are relaxed', and so on. This can be especially effective for those who struggle to stop the relentless mental chatter – the brain is focused on the Body Scan, not the mental activity. See Chapter 10: Mindspace for more.

Sleep apps

There are many sleep apps available that use a plethora of musical arrangements, guided meditations and other effects to help soothe the senses and induce sleep. Many of these come with sound scientific support like the guided sleep meditations on Headspace (see page 188). This said, some experts are cautious about having any form of technology to hand when trying to sleep.

Let go

Most of us think in terms of 'going to sleep' at bedtime. We forget that sleep is not a place. You cannot will yourself to sleep and worrying about it simply increases anxiety. Sleep is about letting go and should be something that comes automatically. Experts tell us that it is often our subjective reaction to not falling asleep quickly that makes us more anxious. For many people, this means detaching themselves from the myriad thoughts running through their heads. If your brain is still working overtime as you lie in bed, practise the meditation techniques outlined on the previous page or try jotting down ideas that come to mind and jobs that need to be done in a notepad kept by your bed, instead of mulling them over and hoping they won't be forgotten. Most importantly, don't worry about not sleeping. Sleep will come.

Apply the quarter-of-an-hour rule

You may notice that you spend a lot of time lying in bed awake, so your bed may become connected with being awake, rather than asleep. To promote your bed–sleep connection, follow the quarter-of-an-hour rule recommended by the Sleep and Circadian Neuroscience Institute at Oxford University: if you are not asleep within around 15 minutes of going to bed, try getting out of bed, go to another room, wind down until you are feeling sleepy-tired and ready to sleep. But don't clock-watch – just estimate that quarter of an hour. See www.scni.ndcn.ox.ac.uk for more.

Set the scene

▸ **Darkness:** This is a prerequisite for melatonin production, so your close curtains/blinds and minimise or remove glowing indicator lights from alarm clocks and charging indicators on cordless phone, etc.

▸ **Temperature:** Lowering ambient temperature to about 18–21°C is believed to suit most people, even during cooler months. Use a floor or ceiling fan in hot weather to create a breeze or an air-conditioner set to 21°C, if available.

▶ **Bedding:** Invest in a comfortable mattress and pillows made from natural rather than synthetic fibres that are designed for breathability. Your mattress should be firm enough to support your spine in correct alignment (but not too hard). Replace any pillows that are floppy or out of shape.

▶ **Essential oils:** Aromatherapy stimulates the limbic system in the brain and can affect how we feel and experience emotions. Essential oils like lavender, camomile, bergamot and ylang-ylang create a sense of calm, making it easier to drift off. These can be added to a burner or diffuser, applied to the pulse points on the body before going to bed, added to a bath or used as pillow sprays. There are many sleep-inducing essential oil blends available but always choose reputable brands and check the labels for quality.

Listen to soothing sounds

Certain types of music have been shown to calm the mind and help induce sleep. A 2014 analysis of 10 published studies all measuring how well music could alleviate acute and chronic sleep disorders found that music promoted significant improvements in overall sleep quality.

While the genres of music in the individual studies varied, all the selections had a tempo between 60 and 80 BPM, a regular rhythm, low pitches and tranquil melodies. The researchers also found that the positive effects of listening to music accumulated over time, meaning that the longer you listen to music, the more beneficial it is to overall sleep quality. Many people find the often-monotonous repetition of sounds helps distract constant thoughts and relax muscles.

Be thankful

While this may sound somewhat 'new agey', thinking of four or five things during the day for which you can be thankful (regardless of how difficult your life may be at the time) helps focus the mind on the positive, rather than encouraging that wakeful tossing and turning associated with negative thoughts.

Breathe

In Indian and Tibetan yoga philosophy, our thoughts and breath are inextricably linked. Try the following when lying on your back in bed:

focus both your mind and body on taking slow, deep breaths. With lips lightly touched, breathe in through your nose for a count of five, hold for three seconds, breathe out through your nose for a count of five, then hold for three seconds. Repeat this four times without letting the mind wander. Work slowly up to eight repetitions. If the mind wanders, gently bring it back to the breath. If it continues to wander, then begin the exercise again. With slow breathing, the rib cage expands, allowing the lungs to fill completely, before emptying naturally on the exhale. By training your mind to focus on the breath, the rest comes naturally.

WARNING!

Taking sleeping pills will not resolve underlying sleep issues. Numerous studies have concluded that long-term use of sleeping pills, whether prescription or over-the-counter, does more harm than good. They can also be highly addictive. If you have been taking them for a long time, ask your doctor to help break the habit.

Instead of sleeping pills or alcohol, try supplements or herbal teas that help induce an inner calm – camomile, valerian root, lemon balm and numerous mixed blends are widely available.

Melatonin supplements can help realign natural circadian rhythms when taken at the right time and based on each individual's body rhythms. They are only a short-term remedy though. If using on an ongoing basis, seek advice from a qualified health practitioner.

PAULA'S TIPS FOR GETTING MORE ZZZZZZZ

We all know getting enough sleep is critical for beating fatigue and for recovery. People who sleep less than six hours per night tend to have higher blood pressure, higher blood sugar and greater inflammation, and to be more obese than those who sleep longer. They also have a poorer immunity.

Check your eating and drinking habits to improve sleep hygiene.

▶ **Avoid big heavy meals at night.** Lean proteins such as white fish, shellfish, chicken and eggs are easy to digest when meal time is delayed.

▶ **Magnesium and iron deficiencies may cause restless leg syndrome,** which can disrupt sleep, so include food sources of these minerals in your diet.

▶ **Cut down on fluid.** Drinking too much of anything will disrupt your sleep if you have to get up several times to go to the bathroom.

▶ **Stop drinking earlier** when attending functions. Alcohol may help you fall asleep faster, but you may wake up more often and experience less restful sleep.

▶ **If you're 'starving' before bed.** a light snack – cereal with hot milk, a banana or yogurt – can help promote sleep. Milk contains tryptophan, the raw material the brain uses to build both serotonin and melatonin. These are compounds that help us relax and prepare for sleep. While the amount of tryptophan in a glass of milk may not be enough to cause any real drowsiness, a glass of warm milk warms the body and has comforting associations with childhood. People sleep better when they are warm because the muscles relax more, so if you have to drink something, it's not a bad option before bed.

▶ **Don't be fooled by the notion of a 'relaxing' smoke.** Nicotine is a stimulant, with effects similar to those of caffeine.

CHAPTER 12
Sex

Love is the answer, but while you are waiting for the answer, sex raises some pretty good questions.

Woody Allen, director

Sex is intrinsically linked with youth in our society. The idea that older women might still enjoy sex is just not entertained. It's as if we couldn't or shouldn't be up for it! But in spite of diminishing hormones and the end of our fertile years, many women remain interested in sexual pleasure in the years after menopause.

YOU ONLY HAVE ONE SEX LIFE. CHALLENGE ANY THOUGHTS THAT ARE HOLDING YOU BACK.

Illusions abound and need to be challenged. Many of us still have sex in our middle years. We still feel desire, enjoy fantasies and have orgasms. In fact, research suggests that older women have as much sex as they used to in their 40s.

Sex can even be better in later life. Is this because we feel less inhibited or less restrained? Is it because of a new-found confidence or a couldn't-care-less attitude? Do we relax more, knowing that we can't get pregnant or that we won't be interrupted? Whatever the reason, it's a myth that all of us stop wanting sex after the menopause.

Of course, if you have never enjoyed sex, you certainly can't expect to desire it in later life unless something changes radically, such as your attitude or your partner!

A LOSS OF DRIVE AND DESIRE FOR SEX AFFECTS SOME 20 TO 40 PER CENT OF WOMEN. THERE MAY BE ONE OR MANY FACTORS CONTRIBUTING TO THE PROBLEM.

Menopausal symptoms can, however, diminish many a woman's curiosity and enthusiasm for sex in her middle years. In this chapter, we look at some common issues surrounding our sexuality and explore sexologist Emily Power Smith's 'three golden rules' for a healthy sex life.

COMPLETE LACK OF INTEREST IN SEX?

Many factors can contribute to a loss of libido. The psychological, physical, inter-relational and hormonal lists are long, making it a complex issue that can be difficult to manage.

Identifying why you have lost your libido is the key however. Then you can develop strategies to deal with the cause(s).

FAST FACTS ▸▸

Physical causes of lost libido:

- ▸ Pain-related condition
- ▸ Side effect of medication
- ▸ Vaginal dryness
- ▸ Night sweats
- ▸ Diabetes
- ▸ Heart disease
- ▸ Anaemia
- ▸ Chronic disease.

Psychological causes of lost libido:

- ▸ Excess stress
- ▸ Fatigue and exhaustion
- ▸ Low self-esteem
- ▸ Poor body image
- ▸ Feelings of boredom
- ▸ Depression/anxiety.

Inter-relational causes of lost libido:

- ▸ Poor sexual history with partner
- ▸ Lack of communication and trust in partner
- ▸ Partner is ill
- ▸ Partner has low sex drive
- ▸ Major life changes (such as looking after elderly parents).

THE MAIN CAUSE OF LANGUISHING LIBIDOS

You've guessed it – hormones again! Decreasing levels of three major hormones contribute to the reduction of sexual drive and energy in midlife:

- ▶ **The drop in oestrogen** leads to hot flushes, night sweats, irregular periods and vaginal dryness.

- ▶ **The drop in progesterone** results in irregular periods, fatigue and loss of libido.

- ▶ **The drop in androgens** such as testosterone also causes a loss of libido.

VAGINAL DRYNESS

Studies report that 40 to 60 per cent of women develop vaginal dryness during the menopausal years. Lack of interest in sex is an understandable side effect. These symptoms affect the way women feel about their changing bodies and sex.

Reduced oestrogen levels cause the vulval and vaginal tissues to become thinner, dryer and less elastic. This decrease in oestrogen is the primary cause of vaginal dryness during menopause.

Associated symptoms include general discomfort, itching, a burning sensation, stinging and painful intercourse. Men have something to say about this too.

A recent study found that men ranked 'mood swings' and 'vaginal pain during intercourse' among their top five complaints related to menopause, while for women, disrupted sleep and weight gain were more important.

The good news is that abstinence doesn't have to be your only coping strategy. There are effective ways of managing vaginal dryness and ensuring that sex remains pleasurable and pain-free.

Check out your head as well as your hormones. Excessive stress can cause or increase the severity of vaginal dryness. Other emotional problems, including anxiety and depression, can lead to lack of arousal and vaginal dryness. Unresolved relationship problems can result in decreased vaginal lubrication during sexual activity, loss of libido and problems with arousal. A visit to a relationship counsellor or a sexologist may help here.

There may be underlying causes that contribute to vaginal dryness other than the hormonal, physiological and emotional factors. Discuss the following issues with your doctor if they are applicable:

▶ Certain medications such as blood pressure drugs, anti-depressants, anti-histamines, certain cancer therapies

▶ Autoimmune diseases such as Sjogren's syndrome

▶ Infections (bacterial and viral)

▶ Smoking and/or excessive alcohol intake.

Fortunately, vaginal dryness doesn't have to be a permanent torment. There are many self-management techniques and treatment options available.

It's best to start with the least invasive approach and continue with the more drastic treatments if symptoms remain unchanged.

▶ For sexual comfort, over-the-counter vitamin E oils, vaginal moisturisers or water-based vaginal lubricants may help.

▶ A topical vaginal oestrogen cream might be worth considering too. This is an alternative to hormone therapy, with minimal absorption into the bloodstream and fewer side effects. Discuss options with your doctor.

EXPERT OPINION: THE THREE GOLDEN RULES ◀ ·······················

Emily Power Smith, leading clinical sexologist (www.empowersme.com)

All around us, every day, is the pressure to be thinner, richer, younger, fitter, happier ... the list goes on. We're expected to prioritise how we look over how we feel sexually by having bigger boobs, flatter tummies, longer legs, better tans, neat, hairless vulvas and rejuvenated vaginas.

If we buy into all this, we get waxed, lasered, bleached, cut, nipped, tucked, injected and poured into Spanx, all before striding confidently in stripper heels to the helipad where we are supposed to become insatiable, adventurous and uninhibited 'sexperts' whose aim is to meet our lover's needs instantly – before we even take off!

Hmmm. No wonder the idea of the innocent, natural girl being seduced and 'educated' sexually appeals to so many women. We're tired, busy, bored, out of shape, narky and we don't feel desired, so of course we fantasise about being irresistible just as we are – and this is a very important clue as to what women actually want.

As we get older, we need to feel sexy and turned on. We need reminders that we are beautiful, desired, interesting and appreciated in non-sexual ways before we can engage with our sexual selves. Once we're getting that, we can begin to look at what we need to do for our mojos.

What follows are some solid, reliable suggestions to help women get their mojo back. But if your relationship doesn't provide closeness, intimacy and trust, you may want to work on (re-)building those components before you feel motivated to engage sexually with your partner. The good news is that no matter what your relationship status is, the tips here will go a long way to enlivening your sexual energy, body confidence and sexual know-how.

No matter what your situation, my three golden ingredients for great sex are crucial: lubrication, masturbation, communication.

1. LUBRICATION
Whatever your age, lubrication is important for all sexual play, whether alone or with a partner, but it is vital as we age.

There are many reasons for not lubricating naturally:

- ▶ Lack of arousal due to poor skills, lack of time or intimacy
- ▶ Surgical removal of ovaries (removal of womb alone does not cause dryness)
- ▶ Menopause (significant drop in oestrogen production)
- ▶ Use of hormonal contraceptives (oral, patch, implant, etc.)
- ▶ Poor hydration
- ▶ Smoking pot (dry mouth = dry vagina)
- ▶ Taking cold/flu or hay fever medication (dries up your vaginal mucus).

Why do you need lube?

The skin in your vulva (vulva is the correct name for your external genitals and encompasses the labia, clitoris, urethra and vagina) is very delicate and easily damaged. Adding a touch of lube for external stimulation allows fingers and toys to slip and slide without pulling or irritating the skin. Internally, it allows the delicate vaginal (or anal) tissue to be stimulated without causing damage or tearing.

Lubrication can be a sign of arousal. Yet it's quite common for a woman to feel aroused and sexy and be as dry as the Gobi Desert, which makes lube invaluable.

Certain sexual practices such as vaginal or anal penetration (with finger, penis or toy) need lubrication. Without lube, you can experience tiny lesions, cuts, irritation, pain or burning and if you keep trying to push yourself through this pain, it can lead to ongoing sexual pain. You will need the help of a professional.

WHILE LUBE IS FABULOUS AND CAN FACILITATE ALL SORTS OF SEX PLAY AND PENETRATION (INCLUDING HOT QUICKIES WITH MINIMAL WARM-UP), IT IS NOT A REPLACEMENT FOR THE KIND OF SKILLED AND CARING SEX PLAY WOMEN NEED TO FEEL REALLY AROUSED!

Tips for all lube users

▶ Avoid cheap over-the-counter lubes as they often contain parabens, petroleum and glycerin, which causes yeast infections.

▶ Choose a lube with simple, natural ingredients.

▶ Avoid flavoured, scented, numbing or tingling lubes as they contain ingredients that may damage your body.

▶ Apply plenty.

▶ Reapply often.

▶ Keep wet wipes and/or towel nearby.

▶ Always do a patch test first.

Organic or non-organic?

Organic is better for your body. If you wouldn't put it in your mouth, don't put it in your vagina, as it will absorb into your bloodstream through the super-absorbent tissue.

Popular natural lubes

Easily sourced and good value, these oils don't need to be hidden, are great for massage are not as slippery as purpose-made lubes, which makes them perfect for non-penetrative and solo sex. However, they may stain and should be wiped off your genitals after use and are not safe with latex condoms.

▸ Try solid organic coconut oil (for cooking); sweet almond oil.

Artificial oil-based lubes

These work the same as natural lubes but remain slippery for longer. They have all the same benefits and problems as natural lubes. However, there is research showing that oils can harbour bacteria in the thin film they leave inside the vagina (or anus) and can also cause irritation if left on.

▸ Try Sliquid; Yes Yes Yes; Pjur.

Silicone-based lubes

I don't recommend them as they are chemical-based and most likely to cause irritation. They are not safe with silicone toys.

Water-based lubes

Water-based lubes are safe with all toys and condoms, easy to wash off and don't stain. They can be sticky or can dry quickly but can be refreshed with a few drops of water or saliva. These are the best choice as they are the least likely to cause irritation.

▸ Try Yes Yes Yes (organic); Sliquid (organic or not); Liquid Silk (non-organic).

It can be fun to have an array of lubes (a 'lubrary') for different occasions and moods. For example, if you plan on some anal loving, you will need Sliquid lubricating gel rather than Yes Yes Yes because it is thicker and better for anal play.

2. MASTURBATION, SELF-PLEASURE OR SELF-LOVE

Whether you have never masturbated or have been taking a masturbatical (sabbatical from masturbation), nothing will get your mojo back quicker than some good old self-loving.

Masturbation is a very clear term but has negative connotations for many. I prefer self-love or self-pleasure, though my BFF likes to refer to it as 'polishing her jelly-tot'. To ensure people know what I'm talking about, however, I like to get my words right. Using the correct words doesn't make the pet names people have any less funny or cute though. Use whatever language you like – as long as your partner knows what you're referring to when you say 'lady garden' or 'vertical smile'.

Self-exam

You can't expect to drive to Donegal without looking at a map and planning your route. The journey to delicious orgasms is no different, so have a good look at your genitals (use a mirror) so you know where everything is.

TRY THIS ▼

Some tips for 'intimate housekeeping':

▶ Spend a few minutes transitioning from your busy world to your world of self-love.

▶ Bathe, light candles, put on some music, read or watch something sexy to get you in the mood. Make this a ritual based on what you would like from your lover.

▶ Breathe deeply for a few minutes and then start touching yourself with curiosity.

▶ This part can be a battle between your shame and your empowerment and you need to take it very seriously. The more you engage in negative self-talk the further from orgasm you will be. Keep focused on the sensations you're feeling, your fantasies and your breathing.

▶ Give yourself 20 minutes of self-loving before bringing yourself to orgasm.

▶ If you don't know how to bring yourself to orgasm, have forgotten or want to up-skill and try new ways to come, read *The Elusive Orgasm* by Dr Vivienne Cass and *Sex for One* by Betty Dodson, or go to www. dodsonandross.com.

A minimum of 20 minutes three times a week will fuel your desire levels, as long as you're enjoying yourself. If there are bigger problems in your relationship or if you feel bad about touching yourself, you may need extra help.

Fantasise

Recall your sexiest encounters or imagine what you'd like to try. Another tip is to use your favourite sex or love scene from a book or movie to whet your appetite before, during or in between self-love sessions. Imagine yourself in the scenes, and if that incorporates your partner, great! But if it doesn't, don't worry. Fantasies are just that. They are not plans, so you don't have to feel bad that when you fantasise, the person in your dreams looks more like Magic Mike than Mickey Joe.

Toys

Get some! If you are a woman in your 40s or older and you find it hard or impossible to orgasm with your hands or if you simply want a boost, treat yourself!

Ninety per cent of women need external clitoral stimulation to reach orgasm (with or without penetration). So, when choosing a toy, I recommend an external, easy-to-use toy that fits in the palm of your hand or is easy to hold. If you feel you'd like penetration as well, get a separate device, though not a rabbit; they're expensive and rarely get used as advertised due to being too complicated and fitting just one body type.

Tips for toys

- **Get a powerful external clit stimulator** with a variety of speeds.

- **If the low speed is too much,** pop a flannel between it and your genitals while you get used to it.

- **If you want a toy for penetration** and aren't sure about size, start with a carrot or courgette and carve it into the size you think you like, pop a condom over it and give it a try with plenty of lube. When you've got the size right, you can buy the real thing (saves a fortune).

- For penetration, **you can go for a vibrator** (which vibrates) **or a dildo** (which doesn't). Some women enjoy the feeling of vibrations inside them and others prefer a dildo with a curve so they can stimulate their own G-spot without vibrations.

- **Get body-safe toys.** They are more expensive but they last longer and won't leach nasty petro-chemicals into your body, degrade over time or attract dust and fluff.

- **Rubber absorbs bacteria and yeast** and can re-infect you with urinary tract infections. So the less porous the material, the better. If it has an unpleasant smell before you use it, it's bad for your body.

- Materials such as **medical-grade silicone, stainless steel or glass** are great.

- **Brands to look for:** Lelo, Fun Factory, We-vibe, Vibratex Mystic Wand (my favourite – powerful and quiet), Tantus, Jimmy Jane, Minna, Njoy.

3. COMMUNICATION

Now you have your lube, are masturbating to orgasm and taking your time to do so and are armed with the perfect toys, it's time to teach your partner how to please you.

Here are some tips I've learned regarding successful communication:

- **Consider in advance** what you want to say (make notes if necessary).

- **Book a chat time** that suits both parties (avoid bed-times, social occasions, car journeys with kids or when either of you is busy).

- **Time your talk,** keep it short and stick to one topic per conversation. Adding more examples won't make your message clearer.

- **Be very clear** and don't contradict yourself just to make your partner feel better or avoid rows.

- To avoid 'I said, you said' arguments, **use 'I' statements** rather than telling your partner what they are doing/thinking/saying.

- **Think about your delivery** so your message isn't lost. Be calm and keep breathing.

- **If you feel yourself getting upset,** angry or fearful, stop and take a break. But tell your partner you will return and make sure you do so. If your partner needs to leave, ask for a return time.

- **Keep bringing it back to you** and your needs. Your needs and feelings are yours, so they're not wrong. Your partner only needs to understand them, not to agree with you or meet your needs. That should be a separate conversation.

- **Reminisce with your partner** about when things were hot between you both and see what you can resurrect or build on from that.

Say it loud

If you find saying sexual words out loud a challenge, then practise it during your self-love sessions. Describe what you're doing and how it feels. Get used to hearing the words coming out of your mouth when you're alone. This can be a real challenge, as many women feel 'dirty' and embarrassed. If you prefer 'pussy' to 'vulva', use it. Use what feels sexy. Don't give up without practising for 30 days. When that becomes easy, do it in the mirror. You can also communicate with a text or note in your partner's pocket or by his bed.

Slow down

When in bed with your partner, slow things down and give clear, specific direction and feedback. For example, if he circles the entrance to your vagina with his tongue at just the right speed and pressure, say, 'That pressure and speed is perfect. Keep doing that.' While 'that's nice' is encouraging, it's too vague to ensure a repeat of the same move because too much is left open to interpretation.

Ask for feedback too so that you can learn exactly what your partner likes. Don't be surprised to learn that something you've been doing for years can be improved upon. Don't take it personally. If verbal instruction is still proving tricky, you can show each other what to do with your own hands either by guiding or by showing how you touch yourself. Talk about it afterwards and share what was hot (or not) so you can build on it the next time.

IF YOU KNOW HOW TO PLEASURE YOURSELF, WHAT YOU NEED TO FEEL COMFORTABLE WHEN BEING SEXUAL AND HOW TO COMMUNICATE YOUR SEXUAL NEEDS, YOU ARE SET FOR VICTORY!

Tell your partner you want this because you love them and you miss having intimate time together and feel that you have both lost your way a bit. It's hard to take that the wrong way. If your partner is not into that idea, you'll need to find out why they're backing out of something that will help you to get back on track. Maybe there's more going on than you are aware of.

In a world that insists that we need to constantly adjust, hide or camouflage ourselves because we aren't good enough as we are, it turns out that the sexiest 'us' we can be is the authentic us. The best sex is authentic sex. The sexiest women are those who are comfortable enough in their own skins to 'be' themselves. So forget the media imagery of photo-shopped girls in disconcertingly sexualised poses and get back to the reality that sex is noisy, messy and funny. Your hair will get messed up, you'll fanny fart and maybe even normal fart, and some sexual positions that feel great *will* make your tummy look fat. But really ... who are you trying to please? Because as well as the person(s) you're having sex with, the person you are trying to please should be you.

WARNING!

Your periods may be irregular and you might think they have stopped, but that doesn't always mean you are infertile. It can be particularly difficult to know if you are post-menopause when you are on hormone therapy.

TRY THIS ▾

Your homework for better sex:

▸ Get regular exercise (see Chapter 9: Movement).

▸ Eat a well-balanced diet, including phytoestrogen-rich foods such as edamame dip, tofu, miso, soya milk. Include oysters for zinc and almonds and leafy greens for magnesium (see Chapter 2: Food).

"There's a sense of liberty associated with the end of menstruation. Finally, I'm free of monthly periods! In fact there's more of a sense of freedom surrounding this stage in life than others. All around me, I see more independent and financially-secure women, enjoying better lives than previous generations of women. We are experienced and know what we really want. We enjoy more spontaneous sex. We are free and happy if we choose to be!"
– Paula

RECIPES

PRANNIE RHATIGAN'S SUPER

GREEN SMOOTHIE

Serves 1	210 calories per portion

7-cm piece Alaria, Asco or bladderwrack or 3 pieces sea spaghetti, rinsed, snipped finely and soaked overnight in just enough water to cover (or ½ tsp mixed seaweeds, dried and ground)

1 chilled pear or banana (you can peel, chop and freeze overnight if you like)

¼–½ ripe pineapple, including core

300ml cold water

6 large Swiss chard, spinach or kale leaves

local honey or a chopped fig to sweeten, if needed

- Put all the ingredients, including the soaking water, into a blender and blend until smooth.
- Serve immediately.

TIP
It is important to vary the ingredients in the recipe, choosing small amounts of seaweeds from a wide variety. These green smoothies also freeze well in lollipop moulds for summer time.

BERRY GOOD SMOOTHIE

Serves 1	50 calories per portion	Immune-boosting recipe

25g frozen raspberries
25g fresh blueberries
1 tsp honey
5–6 ice cubes

- Put all the ingredients into a blender and blend until smooth.
- Serve immediately.

BREAKFAST BERRIES WITH GREEK YOGURT AND MILLED SEEDS

Serves 1	267 calories per portion

1 small banana, chopped
25g blueberries
55g raspberries
150g Greek yogurt
1 tsp honey
1 tbsp of milled mixed
  seeds (flaxseed,
  sunflower, goji berries)

- Combine the fruit, top with the yogurt, drizzle with honey and sprinkle with the seeds.
- Serve immediately.

POACHED EGGS

ON A BED OF SPINACH

Serves 1	365 calories per portion

2 large free range eggs
1 tablespoon olive oil
large handful baby
  spinach leaves
1 slice of granary or
  wholemeal bread,
  toasted
black pepper

- In a medium-sized saucepan, bring some water to the boil or pour some boiling water from the kettle directly into the saucepan. Bring it to a light simmer over a medium heat.

- Crack an egg into a cup and gently pour it into the water. Repeat with the other egg. They will begin to cook straight away. Reduce the heat to a simmer and cook the eggs to your taste. A really runny egg will take 2 minutes and a firmer egg will take 4 minutes (it depends on whether the eggs are at room temperature to start).

- Meanwhile, add the oil to a hot frying pan and add the spinach – it will shrink in the cooking process. Once it has wilted, remove from the heat.

- To check when the eggs are done, remove one carefully from the pan with a slotted spoon and give it a gentle push with a teaspoon. If it feels too soft, put it back in the water and cook for a further 1–2 minutes.

- Transfer the eggs to kitchen paper to dry off, then serve on a bed of wilted spinach with a sprinkling of pepper and a slice of granary toast.

RED LENTIL AND TOMATO SOUP

| Serves 6 | 110 calories per portion |

1 tsp olive oil
1 large onion, roughly
  chopped
2 small garlic cloves,
  crushed
2 celery sticks, chopped
2 tsp ground cumin
¼ tsp red chilli flakes
40 g canned chopped
  tomatoes
140g red lentils
1 litre vegetable stock,
  plus extra if needed
black pepper

- Add the oil to a large saucepan, then add the onion, garlic and celery with salt and pepper to taste and sweat for 6–8 minutes until soft. Sprinkle over the cumin and chilli flakes and sauté for 1–2 minutes to cook out the spices

- Tip the tomatoes into the saucepan.

- Stir in the lentils, then pour in the stock and bring to the boil. Cook over a high heat for 10 minutes, then reduce the heat and simmer for about 20–30 minutes until the lentils are soft. Add more stock if the soup is too thick.

- Remove the pan from the heat, leave the soup to cool slightly, then blend until smooth.

- Return to the heat to warm through, check the seasoning and serve.

SCRAMBLED EGG MUFFIN

Serves 1	325 calories per portion	1500 calorie meal plan

1 egg
3 sundried tomatoes, chopped
4 fresh basil leaves, torn
1 wholemeal English muffin, split and toasted

- Scramble the eggs without butter or cream and stir in the sundried tomatoes and basil.
- Pile on the toasted muffin halves and serve.

CRUSHED BROAD BEAN AND

MINT BRUSCHETTA

Serves 4	182 calories per portion

250g cooked broad beans
small handful grated Parmesan cheese
small bunch mint, leaves only, chopped
dash of extra virgin olive oil, plus extra for drizzling
1 French stick or small ciabatta, cut into 8 thin slices and toasted
1 garlic clove, halved
chilli flakes or black pepper

- Put the broad beans in a bowl and lightly crush.
- Season with chilli flakes or black pepper, then mix in the cheese, mint and a dash of oil.
- Rub the slices of toasted bread with the garlic.
- Top with the broad bean mix, drizzle over a little more oil and serve.

CREAMY GUACAMOLE

Serves 5	173 calories per portion

2 large ripe avocados,
  roughly mashed
1 large tomato, deseeded
  and finely chopped
½ red onion, finely
  chopped
125g low-fat probiotic
  natural yogurt
1 tbsp chopped coriander
juice of 1 lime
rye or wholemeal
  crackers, to serve

- Combine all the ingredients for the guacamole in a bowl.
- Serve immediately with rye or wholemeal crackers.

TIP
This recipe would also work well as a dip for crudités.

BEETROOT AND APPLE SOUP

Serves 6	87 calories per portion

1 tbsp olive oil
1 tsp caraway seeds or cumin seeds
2 onions, roughly chopped
2 large apples, peeled, quartered and cored
500g cooked, vacuum-packed beetroot, cut into 2.5-cm chunks
1 litre vegetable stock
2 star anise
black pepper
snipped fresh chives (optional) and 125g natural yogurt, to serve

- Heat a wide, heavy-based saucepan over a low–medium heat and add the oil and seeds.
- Add the onions and sweat, covered, taking care not to let them burn.
- Add the apple quarters and beetroot.
- Pour in the stock and bring to the boil.
- Drop in the star anise and put the lid back on. Season to taste with pepper.
- Reduce the heat and simmer for 15 minutes. Remove and discard the star anise.
- Purée the soup with a blender. Serve with the chives, if using, and a swirl of yogurt.

CARROT AND GINGER SOUP

Serves 6	85 calories per portion

1 tsp olive oil
1 onion, roughly chopped
1 tsp mustard powder
2 garlic cloves, peeled and crushed
2.5-cm piece fresh root ginger, peeled and grated
1 litre vegetable stock
6 carrots, peeled and chopped
2 celery sticks, finely sliced
black pepper
chopped fresh parsley (optional) and 125g natural yogurt, to serve

- Heat the oil in a saucepan, add the onion and sweat until soft, then add the mustard powder, garlic and ginger and season to taste with salt and pepper.

- Add 2–3 tablespoons of stock after 1–2 minutes and cook for a further 5 minutes, or until everything is soft and fragrant.

- Add the carrots and celery and stir well. Pour in the remaining stock and simmer gently for 30–40 minutes

- Blend the soup until smooth.

- Serve with parsley, if using, and a swirl of yogurt.

COURGETTE AND SPINACH SOUP

Serves 6	106 calories per portion

2 tbsp olive oil
2 onions, roughly
  chopped
2 garlic cloves, crushed
pinch of salt
2 potatoes, cut into 1-cm
  cubes
600g courgettes, roughly
  chopped
1 litre vegetable stock
200g fresh spinach leaves
juice of 1 lemon
chopped fresh coriander
  and natural yogurt, to
  serve (optional)

- Heat the oil in a large saucepan, add the onions and sweat until soft. Add the garlic and salt and sweat for 1 minute.

- Stir in the potatoes and courgettes. Add the stock, bring to a simmer and cook for 10–15 minutes until the potatoes are soft.

- Stir in the spinach and wilt for about 10 seconds.

- Purée the soup with a hand blender until smooth. Whisk in the lemon juice.

- Serve with fresh coriander and a dollop of yogurt, if using.

MINESTRONE SOUP

Serves 6	179 calories per portion

1 litre vegetable stock
1 onion, chopped
2 garlic cloves, crushed
2 carrots, chopped
225g other vegetables
  of choice such as
  courgettes, peas, green
  beans
2 tsp dried basil
400g canned haricot
  beans
100g small pasta shapes
600ml passata or canned
  chopped tomatoes

- Put half the stock into a large saucepan over a high heat, add the onion and garlic and bring to the boil. Reduce the heat and simmer for 5 minutes.

- Add the carrots and other vegetables, basil and remaining stock and simmer for a further 10 minutes.

- Add the haricot beans, pasta shapes and passata and continue to cook for a further 10 minutes.

- Serve hot.

BROCCOLI, CHERRY TOMATO
AND FETA SALAD

| Serves 4 | 305 calories per portion | 1500 calorie meal plan |

50g pumpkin seeds,
 sunflower seeds and
 poppy seeds
500g broccoli florets
100g cherry tomatoes,
 halved
110g feta cheese, cut into
 bite-sized chunks
black pepper

For the French dressing:
50ml red wine vinegar
50ml extra virgin olive oil
100ml rapeseed oil
1 tbsp wholegrain
 mustard
¾ tsp clear honey

- To make the dressing, whisk all the ingredients together in a jug.
- Toast the seeds in a dry frying pan for about 5 minutes until crunchy.
- Put into a bowl with the broccoli and tomatoes.
- Pour over 4 tablespoons of the dressing and season to taste with pepper.
- Top with the cheese and serve.

TIP
Keep an eye on the seeds while toasting them as they will burn very quickly. Store the leftover French dressing in the fridge.

SMOKED SALMON AND
CREAM CHEESE WRAP

Serves 1	380 calories per portion	1500 calorie meal plan

1 wholemeal wrap
1 tbsp low-fat cream
cheese
small handful rocket
leaves
2 standard slices smoked
salmon
1 tsp capers (optional)
dash of lemon juice
black pepper

- Microwave the wrap for a few seconds, so it is easier to roll.
- Spread the wrap with the cheese, then add the rocket and smoked salmon.
- Finish with the capers, if using, lemon juice and some pepper to taste.
- Roll up the wrap and serve immediately.

MARINATED FIG
AND MOZZARELLA SALAD

Serves 4	364 calories per portion	1500 calorie meal plan

8 ripe figs, stalks removed
4 tbsp balsamic vinegar
2 tbsp extra virgin olive oil, plus extra for drizzling
finely grated zest and juice of 1 lemon
1 tbsp chopped fresh thyme
handful fresh mint leaves
300g mozzarella cheese
50g wild rocket leaves, lightly torn
black pepper

- Cut each fig lengthways into four wedges. Make a marinade by whisking together the vinegar, oil and lemon juice with pepper to taste.

- Stand the fig wedges in the middle of a large shallow serving dish, keeping them close together. Scatter over the lemon zest and thyme, then drizzle with the marinade. Leave to stand at room temperature for 30 minutes.

- Roughly chop the mint. Drain and slice the mozzarella, toss with half the mint and season to taste with pepper.

- To serve, arrange the mozzarella and mint mixture round the figs, scatter with the rocket and the remaining mint, and drizzle with a little oil.

BUTTERNUT SQUASH SALAD

| Serves 4 | 266 calories per portion | 1500 calorie meal plan |

1 butternut squash, peeled, deseeded and diced
2 tsp olive oil
50g wild and brown rice
50g Puy lentils
1 head broccoli, cut into florets
50g dried cranberries
25g pumpkin seeds
juice of 1 lemon
black pepper

- Heat oven to 200°C/Fan 180°C/Gas Mark 6. Spread the squash over a large baking sheet in a single layer, drizzle over the oil and bake in the preheated oven for 30 minutes or until tender.

- Meanwhile, bring a saucepan of lightly salted water to the boil, add the rice and lentils and cook for 20 minutes, adding the broccoli for the final 4 minutes of cooking.

- Drain well, then stir in the cranberries and pumpkin seeds with pepper to taste. Add the squash, pour over the lemon juice and serve.

SMOKED TROUT AND PEA PASTA

Serves 2	445 calories per portion	1500 calorie meal plan

175g fusilli or other pasta
100g frozen peas
125g smoked trout fillets
3 heaped tbsp Greek
  yogurt
2 heaped tsp horseradish
  sauce
black pepper

- Cook the pasta according to the instructions on the packet, adding the peas for the last 3 minutes.

- Meanwhile, flake the trout and set aside, then mix the yogurt with the horseradish and pepper to taste.

- Drain the pasta, then return to the pan and stir in the trout and yogurt, allowing the heat of the pasta to warm the sauce. Serve with a green salad.

CHICKEN BIRYANI

| Serves 4 | 592 calories per portion, 12g fat | 1500 calorie meal plan |

300g basmati rice
1 tbsp olive oil
1 large onion, finely sliced
1 bay leaf
3 cardamom pods
small cinnamon stick
1 tsp turmeric
4 skinless chicken breasts,
  cut into large chunks
4 tbsp curry paste
85g raisins
850ml chicken stock
handful coriander,
  chopped
toasted flaked almonds,
  to garnish

- Soak the rice in warm water, then wash under cold running water until the water runs clear.

- Heat the oil in a saucepan, add the onions, bay leaf, cardamom pods and cinnamon and cook for 10 minutes. Sprinkle in the turmeric, then add the chicken and curry paste and cook until aromatic.

- Stir the rice into the pan with the raisins, then pour over the stock. Place a tight-fitting lid on the pan and bring to a fast boil, then reduce the heat to low and cook the rice for a further 5 minutes. Turn off the heat and leave for 10 minutes.

- Stir well, mixing through half the coriander. To serve, scatter over the remaining coriander and some flaked almonds.

PRAWN CREOLE

Serves 1	301 calories per portion	1500 calorie meal plan

1 tsp olive oil
1 celery stick, chopped
½ red onion, chopped
½ red pepper, chopped
1 tsp Tabasco sauce
200g canned chopped tomatoes
115g cooked peeled prawns
100g cooked basmati rice, to serve

- Heat the oil in a frying pan over a medium heat, then add the chopped vegetables and cook, stirring occasionally, until softened.
- Add the Tabasco sauce and tomatoes and simmer for 20 minutes.
- Add the prawns and heat through.
- Serve with basmati rice.

ORIENTAL PRAWN

NOODLE SALAD

| Serves 4 | 236 calories per portion | 1500 calorie meal plan |

3 tbsp soya sauce
2 garlic cloves, crushed
1 tbsp oil (preferably sesame)
300g prawns, peeled and deveined
350g noodles
400g mangetout
225g beansprouts
225g carrots, grated
200g Chinese leaves, chopped
1 tsp lemon juice

- Combine the soy sauce, garlic and oil in a large bowl.
- Add the prawns, stir to coat and leave to marinate in the fridge for at least 1 hour.
- Cook the noodles according to the directions on the packet. Drain.
- In a large bowl, combine the noodles, mangetout, beansprouts, carrots and Chinese leaves.
- Transfer the prawns and marinade to a frying pan or wok and stir-fry until cooked through.
- Add to the bowl of noodles and vegetables, season with the lemon juice and serve immediately.

ABC SALAD

| Serves 2 | 184 calories per portion | 1500 calorie meal plan |

30-cm piece of cucumber, chopped into chunks
4 cherry tomatoes, halved
400g canned haricot beans, drained and rinsed
handful mixed salad leaves
½ tbsp olive oil
1 tbsp orange juice
1 small avocado or ½ large avocado
7 raw cashew nuts
10 black olives

- Mix together the cucumber, tomatoes, beans and leaves.
- In a screw-top jar, combine the oil and orange juice to make a dressing.
- When ready to eat, place the vegetables and beans in a bowl and toss with the dressing.
- Peel and dice the avocado and scatter over the top of the salad with the nuts and olives.
- Toss and serve.

TIP
This salad may seem high in fat but most of the fat is monounsaturated good fat from the olives, nuts and avocado.

BASIC PUY LENTIL SALAD

Serves 4	244 calories per portion	1500 calorie meal plan

10 cherry tomatoes or 4
   medium plum tomatoes,
   halved
3 tbsp olive oil
300g Puy lentils
juice of 1 lemon
1 garlic clove, crushed
1 small red onion, thinly
   sliced
handful flat-leaf parsley
   leaves, roughly chopped
black pepper

- Preheat the oven to 160°C/Fan 140°C/Gas Mark 3.
- Put the tomatoes cut-side up on a small baking tray. Drizzle over 1 tablespoon of the oil and season with pepper. Roast in the preheated oven for 45 minutes until just starting to brown at the edges
- Meanwhile, put the lentils into a saucepan, cover with cold water and bring to the boil, then simmer for 15–20 minutes until just tender. Drain.
- Toss the lentils while still warm with the lemon juice, garlic and the remaining oil and season with pepper.
- Fold the tomatoes, onion and parsley through the lentils and serve at room temperature or leave to cool and keep in the fridge until needed.

Variations

- Roast red peppers along with the tomatoes.
- Try basil leaves instead of parsley.
- Add crumbled feta cheese and beetroot quarters with a French salad dressing.
- Add some blanched broccoli florets.

BROCCOLI, CARROT AND
MIXED SEED SALAD

Serves 4	89 calories per portion

1 head of broccoli, divided into small florets

4 carrots, peeled and coarsely grated

juice and grated zest of 1 orange

4 tbsp reduced-fat French dressing

2 tbsp mixed seeds (poppy, pumpkin, sesame), roasted

- Combine the broccoli florets in a bowl with the carrot, orange juice and zest and dressing
- Sprinkle with the mixed seeds and serve.

Variation

- The salad can be served with served with 25g goat's cheese per portion.

MANGO AND AVOCADO SALAD

WITH CHICKEN

Serves 1	317 calories per portion	Immune-boosting recipe

½ ripe avocado
1 tsp lemon juice
1 tbsp olive oil
1 tsp wholegrain mustard
1 tsp clear honey
½ tsp cider vinegar
handful watercress
25g cooked beetroot
½ small mango, peeled,
  stoned diced
55g cold smoked chicken,
  thinly sliced
black pepper

- Peel and stone the avocado, slice thickly and place a plate. Sprinkle with the lemon juice and set aside.

- Put the oil into a jug with the mustard, honey and vinegar, season with pepper and mix well.

- Remove the avocado from the lemon juice and mix the juice into the dressing.

- Arrange the watercress and beetroot on a plate or in a salad bowl and add the avocado and mango flesh.

- Drizzle the vinaigrette over the salad, top with the slices of smoked chicken and serve.

SPICY INDIAN FISH BAKE

Serves 4	358 calories, per portion

400g sweet potatoes or waxy potatoes
1 tbsp olive oil
400g canned chopped tomatoes
100ml vegetable stock
2 tsp garam masala
1 tsp each ground turmeric, ground coriander and cumin seeds
pinch of hot chilli powder or chilli flakes
1 tbsp grated fresh ginger
2 crushed garlic cloves
sugar, to taste
400g canned chickpeas, drained and rinsed
4 thick white fish fillets such as cod, haddock or pollock
handful fresh coriander leaves
black pepper

- Preheat the oven to 200°C/Fan180°C/Gas Mark 6.
- Cut potatoes into small cubes, then drizzle with the oil.
- Pour over the tomatoes and stock.
- Sprinkle over the garam masala, turmeric, ground coriander, cumin seeds and chilli powder.
- Add the ginger, garlic and a little sugar to taste.
- Season well with pepper, toss to combine, then roast in the preheated oven for 25–30 minutes.
- Remove from the oven and stir through the chickpeas.
- Season the fish fillets with pepper, place on top of the potato and chickpeas and roast for a further 10–12 minutes.
- Sprinkle with fresh coriander leaves and serve with steamed greens or a side salad.

TIP
Waxy potatoes may need a longer roasting time than sweet potatoes.

SEABASS WITH FENNEL AND WILD RICE

Serves 1	443 calories per portion	1500 calorie meal plan

100g cooked wild rice
200g sea bass, steamed
½ fennel bulb, chopped
handful fresh basil
small handful stoned
  black olives
1 tbsp lemon juice
1 tbsp olive oil

- Preheat the oven to 180°C/Fan 160°C/Gas Mark 4.
- Spread the rice over the base of a small baking dish, then place the fish in top.
- Scatter over the fennel, basil and olives, then drizzle with the lemon juice and oil.
- Bake in the preheated oven for 30 minutes.

GREEK MEATBALLS WITH

TOMATO SAUCE

Serves 4	361 calories per portion

3 thick slices brown
bread, crusts removed
and torn into pieces
110ml cooled beef stock
1 tbsp balsamic vinegar
500g fresh lamb or beef
mince
1 small onion, grated
1 garlic clove, crushed
1 egg, beaten
1 tbsp chopped fresh
parsley, plus extra to
garnish
1 tsp ground cumin
½ tsp ground cinnamon
salt and black pepper

For the tomato sauce:
500ml tomato passata
2 tbsp tomato purée
2 tbsp tomato ketchup
1 tbsp olive oil
1 garlic clove, crushed
1 tsp sugar
1 bay leaf

- Preheat the oven to 180°C/Fan 160°C/Gas Mark 4. Put the bread into a bowl with the stock and vinegar and leave to soak for 5 minutes.

- Lightly squeeze out the stock and vinegar – reserving it for the sauce – and put the bread pieces into a bowl with the mince, onion, garlic, egg, parsley, cumin and cinnamon. Season with salt and pepper and mix well.

- Shape the mixture into 12 medium-sized balls, each slightly bigger than a golf ball. Put on a large, non-stick baking sheet and cook for 20 minutes, until golden.

- Meanwhile, combine the reserved stock with all the sauce ingredients in a wide saucepan. Place over a medium heat and simmer for 20 minutes, until thickened. Season to taste with salt and pepper.

- Add the meatballs to the sauce and simmer for a further 10 minutes, turning halfway to coat. Discard the bay leaf.

- Divide the meatballs and sauce between serving plates and serve.

CHICKEN AND PUY LENTIL

ONE POT

Serves 2	142 calories per portion

1 tsp olive oil
2 large skinless chicken thighs, bone-in
1 onion, thinly sliced
1 garlic clove, crushed
2 tsp plain flour
2 tsp tomato purée
150ml dry white wine
250ml chicken stock
75g Puy or green lentils
1 tsp fresh thyme leaves
100g button or chestnut mushrooms, halved if large
1 carrot, cut into small chunks
1 parsnip, cut into small chunks
black pepper

- Heat the oil in a wide, shallow, non-stick saucepan, add the chicken to the pan and fry on each side until lightly browned. Remove from the pan and set aside.

- Reduce the heat, add the onion and fry for 3–4 minutes, then add the garlic and cook for a further 2 minutes.

- Stir in the flour and tomato purée, then cook, stirring, over a low heat for 2–3 minutes.

- Add the wine, stock, lentils and thyme. Bring to the boil, then reduce the heat, cover and simmer for about 15 minutes.

- Stir in the mushrooms, carrot and parsnip. Add the reserved chicken, pushing it under the liquid.

- Cover and simmer gently for 30 minutes, or until the lentils are tender. Season with salt and pepper and serve with seasonal vegetables.

TIP
If you prefer, replace the wine with the same quantity of stock.

PUY LENTIL SHEPHERD'S PIE

Serves 4

335 calories per portion

1 tbsp olive oil
1 onion, finely chopped
2 celery sticks, finely
  chopped
3 carrots, peeled and
  diced
1 garlic clove, crushed
400g canned chopped
  tomatoes
1 tbsp tomato purée
large pinch of sugar
1 bay leaf
1 tsp paprika
200g Puy lentils
500ml vegetable stock

For the topping:
800g sweet potato,
  peeled and cut into
  large chunks
pinch of freshly grated
  nutmeg
1 tbsp grated Parmesan
  cheese
handful fresh chives
  (optional)
black pepper

- Preheat the oven to 180°C/Fan 160°C/Gas Mark 4. Heat the oil in a saucepan, then add the onion, celery, carrots and garlic and cook over a low heat until softened.

- Add the tomatoes, tomato purée, sugar, bay leaf, paprika, lentils and stock, stir and simmer gently for 20–25 minutes. You may need to add more water as lentils absorb a lot of liquid.

- Meanwhile, bring a saucepan of lightly salted water to the boil, add the sweet potato chunks and simmer for 15 minutes, or until soft.

- Drain the sweet potatoes and mash with the nutmeg, cheese and chives, if using, and season with pepper.

- Add pepper to the lentils and spoon into a large pie dish.

- Spoon the mash over the top and use a fork to smooth over. Bake in the preheated oven for 20 minutes, then leave to cool a little before serving.

CHICKEN TAGINE

Serves 4	473 calories per portion

2 tbsp olive oil
8 skinless chicken thighs, bone-in
2 onions, finely sliced
2 garlic cloves, crushed
1 tsp each ground cumin, ground cinnamon and turmeric
1½ tsp ground ginger
1½ tsp paprika
500ml apple juice
500ml hot chicken stock
100g ready-to-eat dried apricots
100g canned chickpeas, drained and rinsed
large bunch of fresh mint or coriander, chopped

- Heat the oil in a heavy-based flameproof casserole over a medium heat, then add the chicken and cook, turning, until browned all over. Reduce the heat, add the onions and garlic and fry for 3-4 minutes.

- Add the spices, cook for 2 minutes, then pour in the apple juice and stock to cover the meat. Bring to the boil and simmer for 15 minutes, stirring occasionally.

- Add the apricots and chickpeas and cook for a further 10-15 minutes until the chicken is tender and the liquid has reduced and thickened a little.

- Before serving, stir in the mint, reserving some to garnish.

- Serve with cooked couscous or rice, garnished with the reserved mint.

TIP
We like to use skinless chicken thighs with bone-in for this recipe, but if you can only get boneless, don't worry.

RED PEPPER CHINESE SCALLOPS

| Serves 4 | 214 calories per portion |

2 tbsp light soy sauce
1 tbsp lemon juce
½ tsp ground ginger
¼ tsp mustard powder
5 sprays cooking spray
1 large green pepper
1 large red pepper
340g scallops
1 large tomato
400g cooked basmati
 rice, to serve

- Combine the soy sauce, lemon juice, ginger and mustard powder in a jug and pour the mixture over the scallops.
- Cover and leave to marinate for 1-12 hours.
- Drain the marinade and reserve.
- Spray a wok with cooking spray and preheat over a medium-high heat.
- Add the green and red peppers, scallops and tomato to the wok and cook, stirring, occasionally adding some of the reserved marinade, until the scallops are cooked through.
- Serve on a bed of rice.

SPICY CHICKEN AND BEAN WRAP

Serves 1	348 calories per portion	1500 calorie meal plan

1 large wholegrain or seeded flour tortilla wrap

100g cooked chicken, shredded

4 tbsp drained black beans or kidney beans

2 tbsp spicy salsa

dash Tabasco sauce

3 cherry tomatoes, halved

handful spinach or rocket leaves

- Warm the tortilla in the microwave for 10 seconds to soften.
- Place the chicken and beans along the middle of the tortilla.
- Season to taste, then spoon over the salsa and drizzle with Tabasco sauce.
- Lay the tomatoes and leaves on top, then bring the bottom of the tortilla up over the filling. Fold in the sides, then roll into a tight wrap and serve.

MOROCCAN LAMB WITH
APRICOTS, ALMONDS AND MINT

Serves 5	353 calories, per portion	1500 calorie meal plan

2 tbsp olive oil
500g lean lamb, cubed
1 onion, chopped
2 garlic cloves, crushed
700ml lamb or chicken
  stock
grated zest and juice of 1
  orange
1 cinnamon stick
1 tsp clear honey
175g ready-to-eat dried
  apricots
3 tbsp chopped fresh
  mint
25g ground almonds
25g toasted flaked
  almonds
black pepper

- Heat the oil in a large casserole dish. Add the lamb and cook over a medium–high heat for 3–4 minutes until browned all over, stirring frequently. Transfer the lamb to a plate using a slotted spoon.
- Stir the onion and garlic into the casserole and cook gently for 5 minutes until softened.
- Return the lamb to the casserole. Add the stock, orange zest and juice, cinnamon, honey and season with pepper. Bring to the boil, then reduce the heat, cover and cook gently for 1 hour.
- Add the apricots and two-thirds of the mint and cook for 30 minutes until the lamb is tender. Stir in the ground almonds to thicken the sauce.
- Serve with the remaining mint and toasted almonds scattered over the top.

TIP
Serve with
couscous and
broccoli.

WARM CHICKEN SALAD

| Serves 2 | 572 calories per portion | Immune-boosting recipe |

2 chicken breasts, cut into bite-sized pieces
6 sprays light olive oil cooking spray
½ small wholemeal baguette, cut into bite-sized pieces
2 tbsp olive oil
1 tbsp balsamic vinegar
150g mixed salad leaves
250g cooked beetroot, cut into bite-sized pieces
100g goat's cheese
salt and black pepper

- Preheat the oven to 200°C/Fan 180°C/Gas Mark 6. Spread the chicken pieces in a single layer in a shallow roasting tin. Spray with the cooking spray and toss to coat. Season to taste with salt and pepper, then bake in the preheated oven for 15 minutes until the chicken is cooked through.

- Toast the bread until golden and crisp under the grill or in a toaster.

- Whisk together the oil and vinegar to make a dressing. Divide the salad leaves between two serving plates, add the beetroot, then scatter the cheese over.

- Add the warm chicken and toasted bread and toss together, then drizzle with the dressing and serve immediately.

PRANNIE RHATIGAN'S FIG
AND WALNUT DULSE
CHOCOLATE TRUFFLES

Serves 12	133 calories per portion

180g walnuts
1 tbsp flaked or ground dulse seaweed
large pinch of dulse salt
12 dried figs, stemmed and halved, soaked for 30 minutes in water, green tea or brandy
1 tsp vanilla extract
1 tbsp raw cacao butter, grated (optional)
¼ cup raw cacao powder, plus extra for dusting
dash pineapple juice or reserved liquid from soaked figs, if needed

- Blitz the walnuts, dulse and dulse salt in a food processor using an S-blade.
- Drain the figs and reserve the soaking liquid. Add the figs to the processor with the vanilla extract and cacao butter, if using, and pulse until the mixture just comes together.
- Add some pineapple juice or reserved liquid if the mixture is too dry.
- Shape the mixture on a square plate. Chill in the fridge for 1 hour, then cut into squares. Dust with raw cacao powder.

Variation
- Roll the truffle mixture into balls, then roll in grated chocolate until coated.

CONTRIBUTORS

Dr Rosemary Coleman

Rosemary is a consultant dermatologist at Blackrock Clinic in Dublin. Her areas of expertise include aesthetic dermatology, laser therapy, rosacea, acne vulgaris, skin cancer and mole surveillance. She has worked in London and the US and has published extensively in peer-reviewed journals in the areas of geno-dermatoses, paediatric and general dermatology. She also makes regular contributions in the lay press and media on various aspects of dermatology.

Shabir Daya

Shabir is a qualified pharmacist specialising in natural health. He is co-founder of Victoria Health, an online specialist in natural health and beauty products (www.victoriahealth.com). With more than 20 years' experience in the health industry, Shabir is regularly featured in the British and international press and is widely regarded as one of the UK's leading natural health experts.

Josephine Fairley

Jo is a successful businesswoman, journalist and author of more than a dozen books, including the *Green Beauty Bible*. She has also been contributing editor on *YOU Magazine* and former chair of the UK Soil Association committee. With her fingers in many organic and philanthropic pies, Jo co-founded and grew Green and Black – the world's first organic chocolate – before the brand's acquisition by Cadbury's in 2005. She is a long-time lover of perfume and in 2014 co-founded the UK-based The Perfume Society.

Mari Kennedy

Mari is a transformational coach, mindfulness trainer, yoga teacher, speaker, wisdom-seeker and change-maker. She has been exploring and experimenting with transformation and what it means to live fully alive for the past 12 years. In addition to a private coaching practice, Mari facilitates corporate leadership development programmes and leads transformational retreats and workshops in Ireland and abroad. Born in Sligo, she had a 20-year career in the public and private sector before choosing to follow her passion – putting well-being at the centre of our lives and society.

Sunita Passi

London-based Sunita is a qualified Ayurvedic specialist and journalist. She is founder of the Tri-Dosha Ayurvedic Therapy Academy in the UK (www.tri-dosha.co.uk). She is also a qualified meditation practitioner and expert in self-enquiry concepts and energy techniques.

Prannie Rhatigan

Prannie is a medical doctor with a lifetime experience of harvesting, cooking and gardening organically with sea vegetables. Born and raised in the northwest of Ireland where she still lives, she has a lifelong interest in the connections between food and health. She holds a BA honours degree in psychology (NUI Galway), a medical degree (NUI Cork) and is a qualified general practitioner.

Emily Power Smith

Emily has a masters degree in sexology and a post-graduate diploma in art psychotherapy, with years of experience as a facilitator, educator and trainer. She is a professional member of the World Association of Sexual Health (WAS) and is accredited to the Irish Association of Creative Arts Therapists (IACAT). Her mission in life is to make it safe and normal for all people to talk about sexuality; to provide current and factual information about sexuality so that people are equipped to make good choices about their own sexual health, well-being and safety; and to provide science-based, non-religious, non-judgemental and up-to-date sexual health education for children (and all ages) that includes lessons in sexual esteem and sexual boundaries.

Jackie Ryder

Jackie has an honours degree in microbiology and a higher diploma in education, and has taught extensively in Ireland and the UK. She has also worked in the UK as a clinical research associate, conducting clinical trials for major pharmaceutical companies. Her love of fashion has led her to an alternative career as a personal stylist, providing style and fashion advice to both corporate and individual clients.

REFERENCES AND FURTHER READING

CHAPTER 1. FACTS
Brizendine, Louann. *The Female Brain*. Harmony, 2006.
Lu, Dr Nan. *Traditional Chinese Medicine: A Women's Guide to a Hormone-Free Menopause*. TCM World Foundation, 2010.
Northrup, Christiane. *Goddesses Never Age*. Hay House, 2015.
Your Hormones (www.yourhormones.com).

CHAPTER 2. FOOD
The Association of UK Dietitians (www.bda.uk.com).
Centre for Integrative Physiology (www.ed.ac.uk/integrative-physiology).
The Department of Health (www.health.gov.ie).
Drink Aware (www.drinkaware.ie).
EU register of nutrition and health claims made on foods (www.ec.europa.eu/nuhclaims).
Food Safety Authority of Ireland (www.fsai.ie).
Irish Nutrition and Dietetic Institute (www.indi.ie).
Prannie Rhatigan's Irish Seaweed Kitchen (www.irishseaweedkitchen.ie).
Safe Food (www.safefood.eu).

CHAPTER 3. WEIGHT
Ann Twomey, Accredited Cognitive Behaviour Therapist, BABCP (www.cbt.ie).
BBC iWonder. 'The test: What's the right diet for you?' BBC (www.bbc.co.uk/guides/z2csfg8), 2015.
Duval, K. et al. 'Effects of the menopausal transition on dietary intake and appetite: a MONET group study'. *European Journal of Clinical Nutrition*, 68.2 (February 2014).
Harvard Medical School (hms.harvard.edu).
'The Right Diet'. *Horizon*. BBC, 2015.
Wansink, Brian. *Mindless Eating: Why We Eat More Than We Think*. Bantam, 2006.

CHAPTER 4. BONES
Food Safety Authority of Ireland (FSAI). *Healthy Eating and Active Living for Adults, Teenagers and Children over 5 – A Food Guide for Health Professionals and Catering Services*. Food Safety Authority of Ireland, 2012.
Irish Osteoporosis Society (www.irishosteoporosis.ie).
The National Dairy Council (www.ndc.ie).
NHS Osteoporosis (www.nhs.uk/Conditions/Osteoporosis).

CHAPTER 5. IMMUNITY
The Association of UK Dietitians (www.bda.uk.com).
British Nutrition Foundation (www.nutrition.org.uk).
Irish Nutrition and Dietetic Institute (www.indi.ie).
Patient – Trusted Medical Information and Support (www.patient.co.uk).
PEN – Practice-based Evidence in Nutrition (www.pennutrition.com).
World Cancer Research Fund International (www.wcrf.org).

CHAPTER 6. HEART
British Nutrition Foundation (www.nutrition.org.uk).
The Dash Diet Eating Plan (www.dashdiet.org).
Heart UK – The Cholesterol Charity (www.heartuk.org.uk).
Irish Heart Foundation (www.irishheart.ie).
Irish Nutrition and Dietetic Institute (www.indi.ie).

PEN – Practice-based Evidence in Nutrition (www.pennutrition.com).

'Vitamin Supplements: Healthy or Hoax?' American Heart Association
(http://www.heart.org/HEARTORG/Conditions/Vitamin-Supplements-Healthy-or-Hoax_
UCM_432104_Article.jsp#.VmhPxPnhCM8), 2015.

'What is the Mediterranean Diet?' Oldways (http://oldwayspt.org/programs/
mediterranean-foods-alliance/what-mediterranean-diet), n.d.

CHAPTER 7. COMPLEMENTARY THERAPIES

Bommer, S., P. Klein and A. Suter, 'First time proof of sage's tolerability and efficacy in
menopausal women with hot flushes'. *Advances in Therapy*, 28.6 (June 2011).

The British Wheel of Yoga (www.bwy.org.uk).

Chiu, Hsiao-Yean et al. 'Effects of acupuncture on menopause-related symptoms
and quality of life in women in natural menopause: a meta-analysis of randomized
controlled trials'. *Menopause*, 22.2 (February 2015).

Jarry, H., G. Harnischfeger and E. Duker, 'Studies on the endocrine efficacy of the
constituents of Cimicifuga racemosa: 2. In vitro binding of constituents to estrogen
receptors'. *Planta Medica*, 51.4 (August 1985).

Menon Venugopal P. and Adluri Ram Sudheer. 'Antioxidant and anti-inflammatory
properties of curcumin'. *Advances in Experimental Medicine and Biology*, Vol. 595
(2007).

Public Health England (PHE). *National Diet and Nutrition Survey: Results from Years 1–4
(combined) of the Rolling Programme (2008/2009–2011/12)*. Gov.uk
(https://www.gov.uk/government/uploads/system/uploads/attachment_data/file/310997/
NDNS_Y1_to_4_UK_report_Executive_summary.pdf), 2014.

Traditional Chinese Medicine World Foundation (www.tcmworld.org).

Trickey, Ruth. *Women, Hormones and the Menstrual Cycle: Herbal and medical solutions
from adolescence to menopause*. Allen & Unwin, 2003.

Tri Dosha – Living Ayurveda (www.tri-dosha.co.uk.).

Ulven, S.M. et al. 'Metabolic Effects of Krill Oil are Essentially Similar to Those of Fish Oil
but at Lower Dose of EPA and DHA, in Healthy Volunteers'. *Lipids*, 46.1 (January 2011).

Victoria Health (www.victoriahealth.com).

Yoga Ireland (www.yoga-ireland.com).

CHAPTER 8. BEAUTY

Alexandra Soveral (www.alexandrasoveral.co.uk).

Aromatherapy Associates (www.aromatherapyassociates.com).

Elemis (www.elemis.com).

ila (www.ila-spa.com).

Kahina (www.kahina-givingbeauty.com).

Philip Kingsley (www.philipkingsley.com).

Rosemary Coleman, Consultant Dermatologist, MD FRCPI,
(www.drrosemarycoleman.com).

The Perfume Society (www.perfumesociety.org).

'Understanding UVA and UVB'. Skin Cancer Foundation (http://www.skincancer.org/
prevention/uva-and-uvb/understanding-uva-and-uvb), n.d.

CHAPTER 9. MOVEMENT

DoYogaWithMe.com (www.doyogawithme.com).

Knight, India. *In Your Prime: Older, Wiser, Happier*. Fig Trees, 2014.

Chattha, Ritu et al. 'Treating the climacteric symptoms in Indian women with an
integrated approach to yoga therapy: a randomized control study'. *Menopause*, 15.5
(September 2008).

Mansikkamäki, Kirsi et al. 'Physical activity and menopause-related quality of life – A population-based cross-sectional study'. *Maturitas*, 80.1 (January 2015).

Yogaglo (www.yogaglo.com).

CHAPTER 10. MINDSPACE

Brach, Tara. 'Working With Difficulties: The Blessings of RAIN'. Tara Brach (http://www.tarabrach.com/articles/RAIN-WorkingWithDifficulties.html), n.d.

Brach, Tara. *True Refuge: Finding Peace and Freedom in Your Own Awakened Heart*. Bantam, 2013.

Brown, Lydia et al. 'Self-compassion weakens the association between hot flushes and night sweats and daily life functioning and depression'. *Maturitas*, 78.4 (August 2014).

Brown, Lydia et al. 'Investigating how menopausal factors and self-compassion shape well-being: An exploratory path analysis'. *Maturitas*, 81.2 (June 2015).

Calm.com (www.calm.com).

Guided Mindfulness Meditation Practices with Jon Kabat-Zinn (www.mindfulnesscds.com).

Headspace (www.headspace.com).

Isaacson, Walter. *Steve Jobs*. Simon & Schuster, 2011.

Lutz, A. et al. 'Long-term meditators self-induce high-amplitude gamma synchrony during mental practice'. *Proceedings of the National Academy of Sciences*, 101.46, (November 2004).

Mari kennedy (www.marikennedy.com)

Matthieu Ricard (www.matthieuricard.org).

MindApps (www.mindapps.se).

Mindful Self-Compassion – Christopher Germer, PhD (www.mindfulselfcompassion.org).

Plum Village Mindfulness Practice Centre, founded by Thich Nhat Hanh (www.plumvillage.org).

Wax, Ruby. *Sane New World: Taming the Mind*. Hodder, 2013.

CHAPTER 11. SLEEP

Lockley, Steven W. and Russell G. Foster. *Sleep: A Very Short Introduction*. Oxford University Press, 2012.

Nuffield Department of Clinical Neurosciences (www.ndcn.ox.ac.uk).

Sleep.org, powered by National Sleep Foundation (www.sleep.org).

'Slow Wave Sleep Integrity And Cortical Thickness Are Tightly Linked'. BrainProtips (http://www.brainprotips.com/article/slow-wave-sleep-integrity-and-cortical-thickness-are-tightly-linked/), n.d.

Van Cauter, Eve, Racel Leproult and Laurence Plat. 'Age-Related Changes in Slow Wave Sleep and REM Sleep and Relationship With Growth Hormone and Cortisol Levels in Healthy Men'. *The Journal of the American Medical Association*, 284.7 (August 2000).

Wang, Chun-Fang, Ying-Li Sun and Hong-Xin Zang. 'Music therapy improves sleep quality in acute and chronic sleep disorders: A meta-analysis of 10 randomized studies'. *International Journal of Nursing Studies*, 51.1 (January 2014).

CHAPTER 12. SEX

Betty Dodson with Carlin Ross (www.dodsonandross.com).

Cass, Dr Vivienne. *The Elusive Orgasm: A woman's guide to why she can't and how she can orgasm*. Brightfire Press, 2004.

Dodson, Betty. *Sex for One: The Joy of Selfloving*. Three Rivers Press, 1996.

Empowers Me (www.empowersme.com)